Lecture Notes in Artificial Inte

Edited by J. G. Carbonell and J. Siekmann

Subseries of Lecture Notes in Computer Science

Paolo Petta   Jörg P. Müller
Matthias Klusch   Michael Georgeff (Eds.)

Multiagent
System Technologies

5th German Conference, MATES 2007
Leipzig, Germany, September 24-26, 2007
Proceedings

 Springer

Series Editors

Jaime G. Carbonell, Carnegie Mellon University, Pittsburgh, PA, USA
Jörg Siekmann, University of Saarland, Saarbrücken, Germany

Volume Editors

Paolo Petta
Medizinische Universität Wien
Freyung 6/II, 1010 Vienna, Austria
E-mail: Paolo.Petta@MeduniWien.ac.at

Jörg P. Müller
Technische Universität Clausthal
Julius-Albert-Str. 4, 38678 Clausthal-Zellerfeld, Germany
E-mail: joerg.mueller@tu-clausthal.de

Matthias Klusch
Deutsches Forschungsinstitut für Künstliche Intelligenz (DFKI)
Stuhlsatzenhausweg 3, 66123 Saarbruecken, Germany
E-mail: klusch@dfki.de

Michael Georgeff
Monash University
Locked Bag 29, Clayton, Victoria 3168, Australia
E-mail: michael.georgeff@med.monash.edu.au

Library of Congress Control Number: 2007934801

CR Subject Classification (1998): I.2.11, I.2, C.2.4, D.1.12, D.1.3, J.1

LNCS Sublibrary: SL 7 – Artificial Intelligence

ISSN	0302-9743
ISBN-10	3-540-74948-9 Springer Berlin Heidelberg New York
ISBN-13	978-3-540-74948-6 Springer Berlin Heidelberg New York

Springer is a part of Springer Science+Business Media

springer.com

© Springer-Verlag Berlin Heidelberg 2007
Printed in Germany

Typesetting: Camera-ready by author, data conversion by Scientific Publishing Services, Chennai, India
Printed on acid-free paper   SPIN: 12123544   06/3180   5 4 3 2 1 0

Preface

The German conference on Multi-Agent System Technologies (MATES) provides an interdisciplinary forum for researchers, users, and developers to present and discuss the latest advances in research work as well as prototyped or fielded systems of intelligent agents and multi-agent systems. The conference aims to promote theory and applications and covers the whole range of agent- and multi-agent technologies.

For the fifth time, the German special interest group on Distributed Artificial Intelligence in cooperation with the Steering Committee of MATES organized this international conference. Building on the four successful predecessors in 2003, 2004, 2005, and 2006, MATES 2007 took place September 24–26, 2007 under the umbrella of the SABRE (Software, Agents, and Services for Business, Research, and E-Sciences) event organized by the University of Leipzig.

Situated in the lively scene of agent-based computing in Europe that is exemplified by federated events such as Durham Agents'007; SABRE itself —that also included the Central and Eastern European Conference on Multi-Agent Systems (CEEMAS); and the subsequent European Conference on Complex Systems (ECCS 2007) in Dresden, MATES 2007 not only succeeded in attracting 27 submissions, out of which 17 could be accepted for presentation and discussion, but also in holding an edition of the doctoral mentoring programme, an important occasion for both students and established researchers to interact and discuss scientific and managerial aspects of activities. The programme of MATES 2007 was rounded off with invited presentations by the distinguished speakers Michael Georgeff and Rafael Bordini.

Our thanks go to the Programme Committee for their diligent, careful, and constructive work; the local organizers of SABRE for their constant support; and foremost to all authors of submitted papers: the present selection stands to testify the important contribution of the MATES conference series to the rich international agent-oriented systems research landscape.

July 2007

Paolo Petta
Jörg P. Müller
Matthias Klusch
Michael Georgeff

Organization

General Co-chairs

Matthias Klusch   DFKI, Germany
Michael Georgeff   Monash University, Australia

Program Co-chairs

Paolo Petta   Medical University of Vienna and OFAI,
     Austria
Jörg P. Müller   TU Clausthal, Germany

Doctoral Consortium Chair

Franziska Klügl   Universität Würzburg, Germany

Steering Committee

Hans-Dieter Burkhard   Humboldt-Universität zu Berlin, Germany
Stefan Kirn   Universität Hohenheim, Germany
Matthias Klusch   DFKI, Germany
Jörg P. Müller   TU Clausthal, Germany
Rainer Unland   Universität Duisburg-Essen, Germany
Gerhard Weiss   SCCH Hagenberg, Austria

Program Committee

Bernhard Bauer   Universität Augsburg, Germany
Federico Bergenti   Università degli Studi di Parma, Italy
Lars Braubach   Universität Hamburg, Germany
Hans-Dieter Burkhard   Humboldt-Universität zu Berlin, Germany
Cristiano Castelfranchi   Università degli Studi di Siena and CNR Roma,
     Italy
Rosaria Conte   CNR Roma, Italy
Hans Czap   Universität Trier, Germany
Mehdi Dastani   Universiteit Utrecht, The Netherlands
Jörg Denzinger   University of Calgary, Canada
Jürgen Dix   TU Clausthal, Germany
Torsten Eymann   Universität Bayreuth, Germany
Klaus Fischer   DFKI GmbH, Germany

Jean-Pierre Georgé	Université Paul Sabatier, France
Paolo Giorgini	Università degli Studi di Trento, Italy
Rune Gustavsson	Blekinge Institute of Technology, Sweden
Heikki Helin	TeliaSonera, Finland
Wiebe van der Hoek	University of Liverpool, UK
Stefan Kirn	Universität Hohenheim, Germany
Franziska Klügl	Universität Würzburg, Germany
Ryszard Kowalczyk	Swinburne University of Technology, Australia
Daniel Kudenko	University of York, UK
Jürgen Lind	iteratec GmbH, Germany
Gabriela Lindemann	Humboldt-Universität zu Berlin, Germany
Jiming Liu	Baptist University, Hong Kong
Stefano Lodi	Università di Bologna, Italy
Beatriz López	Universitat de Girona, Spain
Volker Nissen	TU Ilmenau, Germany
James Odell	Agentis Software, USA
Andrea Omicini	Università di Bologna, Italy
Sascha Ossowski	Universidad Rey Juan Carlos, Spain
Stefan Poslad	Queen Mary University of London, UK
Von-Wun Soo	National Tsing-hua University, Taiwan
Steffen Staab	Universität Koblenz-Landau, Germany
Ingo Timm	Universität Frankfurt am Main, Germany
Robert Tolksdorf	Freie Universität Berlin, Germany
Adelinde Uhrmacher	Universität Rostock, Germany
Rainer Unland	Universität Duisburg-Essen, Germany
Liászló Zsolt Varga	MTA SZTAKI, Hungary
Danny Weyns	K.U. Leuven, The Netherlands
Cees Witteveen	TU Delft, The Netherlands
Michael Wooldridge	University of Liverpool, UK

Auxiliary Referees

Tina Balke	Alexander Kubias	Fernando Silva Parreiras
Ralf Berger	Ingo Müller	Diemo Urbig
Javesh Boodnah	Michele Piunti	Jian Feng Zhang

Table of Contents

Engineering Multi-agent Systems

Multi-Agent System: A Guiding Metaphor for the Organization of
Software Development Projects 1
  Lawrence Cabac

Model Transformation for Model Driven Development of Semantic Web
Enabled Multi-Agent Systems 13
  *Geylani Kardas, Arda Goknil, Oguz Dikenelli, and
  N. Yasemin Topaloglu*

SmartResource Platform and Semantic Agent Programming Language
(S-APL) 25
  Artem Katasonov and Vagan Terziyan

Multi-agent Planning and Learning

Subgoal Identification for Reinforcement Learning and Planning in
Multiagent Problem Solving 37
  Chung-Cheng Chiu and Von-Wun Soo

Medical Image Segmentation by a Multi-Agent System Approach 49
  Nacéra Benamrane and Samir Nassane

Using DESs for Temporal Diagnosis of Multi-agent Plan Execution 61
  Femke de Jonge, Nico Roos, and Huib Aldewereld

Multi-agent Communication, Interaction, and Coordination

Agent Communication Using Web Services, a New FIPA Message
Transport Service for Jade 73
  Esteban León Soto

Goal-Oriented Interaction Protocols 85
  Lars Braubach and Alexander Pokahr

Multi-agent Resource Allocation

VWM: An Improvement to Multiagent Coordination in Highly
Dynamic Environments 98
  *Seyed Hamid Hamraz, Behrouz Minaei-Bidgoli, and
  William F. Punch*

Dynamic Configurable Auctions for Coordinating Industrial Waste
Discharges 109
    Javier Murillo, Víctor Muñoz, Beatriz López, and Dídac Busquets

Distributed Clustering of Autonomous Shipping Containers by Concept,
Location, and Time 121
    Arne Schuldt and Sven Werner

Coordinating Competitive Agents in Dynamic Airport Resource
Scheduling 133
    Xiaoyu Mao, Adriaan ter Mors, Nico Roos, and Cees Witteveen

Multi-agent Planning and Simulation

Large-Scale Agent-Based Pedestrian Simulation 145
    Franziska Klügl and Guido Rindsfüser

Diagnosis of Plan Structure Violations 157
    Nico Roos and Cees Witteveen

Team Cooperation for Plan Recovery in Multi-agent Systems 170
    Roberto Micalizio and Pietro Torasso

Trust and Reputation

On the Behaviour of the TRSIM Model for Trust and Reputation 182
    Alberto Caballero, Juan A. Botía, and Antonio Gómez-Skarmeta

Implementing ReGreT in a Decentralized Multi-agent Environment 194
    Stefan König, Sven Kaffille, and Guido Wirtz

Author Index 207

Multi-Agent System: A Guiding Metaphor for the Organization of Software Development Projects

Lawrence Cabac

University of Hamburg, Dept. of Informatics, Vogt-Kölln-Str. 30, D-22527 Hamburg
http://www.informatik.uni-hamburg.de/TGI

Abstract. In this work we propose the introduction of multi-agent concepts for the organization of software development projects of (especially multi-agent) application design and implementation. This is expressed by the guiding metaphor (German: Leitbild) of a *multi-agent system of developers*.

Team orientation and concurrent development are two aspects that are crucial in every large development project. Consequently, the organizational structure of the programming team has to take account for both. If the developed application is distributed, concurrent and team-oriented – e.g. a multi-agent application – one approach is to aim for a comparable (homomorphic) structure of a developed system and development team. We achieve this by reintroducing the multi-agent system metaphor into the organizational structure of the development team.

Agent attributes such as autonomy, communication, cooperation, self-organization and the capacity for teamwork are transferred by the guiding metaphor back to team members. Concurrency and distribution of resources and processes is naturally supported by the guiding metaphor.

This guiding metaphor can be applied to any project organization. However, it is best suited for the organization of multi-agent application development, due to the similarity in structure.

Keywords: agents, guiding metaphors, *multi-agent system of developers*, Leitbild, metaphor, project management, software development approach, team organization.

1 Introduction

Multi-agent systems are applications based on encapsulated, autonomous software entities that can flexibly achieve their objectives by interacting with one another in terms of high-level interaction protocols and languages. Agents balance their reactive behavior in response to influences from the environment with their proactive behavior towards the achievement of design objectives.

The agent metaphor is highly abstract and it is necessary to develop software engineering techniques and methodologies that particularly fit the agent-oriented paradigm. Traditional software development techniques such as for example object-oriented analysis and design are inadequate to capture the flexibility and autonomy of an agent's problem-solving capabilities, the richness

P. Petta et al. (Eds.): MATES 2007, LNAI 4687, pp. 1–12, 2007.

of agent interactions and the (social) organizational structure of a multi-agent system as a whole. Many agent-oriented software development methodologies have been brought forward over the last years, many of them already in mature state.

Agent-oriented development methodologies such as GAIA [1,2], MASE [3] or PROMETHEUS [4] are well-established. Similarities can be found in methods and abstractions such as use cases, system structure (organization) diagrams, role models, interaction diagrams and interaction protocols. However, it is not a trivial task to decide on a suitable implementation platform as pointed out by Sudeikat et al. [5].

Similar claims hold for the management of development processes, the organization and guidance of a team as well as for project management. As well as for methodologies and techniques of software development, there also exists a necessity to develop approaches for the management of projects that particularly fit the agent-oriented paradigm. As already proposed by Petrie et al. [6] the organization of projects can be oriented towards the agent concept. The proposal here is to increase even more the symmetry between the project management and the software being build.

We present a guiding metaphor that is capable to dynamically adapt to the needs of the team and development processes. Criteria for a powerful and acceptable metaphor is its simplicity, flexibility and the range of the commonly known concepts. It should take account of the main concepts and design objectives of the developed system; e.g. for a multi-agent application these are concepts such as distribution, concurrency and dynamical structures.

Section 2 introduces the term *guiding metaphor* and explains the guiding metaphor *multi-agent system of developers*[1] for the development of multi-agent-based projects in detail. Section 3 describes the utilization and our experiences with this guiding metaphor.

2   Leitbild: MAS

Before we start with our approach we will elaborate on the notion of the *guiding metaphor*. Then we will describe the guiding metaphor of a *multi-agent system of developers* in regard to three aspects. First, we describe the guiding metaphor in more detail in its role as a Leitbild [7] regarding orientation, notions, strategies and terminology in the environment of multi-agent application development. Second, we go into detail of the guiding metaphor's manifestation in the organizational structure of a (multi-agent application) development project especially in regard to concurrent and distributed development. Third, we focus on communication, coordination, project organization and team management.

---

[1] We include all participants of a development process, such as programmers, users, supporting staff, etc. We could thus also call the metaphor *multi-agent system of participants* but in the context of system development we regard all participants as developers of the system.

2.1 Guiding Metaphor

A guiding metaphor (German: Leitbild [7]) is a strong and well-established concept that can guide the participants of a development team in a general sense. While the term originated in business management, it is also well established in software engineering. A guiding metaphor should have four functions. It should offer orientation and have a strong integrative force. Decision processes should be supported by the guiding metaphor and it should also be a means of coordination. Züllighoven et al. define a guiding metaphor as follows.

> A guiding metaphor in software development defines a frame of orientation for involved groups in development processes as well as during utilization. It supports the design, utilization and the evaluation of software and is based on values and goals. A guiding metaphor can be used constructively or analytically [7, from German, p. 73].

An important feature is that the guiding metaphor is so general and common that every potentially involved person has at least a good idea of the organizational concepts, structures, notions and rules. A good guiding metaphor comes with a whole set of other metaphors that do not have to be named explicitly.[2] In the context of developing software we can distinguish three different forms of guiding metaphor. It can be used to characterize the software systems, the development process and also the team organization (respectively project management).[3] Examples of guiding metaphors are the *tools & material* approach [7] or the *expert work place* [8] for software systems. Guiding metaphors for team organizations are *the factory, the office, the workshop* or the *(free) jazz band* [9].

One interesting approach as to how to define a new guiding metaphor for team organization has been done by Mack [10]. He proposes the guiding metaphor of an *expedition* for the development process and derives some aspects that are useful in everyday (work) life of a software developer. Here we will not go into detail of this guiding metaphor but we would like to elaborate on the notions that are instantly linked to this example to show the potentials of a guiding metaphor.

For a (development) expedition one will need a team (developers, supporting users and other staff) and resources (computers, software, rooms, paper, etc.). There should be a good notion on how much everyone can carry (individual capabilities of team members) on the way. The organizers need to work out a plan in advance that is detailed enough to take as many aspects as possible into account and flexible enough to allow the team members to react to sudden changes and dangers. In an expedition it seems clear that all members have to support each other and that conflicts that are left unsolved can lead to difficulties that can endanger the expedition (software project). A good communication

---

[2] In this way the guiding metaphor can be compared to an *extended metaphor* or even a *parable* as used in literature.

[3] In this work we focus on the function of the guiding metaphor for the team's organizational structures / project management.

between members of the team is essential in all stages of the expedition. We know that an expedition is a socially challenging project that can be adventurous as well as hard work. In addition, the outcome of an expedition is open in the beginning.

The example shows that a strong guiding metaphor offers many notions (common in the team) and a multitude of metaphors. These help team members to find orientation in the project and by this the guiding metaphor succeeds in guiding a team.

In the following sections we describe a guiding metaphor that is well applicable to the development of multi-agent application and is also well known in the multi-agent community. It is the multi-agent system.

2.2 Multi-Agent System of Developers

Our approach of organizing projects for multi-agent application development is described by the guiding metaphor of *multi-agent system of developers*. Developer teams, their members and their actions are characterized by the attributes usually related to agents [11], multi-agent systems [12] and cooperative workflows [13].[4] In the team members are acting in a self-organized, autonomous, independent and cooperative way. They all have individual goals that culminate in a common vision of the system that is to be developed.

Like agents in a multi-agent system, developers are situated in an environment, in which they communicate with other developers and other participants of the development process. Moreover, the environment offers services or restricts the possibilities of actions for the developers.

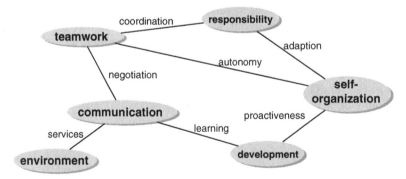

Fig. 1. Agent concepts used in the context of team organization (selection)

---

[4] In the following many agent concepts are used to describe behavior or attributes of members of the development team. These are used for the metaphorical power.

Figure 1 shows a selection of typical multi-agent concepts and their inter-relationships that are utilized in the development project context as metaphors. Lippert et al. [8] identify a selection of key metaphors as shown in the figure as a metaphor design space.

The agent metaphor leads to dynamic and flexible structures in the team's organization. All members can form (sub-)teams with other members during the development process. This is not only encouraged but also a main aspect of the self-responsible and autonomous actions of team members. The structure of a team is not static. Sub-teams are able to decide their own dissolution and to proactively decide on new alliances. From this point of view concurrent and distributed work is a natural phenomenon.

According to the *multi-agent system of developers* metaphor control, project management and organizational matters in the development process are managed through mechanisms typically owned by social agents [14]. Thus social norms, conventions and motivation become important forces in the team's behavioral patterns.

At first glance it seems odd to re-transfer the concept (metaphor) of a multi-agent system, which has been used to define and organize software systems in the manner of (sociological) organizations, back to an organizational structure of people. However, the metaphor of a multi-agent system has grown so strong in recent years that many developers are well acquainted with the notions and key elements of agent concepts. Therefore, the multi-agent system is a reasonable, well-established and powerful guiding metaphor. But even for participants of the team that do not share the concepts of multi-agent systems as paradigm – e.g. users with no technical background – still all the concepts are well known, since they are rooted in social organizations.

In the following two sections we elaborate on two main aspects of agent-oriented development. These are the communication of agents and the concurrency and distribution. Through the guiding metaphor both aspects take a leading role in our vision on the project organization.

2.3   Matrix Organization

In a multi-agent application development project the organizational structure has to be defined, such that responsibilities for certain aspects can be assumed by team members or sub-teams. The general perspectives in the area of a multi-agent system and – therefore also here – for the development process are *structure*, *behavior* and *terminology*. These perspectives are orthogonal with connecting points at some intersections (compare Fig. 2).

The structure of a multi-agent system is given by the agents, their roles, knowledge bases and decision components [15,16]. The behavior of a multi-agent system is given by the interactions of the agents, their communicative acts and the internal actions related to the interactions [17]. The terminology of a multi-agent system is given as a domain-specific ontology that enables agents to refer to the same objects, actions and facts. The agents' common ontology is crucial for their successful interactions.

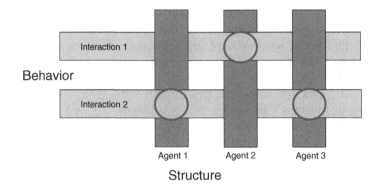

Fig. 2. Two dimensional matrix showing perspectives (*behavior, structure*)

A schematic two dimensional matrix is depicted in Figure 2 showing the independence and interconnections of agents and interactions. Neither is there any direct relationship between any pair of agents, nor between any pair of interactions. Thus these architectural elements are independent and drawn in parallel to each other. Agents and interactions are orthogonal because each agent is involved in some interactions and the same holds the other way around. When an agent and an interaction are coupled, a circle marks the interconnection point.

The general case for any two structural and/or behavioral elements is independence. In the diagram interconnections are explicitly marked. The ontology, which is omitted in the diagram, is the third dimension of perspectives. This perspective is orthogonal to the other two perspectives, but it tends to have many interconnection points because each interaction and each agent needs parts of the ontology definition to fulfill its purpose.

Since the three perspectives are orthogonal and independent within each perspective, it is easily possible to divide the tasks of design and implementation into independent perspectives and independent parts. This means that different interactions can be developed by independent sub-teams and different agents can be designed by other independent sub-teams. Between agent teams and interaction teams, coordination is needed for the crucial parts only (circles).

Following this method, the different parts of the system can be developed independently and concurrently as long as there is enough coordination / synchronization between intersecting groups.

In general it is not a good idea to assign tasks of orthogonal dimensions to the same sub-team because then the responsibilities of the different dimensions might become blurred. However, developers are well advised to look for similarities between independent elements of the same dimension, like for example a set of similar interactions. In such a situation, code reuse becomes possible if a subteam is responsible for multiple parallel elements.

The (agent-based) software system imposes its matrix structure onto the team organization. In the metaphor of *multi-agent system of developers* this is naturally supported.

2.4   Communication, Coordination and Synchronization

We can identify four main phases when applying the guiding metaphor of a *multi-agent system of developers* to the time schedule: (1) the requirements analysis, (2) the (coarse) design of ontology/roles/interactions, (3) the concurrent and highly interactive implementation of ontology/agents/interactions and (4) an intense and concurrent integration and testing phase. The time schedule is iterative in all phases, however, in normal settings iterations in phases two to four would suffice.

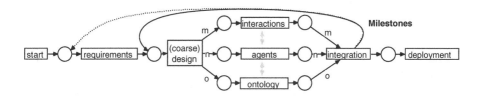

Fig. 3. Schematic and coarse Petri net model of the PAOSE development process

Figure 3 shows a schematic Petri net model of the development process. The design phase results in several independent tasks for interaction, agent and ontology implementation.

The synchronizations between concurrent processes during implementation in the form of communication between the groups have to be supported during development, both through synchronous and asynchronous communication. This is achieved by physical meetings (synchronous), through (web-based) tool support (synchronous and asynchronous) and implicit communication in documentation of activities and code (asynchronous). At the end of the implementation phase a thorough integration phase is necessary to obtain a milestone / running system. Each phase in itself is a process with its own structure.

While the processes of independent activities are concurrent, some synchronizations are necessary during implementation between orthogonal groups (gray arrows). Also phase shifts should be coordinated. This is implied in Figure 3 and explicitly shown at integration, which should be entered synchronously by the whole team.

All team members are attributed with the sociality of communicating agents. The team structure is self-organized and controlled through participating developers by observation, negotiation, rules and norms.

Awareness of participants is an important factor in avoiding problems resulting from miscoordination. Unfortunately, the support for user awareness in our tool-set is not sufficient yet. Thus, we have to compensate with extensive communication about changes in design and implementation. Nevertheless, some simple elements in our communication platform exist, which enable us to track recent changes. Improvements are being discussed.

3 MAS of Developers in the Project Context

The concept of the guiding metaphor has to be backed up with the utilization in the context of a multi-agent application development project. Here the guiding metaphor can unveil its usefulness.

3.1 Employing the Guiding Metaphor

Following the guiding metaphor of *multi-agent system of developers* project organizers or initiators will be able to anticipate the needs of the team members during the development. Good equipment, enough resources and an adequate team composition are essential to any project. Here also the means of communication, coordination, learning, reorganization and the possibility to take responsibility are important parts in the development process. These processes have to be supported by adequate means, for example regular meetings for direct communication and teamwork sessions and/or a (web-based) communication system for asynchronous (and synchronous) communication. These communication means have to be integrated into the environment (platform) of the developers (agents).

The organizers have a powerful means to guide the actions, the way of thinking and the general behavior of participants in the context of the project. Here the main responsibility is that the metaphor is well conveyed to all participants. If all participants have a good notion of agent concepts, everyone will be able to live the metaphor (and the team will profit from that). This means that all participants are aware of the fact that participation (coordination, negotiation) in the development process and in the decision processes of team members as well as the possibility for the team to exercise the sociological prosperity is of importance. The ease of the adaption to the guiding metaphor – borrowed from sociological theories about organizations – can lead to higher motivation, integration and identification with the group and the common goals, which in turn leads to quicker orientation in the project and higher productivity.

In addition to the metaphor's inherent organizational powers, the developers can benefit from a structural organization of the development process that resembles the structure of the developed system.

3.2 Homomorphic Structure

The advantages to work with a homomorphic – similar – structure in software organization and project organization are manifold. In general, they are the same advantages as those of multi-agent systems over conventional paradigms.

The multi-agent system organization of the development team allows for and supports distributed as well as concurrent development. In this context it is important that developers act self-responsible and consider self-reorganization if necessary. Structures in the team should emerge from the processes during development. Thus independence and flexibility as well as means for communication and mobility are supported in this approach as first-order concepts. One main advantage of the similar structure for the developed software – and a successful project – is that the same principles, concepts and organization help the developers also to design a truly agent-oriented software system. Distribution, autonomy and concurrency in the organizational structure will automatically foster the same attributes in the designed system.

Some disadvantages also exist and – not surprising – these are the same disadvantages as those of multi-agent systems again. To succeed with the project by employing the *multi-agent system of developers* metaphor a strong emphasis on communication and adaptive processes has to be made. This leads to a large communication overhead. Due to the flexible and dynamical organization, the inherent concurrency and distribution, the complexity of the project organization is very high. This leads to more management overhead (compared to a non-distributed and non-concurrent development).

3.3   Experiences

Especially in our teaching projects the guiding metaphor of *multi-agent system of developers* works extremely fine. This results to some extend from the fact that our students have a well-founded background knowledge of basic and advanced agent concepts. Usually these concepts are conveyed through conceptualized object Petri net models, which have a strong graphical representation for concurrency, locality and hierarchical nesting.

The main aims of multi-agent system development (concurrent, independent development) are reached with the support of the guiding metaphor. However, it is still useful to gather the source code in a central repository even if parts of the system are run exclusively in disjunct places. This eases the deployment of system and framework.

In addition, common elements have to be made available to all members. Many documents like overview diagrams (multi-agent system structure) or ontology definitions respectively models are also still designed in a central (non-distributed) fashion. Here, still more flexibility can be added to the development process. However, it is not essential to work concurrently (of independently) on these elements, since the ontology for instance is meant to be common to all agents as well as common to all developers. Moreover, these *central* specification elements (especially ontology) can be used by the project leaders to actively control the direction of the development. The software MAS ontology becomes a common language for the developer MAS as well.

Many improvements in support of the development team, communication means and increase of flexibility are possible and the extend of the guiding metaphor has not reached its limits, yet. We would like to include direct and indirect communication, inline documentation and workflow capabilities into our development environments (RENEW [18], MULAN [15,19,16], Eclipse) to better support the interactive means of the developers in their environment. Web-based documentation and groupware features can also be more heavily exploited.

4 Conclusion

In this work we present a guiding metaphor for the organization of (multi-agent) application development projects. The guiding metaphor itself is taken from agent technologies. It is the multi-agent system metaphor applied to the team of developers (and other participants). By this self-reflective view on the organization of development teams a coherent structure in all parts of the system and all processes is defined.

Guiding metaphors are well suited to give a common orientation in a development team. The multi-agent system is, through its origination from socio-organizational structures, its generality, its ease of accessibility and its recognition of distribution, well suited to serve as the guiding metaphor for project organization. We believe that it is an especially powerful metaphor when it comes to multi-agent application development. And in the spirit of this guiding metaphor we believe that the organizational structure and the teams notion of the guiding metaphor is subject to change, adaption, self-organization and emergence. Thus the power of the metaphor will improve during the development process.

The principle behind the usage of guiding metaphors can add to the socio-organizational processes in the development team. Thus, the project managers have a powerful concept tool[5] that enables guidance on an abstract level.

With the organization of the development team as multi-agent system we have achieved agent-oriented software engineering (AOSE) in two ways. In the original meaning of the term *AOSE* the software system is the objective. In our approach also the development team is oriented (guided) by the multi-agent system metaphor.

Acknowledgements. I thank my colleagues Till Dörges, Michael Duvigneau, Michael Köhler, Daniel Moldt, Christine Reese, Heiko Rölke and Matthias Wester-Ebbinghaus for their participation in our AOSE projects as well as for the fruitful discussions regarding the *multi-agent system of developers* metaphor.

References

1. Wooldridge, M., Jennings, N., Kinny, D.: The Gaia methodology for agent-oriented analysis and design. The International Journal of Autonomous Agents and Multi-Agent Systems 3(3), 285–312 (2000)

---

[5] A tool or concept to guide and organize (or even transmit) one's thoughts. The artificial German term *Denkzeug* [20], a mix of *denken* (to think) and *Werkzeug* (tool), fits better.

2. Zambonelli, F., Jennings, N., Wooldridge, M.: Developing multiagent systems: The Gaia methodology. ACM Transactions on Software Engineering and Methodology 12(3), 317–370 (2003)
3. DeLoach, S.: Engineering organization-based multiagent systems. In: Garcia, A., Choren, R., Lucena, C., Giorgini, P., Holvoet, T., Romanovsky, A. (eds.) Software Engineering for Multi-Agent Systems IV. LNCS, vol. 3914, pp. 109–125. Springer, Heidelberg (2006)
4. Padgham, L., Winikoff, M.: Prometheus: A pragmatic methodology for engineering intelligent agents. In: Proceedings of the OOPSLA 2002 Workshop on Agent–Oriented Methodologies, pp. 97–108 (2002)
5. Sudeikat, J., Braubach, L., Pokahr, A., Lamersdorf, W.: Evaluation of agent–oriented software methodologies - examination of the gap between modeling and platform. In: Odell, J.J., Giorgini, P., Müller, J.P. (eds.) AOSE 2004. LNCS, vol. 3382, pp. 126–141. Springer, Heidelberg (2005)
6. Petrie, C.J., Goldmann, S., Raquet, A.: Agent-based project management. In: Veloso, M.M., Wooldridge, M.J. (eds.) Artificial Intelligence Today. LNCS (LNAI), vol. 1600, pp. 339–363. Springer, Heidelberg (1999)
7. Züllighoven, H.: Object-Oriented Construction Handbook. dpunkt Verlag/Co-publication with Morgan-Kaufmann, San Francisco (2004)
8. Lippert, M., Schmolitzky, A., Züllighoven, H.: Metaphor design spaces. In: Marchesi, M., Succi, G. (eds.) XP 2003. LNCS, vol. 2675, pp. 33–40. Springer, Heidelberg (2003)
9. Wikström, K., Rehn, A.:   Playing the live jazz of project management (2002), online http://www.reformingprojectmanagement.com/docs/playing-the-live-jazz-of-Project-management.pdf
10. Mack, J.: Softwareentwicklung als Expedition: Entwicklung eines Leitbildes und einer Vorgehensweise für die professionelle Softwareentwicklung. PhD thesis, Universität Hamburg, Fachbereich Informatik (2001)
11. Wooldridge, M., Jennings, N.R.: Intelligent agents: Theory and practice. Knowledge Engineering Review 10(2), 115–152 (1995)
12. Ferber, J.: Multi-agent Systems: An Introduction to Distributed Artificial Intelligence. Addison-Wesley, Harlow [u.a.] (1999)
13. WfMC: Workflow reference model (2005), http://www.wfmc.org/standards/model.htm
14. Lüde, R.v., Spresny, D., Valk, R.: Sozionik: Modellierung soziologischer Theorie. In: Lüde, R.v., Moldt, D., Valk, R. (eds.) Sozionik: Modellierung soziologischer Theorie. Reihe: Wirtschaft—Arbeit—Technik, vol. 2, pp. 9–45. Lit-Verlag, Münster, Hamburg, London (2003)
15. Köhler, M., Moldt, D., Rölke, H.: Modelling the structure and behaviour of Petri net agents. In: Colom, J.-M., Koutny, M. (eds.) ICATPN 2001. LNCS, vol. 2075, pp. 224–241. Springer, Heidelberg (2001)
16. Rölke, H.: Modellierung von Agenten und Multiagentensystemen—Grundlagen und Anwendungen. Agent Technology—Theory and Applications, vol. 2. Logos Verlag, Berlin (2004)
17. Cabac, L., Moldt, D., Rölke, H.: A proposal for structuring Petri net-based agent interaction protocols. In: van der Aalst, W.M.P., Best, E. (eds.) ICATPN 2003. LNCS, vol. 2679, pp. 102–120. Springer, Heidelberg (2003)

18. Kummer, O., Wienberg, F., Duvigneau, M.: Renew—The Reference Net Workshop. Release 2.1. (March 2007), http://www.renew.de
19. Köhler, M., Rölke, H.: Modelling mobility and mobile agents using nets within nets. In: Moldt, D. (ed.) MOCA'02. Proceedings of the Workshop on Modelling of Objects, Components, and Agents. Computer Science Department, Aarhus University (2002)
20. Moldt, D.: Petrinetze als DENKZEUG, Vogt-Kölln Str. 30, 22527 Hamburg, Universität Hamburg, Fachbereich Informatik, pp. 51–70 (August 2005)

Model Transformation for Model Driven Development of Semantic Web Enabled Multi-Agent Systems

Geylani Kardas[1], Arda Goknil[2], Oguz Dikenelli[3], and N. Yasemin Topaloglu[3]

[1] Ege University, International Computer Institute, 35100 Bornova, Izmir, Turkey
geylani.kardas@ege.edu.tr
[2] Software Engineering Group, University of Twente, 7500 AE, Enschede, The Netherlands
a.goknil@ewi.utwente.nl
[3] Ege University, Department of Computer Engineering, 35100 Bornova, Izmir, Turkey
{oguz.dikenelli, yasemin.topaloglu}@ege.edu.tr

Abstract. Model Driven Development (MDD) provides an infrastructure that simplifies Multi-agent System (MAS) development by increasing the abstraction level. In addition to defining models, transformation process for those models is also crucial in MDD. On the other hand, MAS modeling should also take care of emerging requirements of MAS deployment on the Semantic Web environment. Hence, in this paper we propose a model transformation process for MDD of Semantic Web enabled MASs. We first define source and target models for the transformation regarding the modeling of interactions between agents and semantic web services and then grant mappings between these source and model entities to derive transformation rules and constraints. Finally we realize the whole transformation for a real MAS framework by using a well-known model transformation language named ATL.

1 Introduction

The design and implementation of Multi-agent Systems (MAS) becomes more complex and hard to implement when new requirements and interactions for new agent environments such as Semantic Web [2] are considered. To work in a higher abstraction level is of critical importance for the development of MASs since it is almost impossible to observe code level details of MAS due to their internal complexity, distributedness and openness.

Model Driven Development (MDD) [20], which aims to change the focus of software development from code to models, provides an infrastructure that simplifies the development of future's MASs. Such MDD application increases the abstraction level in MAS development. Although there are ongoing efforts in model driven MAS development, a significant deficiency exists in current studies when we consider modeling of agent systems working on Semantic Web environment. The main challenge in here is to provide new entities and define their relations with the traditional MAS entities for MAS metamodels pertaining to the Semantic Web and employ those new metamodels in a neatly presented model transformation process within the scope of MDD.

P. Petta et al. (Eds.): MATES 2007, LNAI 4687, pp. 13–24, 2007.

In our previous work, we first provided a conceptual MAS architecture [13] in which autonomous agents can also evaluate semantic data and collaborate with semantically defined entities such as semantic web services by using content languages and then we derived entities of a MAS metamodel from the introduced architecture and defined their relations [14]. This new MAS metamodel paves the way for MDD of Semantic Web enabled agent systems in our studies by presenting an alternative for platform independent metamodel of such agent systems.

Definition of such a model is a prerequisite to conduct model transformation which is the key activity in MDD. Hence in this paper, we present a model transformation process for MDD of agent systems working on Semantic Web. A model conforming to above MAS metamodel is transformed into another model conforming to model of a real agent platform within the introduced process. The designed Semantic Web enabled MAS can be implemented on this real platform by applying the transformation. To accomplish this, we first define source and target metamodels for the transformation and then provide mappings between entities of these models to derive transformation rules and constraints. Finally we realize the whole transformation by using a pretty known model transformation language.

The paper is organized as follows: In Sect. 2, we briefly discuss how MDD can be applied for the development of the Semantic Web enabled agent systems. Models for the related transformation are introduced in Sect. 3. Application of the model transformation is discussed in Sect. 4. Section 5 covers related work on MDD of agent systems. Conclusion and future work are given in Sect. 6.

2 MDD for Semantic Web Enabled MAS Development

MDD approach considers the models as the main artifacts of software development. We use *Model Driven Architecture (MDA)* [15] which is one of the realizations of MDD to support the relations between platform independent and various platform dependent agent artifacts to develop semantic web agents.

MDA defines several model transformations which are based on the Meta-Object-Facility (MOF) [15] framework. These transformations are structured in a three-layered architecture: *the Computation Independent Model (CIM)*, *the Platform Independent Model (PIM)*, and *the Platform Specific Model (PSM)*. A CIM is a view of a system from the computation independent viewpoint [15]. CIM requirements should be traceable to the PIM and PSM constructs by marking the proper elements in CIM. For instance, although the CIM does not have any information about agents and semantic web services, entities in CIM are marked in an appropriate notation to trace the agents and semantic web services in the PIM of the Semantic Web enabled MAS. The PIM specifies a degree of platform independency to be suitable for use with a number of different platforms of similar type [15]. In our perspective, the PIM of a Semantic Web enabled MAS should define the main entities and interactions which are derived from the above mentioned conceptual architecture. Finally, PSM combines PIM with additional details of the platform implementation. The platform independent entities in PIM of semantic web agents are transformed to PSM of an implemented Semantic Web enabled agent framework like SEAGENT [3]. The flexible part of this approach is that the PIM enables to generate different PSMs of

Semantic Web enabled agent frameworks automatically. These PSMs can be considered as the realizations of our conceptual architecture.

The development process and the MOF based transformations between the MDA models are given in Fig. 1. In the depicted transformation pattern, a source model *sm* is transformed into a target model *tgm*. The transformation is driven by a transformation definition written in a transformation language [5] [12]. The source model, the target model and the transformation definition conform to their metamodels *SMM*, *TgMM* and *TMM* respectively. The transformations defined from CIM to PIM and PIM to PSM use the metamodels of CIMs, PIMs and PSMs for source and target metamodels in the transformation pattern.

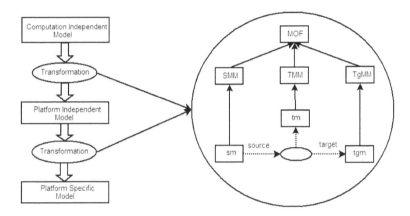

Fig. 1. Transformation Steps in MDA

We applied the transformation mechanism depicted in Fig. 1 for models conforming to our Semantic Web enabled agent metamodel [14] and SEAGENT [3] model respectively. Due to space limitations, the whole transformation process couldn't be discussed in this paper. However, we believe that interaction between semantic agents and semantic web services is crucial for development of such MASs. Hence, rest of the paper describes modeling of this interaction and whole process of the related transformation.

3 Models for Agent – Semantic Web Service Interaction

Model transformation requires syntactical and semantic definitions of models which are provided by metamodels. We introduced a metamodel for Semantic Web enabled MASs in [14] which extends FIPA Modeling TC's Agent Class Superstructure Metamodel (ACSM) [16]. By extending ACSM, we do not need to re-define basic entities of the agent domain. Also, ACSM models assignment of agents to roles by taking into consideration of group context. Therefore, extending ACSM clarifies relatively blurred associations between "Semantic Organization", "Semantic Agent" and "Role" concepts in our metamodel by appropriate inclusion of ACSM's Agent Role Assignment entity. However, ACSM extension is not sufficient and we provide new constructs for our metamodel by extending UML 2.0 Superstructure and Ontology UML Profile [4].

Ontology entities of the metamodel are defined as extensions of the *Ontology* element of the Ontology UML Profile (OUP) defined in [4]. OUP captures ontology concepts with properties and relationships and provides a set of UML elements available to use as semantic types in our metamodel. By deriving the semantic concepts from OUP, there will be already-defined UML elements to use as semantic concepts within the metamodel.

The aim of this study is to present model transformation for developing Semantic Web enabled MAS by employing our metamodel so full specification of the model is beyond the scope of this paper. The specification of the complete model can be found in [14]. In here, we discuss on its zoomed part in which the interaction between agents and semantic web services is elaborated.

The metamodel given in Fig. 2 is the PIM which will be our source metamodel during the transformation process. This metamodel provides modeling the agent – service interaction from the point of entity aspect.

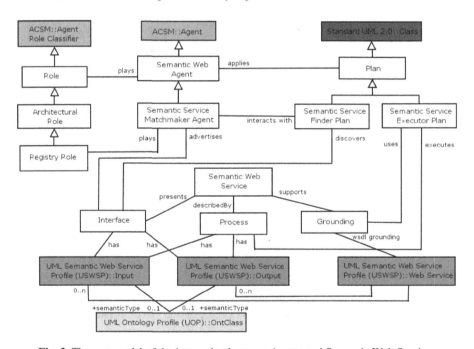

Fig. 2. The metamodel of the interaction between Agents and Semantic Web Services

Semantic Web Agent is an autonomous entity which is capable of interaction with both other agents and semantic web services within the environment. It is a special form of the ACSM's Agent class due to its entity capabilities. It includes new features in addition to Agent classified instance.

The *Role* concept in the metamodel is an extension of Agent Role Classifier due to its classification for roles the semantic agents are capable of playing at a given time.

This conforms to the Agent – Agent Role Classifier association defined in ACSM [16]. In here, we also define its one sub-entity called *Architectural Role*. This role defines a mandatory Semantic Web enabled MAS role that should be played at least one agent inside the platform regardless of the organization context.

Semantic Web Agents have *Plan*s to discover and execute *Semantic Web Service*s dynamically. In order to discover service capabilities, agents need to communicate with a service registry. For this reason, the model includes a specialized agent entity, called *Semantic Service Matchmaker Agent*. This meta-entity represents matchmaker agents which store capability advertisements of semantic web services within a MAS and match those capabilities with service requirements sent by the other platform agents. This agent plays the *Registry Role* which is a specialized Architectural Role.

A *Semantic Web Service* represents any service (except agent services) whose capabilities and interactions are semantically described within a Semantic Web enabled MAS. Each service may be a web service or another service with predefined invocation protocol in real-life implementation. But they should have a semantic web interface to be used by autonomous agents of the platform.

When we consider various semantic web service modeling languages such as OWL-S [21] and WSMO [22], it is clear that services are represented by three semantic documents: *Service Interface*, *Process Model* and *Physical Grounding*. Service Interface is the capability representation of the service in which service inputs, outputs and any other necessary service descriptions are listed. Process Model describes internal composition and execution dynamics of the service. Finally Physical Grounding defines invocation protocol of the web service. These Semantic Web Service components are given in the metamodel with *Interface*, *Process* and *Grounding* entities respectively. Semantic input, output and web service definitions used by those service components are exported from the UML Semantic Web Service Profile proposed in [8].

Semantic Web Agents have two consecutive plans to interact with Semantic Web Services. *Semantic Service Finder Plan* is a Plan in which discovery of candidate semantic web services takes place. During this plan execution, the agent communicates with the service matchmaker of the platform to determine proper semantic services. After service discovery, the agent applies the *Semantic Service Executor Plan* in order to execute appropriate semantic web services. Process model and grounding mechanism of the service are used within the plan.

The input model of our transformation process is an instance model which conforms to the above mentioned interaction metamodel. This source model for the transformation is given in Fig. 3. The model depicts the interaction between a Hotel Client Agent and a Reservation Service within a MAS working in Tourism domain. The client agent is a Semantic Web Agent which reserves hotel rooms on behalf of its human users. During its task execution, it needs to interact with a semantic web service called Reservation Composite Service. Matchmaker Agent is the service matcher of the related agent platform. Hotel Client Agent determines appropriate semantic service by asking the Matchmaker Agent and interacts with the determined semantic service by executing service's process description and using service's grounding.

To realize MDD of the MAS defined in Fig. 3, we employ the transformation between PIM and PSM shown in Fig. 1. We can facilitate implementation of the specified agent system in various Semantic Web enabled agent development

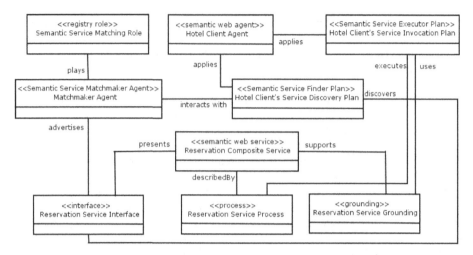

Fig. 3. An instance model for the agent – service interaction within a MAS working in Tourism domain. The model is used in the transformation process as the source model.

environments such as SEAGENT [3] if we provide metamodels of the corresponding frameworks as platform specific metamodels and define transformation rules.

In this study, our target platform for platform specific models is the SEAGENT framework. SEAGENT is implemented in Java and provides libraries to develop Semantic Web enabled MASs also in Java. Java classes and objects are concrete realizations of our PIM entities in the platform specific level and target (output) model of the transformation will be a Java model (composed of SEAGENT classes and their associations). This Java model conforms to the metamodel of Java [9].

Table 1. Mappings between the metamodel entities and SEAGENT classes

Metamodel Entity	SEAGENT Class	Explanation
Role Semantic Web Agent (SWA)	Agent	Both Role and SWA in the metamodel corresponds to the Agent in SEAGENT.
Registry Role Semantic Service Matchmaker Agent (SSMA)	Semantic_Service_Matcher (SSM)	Both Registry Role and SSMA in the metamodel corresponds to the SSM in SEAGENT.
Semantic Service Finder Plan	DiscoverCandidateService	Corresponding SEAGENT entities are Behaviour classes.
Semantic Service Executor Plan	EnactService	
Semantic Web Service	OWL-S_Service	In SEAGENT, capabilities and process models of semantic web services are defined by using OWL-S markup language.
Interface	OWL-S_Profile	
Process	OWL-S_Process	
Grounding	OWL-S_Grounding	

The crucial part of the transformation process is to define transformation rules in a predefined transformation language. Those rules are based on the mappings between source and target model entities. The rules also include formal representation of mapping constraints which are applied during transformation. In our case, we have to define mappings between entities of the interaction metamodel and SEAGENT framework. In Table 1, some of the entity mappings are listed. After execution of the whole transformation process, we achieved platform specific model of our MAS. This output (target) model is given at the end of the following section (in Fig. 4).

4 Application of the Transformation Using ATL

We implemented the whole transformation process discussed in this study by using ATLAS INRIA & LINA research group's ATL (Atlas Transformation Language) [12]. ATL is a widely accepted model transformation language, specified as both a metamodel and a textual concrete syntax. It also provides a development environment as a plugin in Eclipse [6]. These advantages cause us to prefer ATL.

Referring to transformation process depicted in Fig. 1, transformation metamodel (TMM) is ATL and source, target and transformation metamodels conform to Ecore metametamodel [6] in our case. Our source model (SM) is the platform independent model given in Fig. 3 which comforms to metamodel given in Fig. 2. Our target metamodel is the metamodel of the Java language [9].

In order to use ATL engine, we need to prepare Eclipse Modeling Framework (EMF) encodings -ecore files- of both metamodels (SMM and TgMM). EMF provides its own file format (.ecore) for model and metamodel encoding. However manual edition of Ecore metamodels is particularly difficult with EMF. In order to make this common kind of editions easier, the ATL Development Tools (ADT) include a simple textual notation dedicated to metamodel edition: the Kernel MetaMetaModel (KM3) [11]. This textual notation eases the edition of metamodels. Once edited, KM3 metamodels can be injected into Ecore format using ADT integrated injectors. More information about such injections can be found in [11].

Due to space limitations, it is impossible to give whole KM3 representations and ATL rule definitions of our implementation. To give some flavor of the implementation in here, we describe transformation of the Semantic Web Agent source entity into its corresponding entity in Java based SEAGENT framework.

Following is the part of the KM3 file in which Semantic Web Agent is represented with its associations for Role and Plan entities:

```
class SemanticWebAgent {
      attribute name : String;
      reference apply[0-*] : Plan oppositeOf appliedBy;
      reference play[0-*] : Role oppositeOf playedBy;            }
class Role {
      attribute name : String;
      reference playedBy[0-*] : SemanticWebAgent oppositeOf play;   }
class Plan {
      attribute name : String;
      reference appliedBy [0-*] : SemanticWebAgent oppositeOf apply; }
```

According to the entity mappings, heuristic rules for the transformation should be given in ATL. Each ATL rule for the transformation defines a source model element in its source part and has the full definition of constraints to query the whole source pattern in the model. For instance, the Semantic Web Agent class in the source part of SemanticWebAgent2Agent rule needs the full constraint definition of the source pattern to match in the model because the constraint part requires constraints of other source pattern elements related to the Semantic Web Agent class to bind the appropriate model element. The helper rules are required in the constraint part to define the relationships between the pattern elements. Following is the `SemanticWebAgent2Agent` ATL rule:

```
1 rule SemanticWebAgent2Agent {
2       from ag: Agent!SemanticWebAgent(
3                 ag.partofPatternforWebAgent   )
4       to c:JAVA!Class (
5             name<- ag.name,
6             associatedClass<-Sequence{ag.executorPlans, ag.finderPlans} )
7 }
```

In rule `SemanticWebAgent2Agent`, we need to call helper rule for the relations of the SemanticWebAgent Class with its role and plan attributes. We also use another rule in order to realize mapping of the SemanticWebAgent class into its corresponding target model entity (a JAVA class in here). The same helper rules and constraint repetitions may be required for other rules in the transformation. Hence this kind of rule decomposition makes the definitions easier. The helper `partofPatternforWebAgent` called in line 3 of the rule `SemanticWebAgent2Agent` is given below:

```
1 helper context Agent!SemanticWebAgent def:
2   partofPatternforWebAgent : Boolean =
3     if not self.oclIsTypeOf(Agent!SemanticServiceMatchmakerAgent)
4       and not self.play.oclIsTypeOf(Agent!RegistryRole)
5       and self.apply->
6             select(p|p.oclIsTypeOf(Agent!SemanticServiceExecutorPlan))->
7                 forAll(p|p.execute.owner = p.use.owner)
8       and self.apply->
9             select(p|p.oclIsTypeOf(Agent!SemanticServiceFinderPlan))->
10                forAll(p|p.interact.advertise->
11                        exists(intfc|intfc=p.discover))
12      then true
13      else false
14   endif;
```

The helpers correspond to the constraint part of the related rules. There are two types of helper in our transformations. The first type helpers like `partofPatternforWebAgent` are used to check if the model element is the part of the pattern or not. The second type helpers (e.g. `finderPlans` and `executorPlans`) are used to select the appropriate elements for the associations between target elements within the transformation. Following is the `finderPlans` helper which is called in line 6 of the rule `SemanticWebAgent2Agent`:

```
1 helper context Agent!SemanticWebAgent def:
2   finderPlans : Sequence(Agent!SemanticServiceFinderPlan) =
3     self.apply->select(fp|fp.oclIsTypeOf(
4     Agent!SemanticServiceFinderPlan))->select(fndpln|
5        fndpln.appliedBy->forAll(agnt| not
6          agnt.oclIsTypeOf(Agent!SemanticServiceMatchmakerAgent)
7          and not agnt.play.oclIsTypeOf(Agent!RegistryRole))
8          and fndpln.interact.play.oclIsTypeOf(Agent!RegistryRole)
9          and fndpln.interact.advertise->
10               exists(intfc|intfc.discoveredBy=fndpln)
11         and fndpln.discover.advertisedBy.interactedBy=fndpln);
```

The ecore model conforming to source metamodel includes the following model instance in which the Semantic Web Agent called "Hotel Client Agent" is defined. References to the other instances are omitted.

```
<xmi:XMI xmi:version="2.0" xmlns:xmi="http://www.omg.org/XMI" xmlns="Agent">
    <SemanticWebAgent name="Hotel Client Agent" apply="#/2 #/3" play="#/1" />
    <Role name="Hotel Client Role" playedBy="#/0" />
    <SemanticServiceFinderPlan name="Hotel Client's Service Discovery Plan"
                               appliedBy="#/0" interact="..." discover="..." />
    <SemanticServiceExecutorPlan name="Hotel Client's Service Invocation Plan"
                               appliedBy="#/0" execute="..." use="..." />
</xmi:XMI>
```

During the transformation process, the ATL engine applies the above rule (SemanticWebAgent2Agent) in order to transform "Hotel Client Agent" into a SEAGENT Agent class. The ecore representation of this obtained target instance is given below. References to the other instances are omitted again:

```
<xmi:XMI xmi:version="2.0" xmlns:xmi="http://www.omg.org/XMI" xmlns="JAVA">
<Class name="Hotel Client Agent" associatedClass="/1 /2"/>
<Class name="Hotel Client's Service Discovery Plan" superClass=".." associatedClass="/0"/>
<Class name="Hotel Client's Service Invocation Plan" superClass=".." associatedClass="/0"/>
</xmi:XMI>
```

After execution of the whole process in ATL environment, we obtained the platform specific (SEAGENT) model of the tourism MAS given in Fig. 4. Each entity of the model is a Java class. Upper part of the model includes the SEAGENT planner components. In the SEAGENT framework, agents execute their tasks according to Hierarchical Task Networks (HTN) [23]. As a requirement of HTN, tasks might be either complex (called behaviors) or primitive (called actions). Tasks have a name describing what they are supposed to do and have zero or more provisions (information needs) and outcomes (execution results). Classes for the tourism MAS take place beneath the agent plan components. Model includes the Hotel_Client_Agent that discovers hotel reservation services with semantic capability interfaces according to its Hotel_Client_Service_Discovery_Plan. It communicates with the Matchmaker_Agent of the system during execution of this plan. Discovery plan extends DiscoverCandidateService behavior. This behavior is the corresponding entity for the "Semantic Service Finder Plan" meta-entity given in our PIM. Similarly, agent's service execution plan (Hotel_Client_Service_Invocation_Plan) is an EnactService behavior and is the counterpart of our PIM's "Semantic Service Executor Plan" meta-entity. Semantic web services are OWL-S services in SEAGENT. Hence, our reservation service is a subclass of OWL_S_Service class after the transformation as expected.

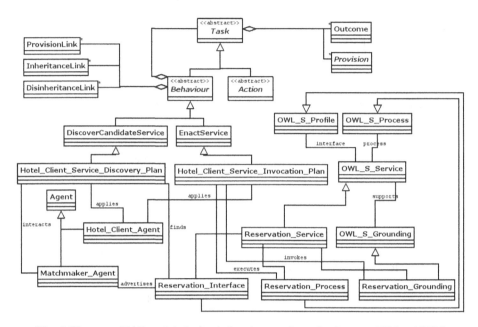

Fig. 4. The target MAS model obtained after the transformation between PIM and PSM

5   Related Work

Recently, model driven approaches have been recognized and become one of the major research topics in agent oriented software engineering (AOSE) community. As briefly mentioned below, some of the studies intend to apply the whole MDD process for MAS development while some of them only utilize either metamodels or model transformation as needed. Conceptual MDA definitions and study on MDA based MAS research directions are also discussed in some of the studies e.g. [1] [7]. Bauer and Odell discuss the use of UML 2.0 and MDA for agent-based systems in [1]. They also discuss which aspects of a MAS could be considered at CIM and PIM. The Cougaar MDA discussed in [7] provides a higher application composition for agent systems by elevating the composition level from individual components to domain level model specifications in order to generate software artifacts. Jayatilleke et al. [10] provide a toolkit for their conceptual framework of domain independent component types in order to make their approach consistent with MDD and use agent models to generate executable codes.

On the other hand, the study defined in [19] is a good example that applies the transformation process of MDA which is depicted in Fig. 1. In that study, Perini and Susi [19] use TEFKAT model transformation language [5] to implement the transformation process in automating conversions from their methodology structures to UML models. In [17], Pavon and his friends reformulate their agent-oriented methodology called INGENIAS in terms of the Model Driven Development paradigm. This reformulation increases the relevance of the model creation, definition and transformation in the context of multi-agent systems. A similar MAS methodology revision is discussed in [18]. Ideas and standards from MDA are adopted both in refining the modeling process algorithm and building tools within this study.

Regarding all of the above studies, it can be said that current application of the MDD on MAS development is in its preliminary phase. Neither a complete MDD process nor a common MAS metamodel has been developed. On the other hand, Semantic Web [2] technology and its required constructs on MASs are not supported within those studies. We believe this shortage in question is crucial when development of future MASs is considered. Therefore providing a Semantic Web enabled MDD process for MAS development is the key difference between our study and those previous studies.

6 Conclusion and Future Work

A model transformation process for the model driven development of Semantic Web enabled MASs is discussed in this paper. The study in here presents description of a whole process in which the source and the target metamodels, entity mappings and the implementation of the transformation for a real MAS framework are all included.

In fact, our aim is to enhance this study by providing code generation (at least in template level) for Semantic Web enabled MAS implementations. That means a MAS developer just creates a model of the MAS conforming to the platform independent model and then chooses the desired physical implementation environment (e.g. SEAGENT) for the system. Finally, our tool generates template codes for the developer by using target environment's metamodel, model and transformations. The developer completes the software for the full deployment of the system. Therefore, in addition to improvement studies on model transformation (e.g. elaborating mappings in entity attribute level, clarifying input/output and precondition/effect representations of semantic web service entities on the model), we are currently working on code generation from target models we gained. We intend to employ a source code generator such as JET (Java Emitter Templates) Engine [6] in order to generate platform specific MAS software as the final product of our MDD process.

References

[1] Bauer, B., Odell, J.: UML 2.0 and Agents: How to Build Agent-based Systems with the New UML Standard. Journal of Engineering Applications of Artificial Intelligence 18(2), 141–157 (2005)
[2] Berners-Lee, T., Hendler, J., Lassila, O.: The Semantic Web. Scientific American 284(5), 34–43 (2001)
[3] Dikenelli, O., Erdur, R.C., Kardas, G., Gümüs, Ö., Seylan, I., Gürcan, Ö., Tiryaki, A.M., Ekinci, E.E.: Developing Multi Agent Systems on Semantic Web Environment using SEAGENT Platform. In: Dikenelli, O., Gleizes, M.-P., Ricci, A. (eds.) ESAW 2005. LNCS (LNAI), vol. 3963, pp. 1–13. Springer, Heidelberg (2006)
[4] Djuric, D.: MDA-based Ontology Infrastructure. International Journal on Computer Science and Information Systems 1(1), 91–116 (2004)

[5] Duddy, K., Gerber, A., Lawley, M.: Model Transformation: A declarative, reusable patterns approach. In: 7th International Enterprise Distributed Object Computing Conference, pp. 174–185. IEEE Computer Society Press, Los Alamitos (2003)

[6] Eclipse Open Development Platform, http://www.eclipse.org

[7] Gracanin, D., Singh, H.L., Bohner, S.A., Hinchey, M.G.: Model-Driven Architecture for Agent-Based Systems. In: Hinchey, M.G., Rash, J.L., Truszkowski, W.F., Rouff, C.A. (eds.) FAABS 2004. LNCS (LNAI), vol. 3228, pp. 249–261. Springer, Heidelberg (2004)

[8] Gronmo, R., Jaeger, M.C., Hoff, H.: Transformations between UML and OWL-S. In: Hartman, A., Kreische, D. (eds.) ECMDA-FA 2005. LNCS, vol. 3748, pp. 269–283. Springer, Heidelberg (2005)

[9] Java Metamodel, http://www.eclipse.org/gmt/am3/zoos/atlanticUMLZoo/#JAVA

[10] Jayatilleke, G.B., Padgham, L., Winikoff, M.: A Model Driven Development Toolkit for Domain Experts to Modify Agent Based Systems. In: Padgham, L., Zambonelli, F. (eds.) AOSE VII / AOSE 2006. LNCS, vol. 4405, Springer, Heidelberg (2007)

[11] Jouault, F., Bezivin, J.: KM3: A DSL for Metamodel Specification. In: Gorrieri, R., Wehrheim, H. (eds.) FMOODS 2006. LNCS, vol. 4037, pp. 171–185. Springer, Heidelberg (2006)

[12] Jouault, F., Kurtev, I.: Transforming Models with ATL. In: Bruel, J.-M. (ed.) MoDELS 2005. LNCS, vol. 3844, pp. 128–138. Springer, Heidelberg (2006)

[13] Kardas, G., Goknil, A., Dikenelli, O., Topaloglu, N.Y.: Metamodeling of Semantic Web Enabled Multiagent Systems. In: Weyns, D., Holvoet, T. (eds.) Multiagent Systems and Software Architecture, Proceedings of the Special Track at Net.ObjectDays, Erfurt, Germany, September 19, 2006, pp. 79–86. Katholieke Universiteit Leuven, Belgium (2006)

[14] Kardas, G., Goknil, A., Dikenelli, O., Topaloglu, N.Y.: Modeling the Interaction between Semantic Agents and Semantic Web Services using MDA Approach. In: O'Hare, G., et al. (eds.) ESAW 2006. LNCS (LNAI), vol. 4457, pp. 209–228. Springer, Heidelberg (2007)

[15] OMG Specifications, http://www.omg.org

[16] Odell, J., Levy, R., Nodine M.: FIPA Modeling TC: Agent Class Superstructure Metamodel, http://www.omg.org/docs/agent/04-12-02.pdf

[17] Pavon, J., Gomez, J., Fuentes, R.: Model Driven Development of Multi-Agent Systems. In: Rensink, A., Warmer, J. (eds.) ECMDA-FA 2006. LNCS, vol. 4066, pp. 284–298. Springer, Heidelberg (2006)

[18] Penserini, L., Perini, A., Susi, A., Mylopoulos, J.: From Stakeholder Intentions to Software Agent Implementations. In: Dubois, E., Pohl, K. (eds.) CAiSE 2006. LNCS, vol. 4001, pp. 465–479. Springer, Heidelberg (2006)

[19] Perini, A., Susi, A.: Automating Model Transformations in Agent-Oriented Modeling. In: Müller, J.P., Zambonelli, F. (eds.) AOSE 2005. LNCS, vol. 3950, pp. 167–178. Springer, Heidelberg (2006)

[20] Selic, B.: The Pragmatics of Model-Driven Development. IEEE Software 20(1), 19–25 (2003)

[21] The Semantic Markup for Web Services (OWL-S), http://www.daml.org/services/owl-s

[22] Web Service Modeling Ontology, http://www.wsmo.org/

[23] Williamson, M., Decker, K., Sycara, K.: Unified Information and Control Flow in Hierarchical Task Networks. In: Baral, C. (ed.) Theories of Action, Planning, and Robot Control: Bridging the Gap. Papers from the AAAI Workshop, Technical Report WS-96-07, pp. 142–150. AAAI Press, Menlo Park CA (1996)

SmartResource Platform and Semantic Agent Programming Language (S-APL)

Artem Katasonov and Vagan Terziyan

Agora Center, University of Jyväskylä
P.O. Box 35, FIN-40014, Jyväskylä, Finland
artem.katasonov@jyu.fi, vagan@it.jyu.fi

Abstract. Although the flexibility of agent interactions has many advantages when it comes to engineering a complex system, the downside is that it leads to certain unpredictability of the run-time system. Literature sketches two major directions for search for a solution: social-level characterization of agent systems and ontological approaches to inter-agent coordination. Especially the latter direction is not yet studied much by the scientific community. This paper describes our vision and the present state of the SmartResource Platform. The main distinctive features of the platform are externalization of behavior prescriptions, i.e. agents access them from organizational repositories, and utilization of the RDF-based Semantic Agent Programming Language (S-APL), instead of common Prolog-like languages.

1 Introduction

When it comes to developing complex, distributed software-based systems, the agent-based approach was advocated to be a well suited one [1]. From the implementation point of view, agents are a next step in the evolution of software engineering approaches and programming languages, the step following the trend towards increasing degrees of localization and encapsulation in the basic building blocks of the programming models [2]. After the structures, e.g., in C (localizing data), and objects, e.g., in C++ and Java (localizing, in addition, code, i.e. an entity's behavior), agents follow by localizing their *purpose*, the thread of control and action selection.

The actual benefit of the agent-oriented approach arises from the fact that the notion of an agent is also appropriate as a basis for the analysis of the problem to be solved by the system. Many processes in the world can be conceptualized using an agent metaphor; the result is either a single agent (or cognitive) description or a multi-agent (or social) description [3]. Jennings [1] argued that agent-oriented decompositions (according to the purpose of elements) are an effective way of partitioning the problem space of a complex system, that the key abstractions of the agent-oriented mindset are a natural means of modeling complex systems, and that the agent-oriented philosophy for modeling and managing organizational relationships is appropriate for dealing with the dependencies and interactions that exist in complex systems.

The problem of crossing the boundary from the domain (problem) world to the machine (solution) world is widely recognized as a major issue in software and systems

P. Petta et al. (Eds.): MATES 2007, LNAI 4687, pp. 25–36, 2007.

engineering. Therefore, when it comes to designing software, the most powerful abstractions are those that minimize the semantic distance between the units of analysis that are intuitively used to conceptualize the problem and the constructs present in the solution paradigm [2]. A possibility to have the same concept, i.e. agent, as the central one in both the problem analysis and the solution design and implementation can make it much easier to design a good solution and to handle complexity. In contrast, e.g. the object-oriented approach has its conceptual basis determined by the underlying machine architecture, i.e. it is founded on implementation-level ontological primitives such as object, method, invocation, etc. Given that the early stages of software development are necessarily based on intentional concepts such as stakeholders, goals, plans, etc, there is an unavoidable gap that needs to be bridged. [4] even claimed that the agent-oriented programming paradigm is *the only* programming paradigm that can gracefully and seamlessly integrate the intentional models of early development phases with implementation and run-time phases. In a sense, agent-oriented approach postpones the transition from the domain concepts to the machine concepts until the stage of the design and implementation of individual agents (given that those are still to be implemented in an object-oriented programming language).

Although the flexibility of agent interactions has many advantages when it comes to *engineering* complex systems, the downside is that it leads to *unpredictability in the run time* system; as agents are autonomous, the patterns and the effects of their interactions are uncertain [2]. This raises a need for effective coordination, cooperation, and negotiation mechanisms. (Those are in principle distinct, but the word "coordination" is often used as a general one encompassing all three; so for the sake of brevity we will use it like that too.) Jennings [2] discussed that it is common in specific systems and applications to circumvent these difficulties, i.e. to reduce the system's unpredictability, by using interaction protocols whose properties can be formally analyzed, by adopting rigid and preset organizational structures, and/or by limiting the nature and the scope of the agent interplay. However, Jennings asserted that these restrictions also limit the power of the agent-based approach; thus, *in order to realize its full potential some longer term solutions are required.* Emergence of such a longer term solution that would allow flexible yet predictable operation of agent systems seems to be a prerequisite for wide-scale adoption of the agent-oriented approach.

The available literature sketches two major directions of search for such a solution:

- D1: *Social level* characterization of agent-based systems. E.g. [2] stressed the need for a better understanding of the impact of sociality and organizational context on an individual's behavior and of the symbiotic link between the behavior of the individual agents and that of the overall system.
- D2: *Ontological* approaches to coordination. E.g. [5] asserted a need for common vocabulary for coordination, with a precise semantics, to enable agents to communicate their intentions with respect to future activities and resource utilization and get them to reason about coordination at run time. Also [6] put as an issue to resolve the question about how to enable individual agents to represent and reason about the actions, plans, and knowledge of other agents to coordinate with them.

Recently, some progress has been made with respect to D1, resulting, e.g., in elaboration of the concept of a *role* that an agent can play in an organization (see Sect. 2).

However, with respect to D2 very little has been done. Bosse and Treur [3] discussed that the agent perspective entails a distinction between the following different types of ontologies: an ontology for internal mental properties of the agent A, MentOnt(A), for properties of the agent's (physical) body, BodyOnt(A), for properties of the (sensory or communication) input, InOnt(A), for properties of the (action or communication) output, OutOnt(A), of the agent, and for properties of the external world, ExtOnt(A). Using this distinction, we could describe the state of the art as following. The work on explicitly described ontologies was almost exclusively concerned with ExtOnt(A), i.e. the *domain ontologies*. MentOnt(A) comes for free when adopting a certain agent's internal architecture, such as Beliefs-Desires-Intentions (BDI) [7]. Also, the communication parts of InOnt(A) and OutOnt(A) come for free when adopting a certain communication language, such as FIPA's ACL. However, BodyOnt(A), i.e. the perceptors and actuators the agent has, sensory part of InOnt(A), i.e. the agent's perception patterns, and action part of OutOnt(A), e.g. the agent's acting patterns, are not usually treated. However, sharing these ontologies is a necessary precondition for agents' awareness of each other's actions, i.e. for D2. Already referred to article by [5] is one of the first endeavors into this direction, which however only introduced and analyzed some of the relevant concepts, such as resource, activity, etc.

In our work, we attempt to provide a solution advancing into both D1 and (especially) D2 and somewhat integrating both. This paper describes the present state of our SmartResource Platform and the central to it Semantic Agent Programming Language (S-APL). The rest of the paper is structured as follows. Section 2 presents some basic thinking leading to our approach and comments on the related work. Section 3 describes the architecture of the SmartResource Platform, while Sect. 4 describes S-APL. Finally, Sect. 5 concludes the paper.

2   Motivation and Related Work

On the landscape of research in agent-based systems, we can identify two somewhat independent streams of research, each with its own limitations. The first stream is the research in multi-agent systems (MAS); the second stream is the research in agents' internal architectures and approaches to implementation.

Researchers in MAS have contributed with, among others, various methodologies for designing MAS, such as Gaia [8], TROPOS [4], and OMNI [9]. For example, OMNI (which seems to be the most advanced with respect to D1) elaborates on the organizational context of a MAS, defines the relationship between organizational roles and agents enacting those roles, discusses how organizational norms, values and rules are supposed to govern the organization's behavior and thus to put restrictions on individual agents' behaviors. However, OMNI touches only on a very abstract level the question about how the individual agents will be implemented or even function; the agents are treated as rather atoms. One reason is that it is (reasonably) assumed that the agent organization's designer may have no direct control over the design of individual agents. The organization designer develops the rules to be followed and enforcing policies and entities, such as "police" agents, while development of other agents is done by external people or companies. One of few concrete implementation requirements mentioned in

OMNI is that a rule interpreter must be created that any agent entering the organization will incorporate, somehow. The OMNI framework also includes explicitly the ontological dimension, which is restricted, however, to a domain ontology only (see Sect. 1), and thus does not provide much new with respect to D2.

The other stream of research, on individual agents, has contributed e.g. with well-known BDI architecture, and introduced *agent-oriented programming* [10] along with several *agent programming languages* (APL) such as AGENT-0 [10], AgentSpeak(L) [11], 3APL [12] and ALPHA [13]. All of those are declarative languages and based on the first-order logic of n-ary predicates. For example, an agent program in ALPHA consists of declarations of the beliefs and goals of that agent and declaration of a set of rules, including belief rules (generating new beliefs based on existing ones), reactive rules (invoking some actions immediately) and commitment rules (adopting a commitment to invoke an action). Perceptors (perceiving environment and generating new beliefs) and actuators (implementing the actions to be invoked) are then pieces of external code, in Java. As discussed in Sect. 1, agent-oriented approach postpones the transition from the domain concepts to the machine concepts until the stage of the design and implementation of individual agents. The advantage of using an APL is that the transition is postponed even further, until the implementation of particular perceptors and actuators.

This advantage seems to be, however, the only one that is considered. We did not encounter in literature approaches that would extend the role of APL code beyond the development stage. APL code is assumed to be written by the developer of an agent and either compiled into an executable program or interpreted in run-time but remaining an agent's intrinsic and static property. APL code is not assumed to ever come from outside of the agent in run-time, neither shared with other agents in any way.

Such export and sharing of APL code would, however, probably make sense in the light of findings from the field of MAS, and also in the light of D2. Methodologies like OMNI describe an organizational role with a set of rules, and an APL is a rule-based language. So, using an APL for specifying a role sounds as a natural way to proceed. The difference is that APL code corresponding to a role should naturally be a property of and controlled by the organization, and accessed by the agents' enacting the role potentially even in the run-time. Run-time access would also enable the organization to update the role code if needed.

The second natural idea is that the agents may access a role's APL code not only in order to enact that role, but also in order to coordinate with the agents playing that role. As one option, an agent can send to another agent a part of its APL code to communicate its intentions with respect to future activities (so there is no need for a separate content language). As another option, if a role's code is made public inside the organization, the agents may access it in order to understand how to interact with, or what to expect from, an agent playing that role.

However, when thinking about using the existing APLs in such a manner, there are at least two issues:

- The code in an APL is, roughly speaking, a text. However in complex systems, a description of a role may need to include a huge number of rules and also a great number of beliefs representing the knowledge needed for playing the role. Also, in a case of access of the code by agents that are not going to enact this role, it is likely that they may wish to receive only a relevant part of it, not the whole thing. Therefore, a more efficient, e.g. a database-centric, solution is probably required.

– When APL code is provided by an organization to an agent, or shared between agents, mutual understanding of the meaning of the code is obviously required. While using first-order logic as the basis for an APL assures understanding of the semantics of the rules, the meaning of predicates used in those rules still needs to be consistently understood by all the parties involved. On the other hand, we are unaware of tools allowing unambiguous description of the precise semantics of n-ary predicates.

As a solution to these two issues, we see creating an APL based on the W3C's Resource Description Framework (RDF). RDF uses binary predicates only, i.e. triples (n-ary predicates can be represented nevertheless, of course, using several approaches). For RDF, tools are available for efficient database storage and querying, and also for explicit description of semantics, e.g. using OWL. Our proposition for such an RDF-based APL is the *Semantic Agent Programming Language (S-APL)* that will be described in Sect. 4.

3   SmartResource Platform

The SmartResource Platform is a development framework for creating multi-agent systems. It is built on the top of the Java Agent Development Framework (JADE, see http://jade.tilab.com/), which is a Java implementation of IEEE FIPA specifications. The name of the platform comes from the name of the research project, in which it was developed. In the SmartResource project (see http://www.cs.jyu.fi/ai/OntoGroup/ SmartResource_details.htm), a multi-agent system was seen, first of all, as a middleware providing interoperability of heterogeneous (industrial) resources and making them proactive and in a way smart.

The central to the SmartResource Platform is the architecture of a SmartResource agent depicted in Fig. 1. It can be seen as consisting of three layers: Reusable Atomic Behaviors (RABs), Behavior Models corresponding to different roles the agent plays, and the Behavior Engine. An additional element is the storage for agent's beliefs and goals. The SmartResource Platform uses the RDF data model, i.e. any belief or goal is a subject-predicate-object triple, e.g. "John Loves Mary".

A *reusable atomic behavior (RAB)* is a piece of Java code implementing a reasonably atomic function. RABs can be seen as the agent's perceptors and actuators. As the name implies, RABs are assumed to be reusable across different applications, different agents, different roles and different interaction scenarios. Obviously, RABs need to be parameterizable.

In the SmartResource Platform, the behavior of an agent is defined by the roles it plays in one or several organizations. Some examples of the possible roles: operator's agent, feeder agent, agent of the feeder N3056, fault localization service agent, ABB's fault localization service agent, etc. Obviously, a general role can be played by several agents. On the other hand, one agent can (and usually does) play several roles.

A *behavior model* is a document that is supposed to specify a certain organizational role, and, therefore, there is one-to-one relation between roles and behavior models. In

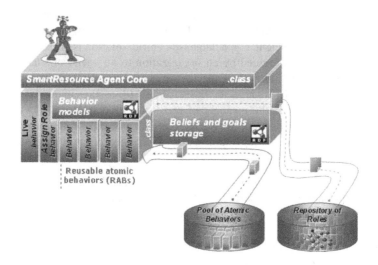

Fig. 1. SmartResource Platform

the SmartResource Platform, behavior models are encoded in a high-level rule-based language, Semantic Agent Programming Language (S-APL). S-APL is based on the RDF data model, i.e. the whole document can be seen as a set of subject-predicate-object triples. A behavior model consists of a set of beliefs representing the knowledge needed for playing the role and a set of behavior rules. Roughly speaking, a behavior rule specifies conditions of (and parameters for) execution of various RABs.

The *behavior engine* is the same for all the SmartResource agents (this of course means that each agent has a copy of it). The behavior engine consists of the agent core and the two core behaviors that we named "Assign Role" and "Live".

The AssignRole behavior processes an S-APL document, loads specified initial beliefs and goals into the beliefs and goals storage, and parses the behavior rules. In addition, it registers the new role with the system Directory Facilitator agent. It is recommended that if a behavior model is to specify the need of interaction with another agent, that agent should be specified by its role, not the name or another unique identifier of a particular agent. Then, DFLookup atomic behavior, provided with the platform, can find with DirectoryFacilitator names of agents playing a particular role. If several agents play the role needed, the behavior model is supposed to include some rules specifying a mechanism of resolving such a situation, e.g. random select, auction, etc. Different such mechanisms can of course be assigned to resolving conflicts with respect to different roles. When an agent is created it has to be given at least one behavior model to start working. Therefore, the agent's core needs to directly engage the AssignRole behavior for the model(s) specified. However, all the later invocations of AssignRole, i.e. adding new roles, are to be specified in some behavior models. Therefore, AssignRole has the duality of being a part of the behavior engine and a RAB in the same time.

The Live behavior implements the run-time cycle of an agent. Roughly speaking, it iterates through all the behavior rules, checks them against existing beliefs and goals, and executes the appropriate rules. Execution of a rule normally includes execution of a RAB and performing a set of additional mental actions, i.e. adding and removing some beliefs. At least at the present stage, if there are several rules that are executable, all of them are executed.

As can be seen from Fig. 1, the SmartResource Platform allows agents to access behavior models from an external repository, which is assumed to be managed by the organization which "hires" the agents to enact those roles. It is done either upon startup of an agent, or later on. Such externalization of behavior models has several advantages:

- Increased flexibility for control and coordination. Namely, the organization can remotely affect the behavior of the agents through modifying the behavior models. Another advantage is that the models can always be kept up-to-date.
- An agent may "learn" how to play a new role in run-time; it does not need to be pre-programmed to do it.
- Inter-agent behavior awareness. How is discussed in Sect. 2, the agents not enacting a particular role can still make some use of the information encoded in its behavior model. One reason is to understand how to interact with, or what to expect from, an agent playing that role.

As can also be seen from Fig. 1, the SmartResource Platform allows agent on-demand access even of RABs. If an agent plays a role, and that role prescribes it to execute an atomic behavior that the agent is missing, the agent can download it from the repository of the organization. In a sense, the organization is able to provide not only instructions what to do, but also the tools enabling doing that. Physically, a RAB is delivered as either .class file or a .zip file (in case when the RAB has several .class files). The obvious additional advantages are:

- An agent may "learn" new behaviors and so enact in a completely new role.
- Agents may have a "light start" with on-demand extension of functionality.

The present version SmartResource Platform provides the behavior model OntologyAgent.rdf along with used in it RAB OntologyLookupBehavior. By starting an agent based on this model, one creates an agent that provides access to both repository of roles and pool of atomic behaviors.

The SmartResource Platform provides the behavior model startup.rdf, which has to be loaded by an agent at startup in order to enable it to remotely access behavior models from an OntologyAgent. For roles specified on startup of the agent, the agent's core takes care of it. In addition, startup.rdf includes the rule for engaging DFLookupBehavior. This rule is obviously needed for resolving the OntologyAgent role. However, it is also enough for any future needs of resolving roles, just a specific convention is to be followed. Figure 2 shows the common process of starting up an agent, when the behavior models are accessed from an OntologyAgent.

The SmartResource Platform provides also the behavior model RABLoader.rdf, which has to be loaded by an agent in order to enable it to remotely access atomic behaviors from an OntologyAgent. It includes rules for requesting, receiving, and (if needed) unzipping the behavior files.

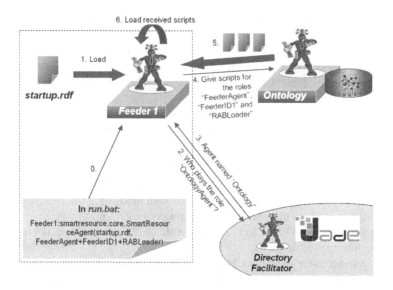

Fig. 2. An agent's start-up

Figure 3 depicts a more complex scenario of auction for selection of a service provider, in this case a fault localization service. The operator's agent behavior model prescribes that in case of several localization services, an auction has to be performed (for other roles, e.g. random select is done). The agent first sends to both localization agents a special request to load the role "AuctionSeller", and then a request to make an offer on, say, price of the service. The agent "Ls1" has loaded the role "AuctionSeller" from the beginning, but the agent "Ls2" did not. So, "Ls2" contacts the OntologyAgent and requests the needed behavior model now. This scenario demonstrates that roles can be loaded also dynamically.

4   Semantic Agent Programming Language (S-APL)

This chapter describes the RDF/XML syntax of the Semantic Agent Programming Language (S-APL) through its three constructs: Belief, Goal and Behavior.

As can be noticed, in defining/referring to beliefs and goals, S-APL does not use the RDF syntax, but has them as literals of the form "subject predicate object". The main reason for this is inability of RDF to restrict the scope of a statement. In RDF, every statement is treated as a global truth. But for describing behavior rules, the statements are specifications of IF and THEN conditions, not facts. Additional reason is a wish to keep S-APL documents concise and human-readable/editable.

In S-APL, all beliefs/goals must be triples. However, at least at present stage, we do not enforce the RDF rule that only the object can be a literal while the subject and the predicate must be URIs. In other words, in S-APL beliefs/goals, the subject and the predicate can be literals as well. When using URIs, a convenient way is to utilize XML's ENTITY construct to simulate the namespaces mechanism (see example below).

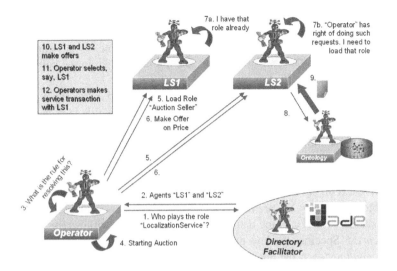

Fig. 3. Scenario: Auction for selection of the service provider

Element <gb:Belief> specifies a belief, with which the agent (in a role) will be initialized. The statement of the belief is given in the <gb:statement> field in the format (whitespace-separated) "subject predicate object". Element <gb:Goal> specifies a goal, with which the agent (in a role) will be initialized. The statement of the belief is also given in the <gb:statement> field.

Element <gb:Behavior> specifies a behavioral rule. The fields trueIf, falseIf, trueIf-GoalAchieved, achievesGoal, and event describe the left side (IF) of the rule, while the rest describe the right side (THEN) of the rule. None of the fields is mandatory. All can appear more than once, with exception of gb:class and gb:event.

- *<gb:trueIf>* Specifies a precondition, i.e. a belief that must be found in the set of the agent's beliefs to make the rule applicable. If several trueIf is given, they all must be found, i.e. they can be seen as connected with AND.
- *<gb:falseIf>* Specifies a negative condition, i.e. such a belief that, when found in the set of the agent's beliefs, makes the rule not applicable. If several falseIf is given, any of them is enough, i.e. they can be seen as connected with OR.
- *<gb:achievesGoal>* Specifies a goal that must be found in the set of the agent's goals to make the rule applicable. In a sense, it specifies an expected rational effect of the rule execution and puts a need for it as a precondition. If several achievesGoal is given, any of them is enough, i.e. they can be seen as connected with OR.
- *<gb:event>* Specifies an interface event (either from GUI or from HTTP server) that must be the current event to make the rule applicable. If a rule has event specified, it will never be executed from the normal Live cycle of the agent, but only from the interface event handling routine.
- *<gb:trueIfGoalAchieved>* Specifies a sub-goal that must be achieved before an applicable rule can be executed. If according to all the other conditions the rule is applicable and only one or more trueIfGoalAchieved is not fulfilled, the agent will

add those to the set of its goals. In other words, the agent will try to eventually execute a rule that is applicable. If several trueIfGoalAchieved is given, they all need to be present in the beliefs to make the rule executable, so they can be seen as connected with AND. Also, all of them that are not present in the beliefs, will be added to the set of goals at once.

- *<gb:addOn<X>>* Specifies a belief that has to be added in the phase <X>. Possible values for <X> are: *Start* – add the belief when the rule is executed, before invoking the actual behavior i.e. RAB, *End* – add the belief when the behavior has ended the execution, *Success* – add when and if the behavior has ended the execution in success, *Fail* – add when and if the behavior has ended the execution in failure.
- *<gb:removeOn<X>>* Specifies a belief that has to be removed in the phase <X>. Possible values for <X> are the same as above. If the specified belief contains "*" and matches several existing beliefs, all matching beliefs will be removed.
- *<gb:class>* Specifies the Java class implementing the behavior.
- *<x:<anything>>* A parameter that is to be passed to the instance of behavior, and has some meaning in the context of that behavior.

Note that explicit adding or removing of goals is not supported. A goal can only be added if it appears in trueIfGoalAchieved of an applicable rule (and not yet in the set of goals), and removed only when either (1) a rule is executed having it among its achievesGoal or (2) in the beginning or a Live cycle, it is found in the set of beliefs.

Note also that an additional implicit condition for whether a rule is executable is presence of the specified Java class. If it is not found, the rule is considered as not executable, so neither beliefs are modified nor goals are removed.

In the statements, "*" can be used with the meaning of "anything", and "*<var>*" can be used as variable. If variables are used, the rule is applicable/executable if the beliefs and goals of the agent provide at least one possible binding of the values. If several bindings are possible, the first found is taken. The left part of the rule is processed in the following order: event, trueIf, achievesGoal, trueIfGoalAchieved, falseIf. This defines the order in which the variables are bind. The possible set of values for a variable is searched when the variable is first encountered. After that, values from this set can only get filtered out but no new ones can be added.

All the fields of a rule are passed as the start parameters to the instance of the behavior, not only <x:<anything>>. Therefore, if needed, the behavior can have access to the context of its execution, e.g. trueIf, addOnStart, etc. Note though that, in all the start parameters, the variables are substituted with their values.

An example of usage follows. Given that the date is 8 of March, if the agent knows a woman and knows something that she likes, start GiftingBehavior to gift her that thing. A sub-goal of this is to buy the needed thing (handled in the rule behavior2). FalseIf statements are used to prevent the behavior to be executed twice. The belief "I Gifting <X>" is added as soon as the rule is executed (note, this happens after the sub-goal is achieved), and removed as soon as GiftingBehavior ends (regardless of the result). If the result is success, belief "I Gifted <X>" is added. This example has only one belief statement using namespaces and thus referring to an ontology. This is done for the sake of simplicity.

An Example of the RDF/XML Syntax of the Semantic Agent Programming Language

```xml
<?xml version="1.0"?>
<!DOCTYPE rdf:RDF [
<!ENTITY  ex "http://www.example.com/ontology#">
]>
<rdf:RDF xmlns:rdf="http://www.w3.org/1999/02/22-rdf-syntax-ns#"
            xmlns:gb="http://www.smartresource.com/rgbdf#"
            xmlns:x="http://www.smartresource.com/atomic_behaviors#">
<gb:Belief rdf:about="belief1">
    <gb:statement>I Know Alice</gb:statement>
</gb:Belief>
...
<gb:Behavior rdf:about="behavior1">
    <gb:class>smartresource.non_existing.GiftingBehavior</gb:class>
    <gb:trueIf>&ex;Date &ex;Is 08.03</gb:trueIf>
    <gb:trueIf>I Know *X*</gb:trueIf>
    <gb:trueIf>*X* Is Woman</gb:trueIf>
    <gb:trueIf>*X* Likes *thing*</gb:trueIf>
    <gb:falseIf>I Gifting *X*</gb:falseIf>
    <gb:falseIf>I Gifted *X*</gb:falseIf>
    <gb:trueIfGoalAchieved>I Bought *thing*</gb:trueIfGoalAchieved>
    <gb:addOnStart>I Gifting *X*</gb:addOnStart>
    <x:receiver>*X*</x:receiver>
    <x:object>*thing*</x:object>
    <gb:removeOnEnd>I Gifting *X*</gb:removeOnEnd>
    <gb:addOnSuccess>I Gifted *X*</gb:addOnSuccess>
</gb:Behavior>
<gb:Behavior rdf:about="behavior2">
    <gb:class>smartresource.non_existing.BuyingBehavior</gb:class>
    <gb:achievesGoal>I Bought *thing*</gb:achievesGoal>
    <x:object>*thing*</x:object>
    <gb:addOnSuccess>I Bought *thing*</gb:addOnSuccess>
</gb:Behavior>
</rdf:RDF>
```

5   Conclusions and Future Work

Although the flexibility of agent interactions has many advantages when it comes to engineering a complex system, the downside is that it leads to certain unpredictability of the run-time system. Emergence of a solution that would allow flexible yet predictable operation of agent systems seems to be a prerequisite for wide-scale adoption of the agent-oriented approach. Literature sketches two major directions for search for a solution: social-level characterization of agent systems (more or less studied) and ontological approaches to inter-agent coordination (not yet studied much).

This paper described our vision and the present state of the SmartResource Platform. In the architecture of the platform, we attempt to provide a solution advancing into both directions mentioned and somewhat integrating both. The main distinctive features of the platform are externalization of behavior prescriptions, i.e. agents access them from organizational repositories, and utilization of the RDF-based Semantic Agent Programming Language (S-APL), instead of common Prolog-like languages.

In the follow-up project called Smart Semantic Middleware for Ubiquitous Computing (UBIWARE) 2007-2010, we are going to continue our work on the platform. At least the following important research questions have to be yet answered:

– Is it important and, if yes, how to implement the separation between a role's capabilities (individual functionality), and the business processes in which this role can be involved (complex functionality)?

- How to realize an agent's roles as higher-level commitments of the agent that restrict its behavior, still leaving freedom for learning and adaptation on lower-levels, instead of totally and rigidly prescribing the behavior?
- What mechanisms are needed for flexibly treating the potential (and likely) conflicts among the roles played by one agent?
- What would be concrete benefits of and what mechanisms are needed for accessing and using a role's script by agents who are not playing that role but wish to coordinate or interact with an agent that does?

Acknowledgments

This work was performed in the SmartResource project, which was financially supported by the National Technology Agency of Finland (TEKES) and industrial partners ABB, Metso Automation, TeliaSonera, TietoEnator, and Jyväskylä Science Park.

References

1. Jennings, N.: An agent-based approach for building complex software systems. Communications of the ACM 44(4), 35–41 (2001)
2. Jennings, N.: On agent-based software engineering. Artificial Intelligence 117(2), 277–296 (2000)
3. Bosse, T., Treur, J.: Formal interpretation of a multi-agent society as a single agent. Journal of Artificial Societies and Social Simulation 9(2) (2000)
4. Bresciani, P., Perini, A., Giorgini, P., Giunchiglia, F., Mylopoulos, J.: Tropos: An agent-oriented software development methodology. Autonomous Agents and Multi-Agent Systems 8(3), 203–236 (2004)
5. Tamma, V., Aart, C., Moyaux, T., Paurobally, S., Lithgow-Smith, B., Wooldridge, M.: An ontological framework for dynamic coordination. In: Gil, Y., Motta, E., Benjamins, V.R., Musen, M.A. (eds.) ISWC 2005. LNCS, vol. 3729, pp. 638–652. Springer, Heidelberg (2005)
6. Jennings, N., Sycara, K.P., Wooldridge, M.: A roadmap of agent research and development. Autonomous Agents and Multi-Agent Systems 1(1), 7–38 (1998)
7. Rao, A., Georgeff, M.: Modeling rational agents within a BDI architecture. In: KR'91. Proc. 2nd International Conference on Principles of Knowledge Representation and Reasoning, pp. 473–484 (1991)
8. Wooldridge, M., Jennings, N., Kinny, D.: The Gaia methodology for agent-oriented analysis and design. Autonomous Agents and Multi-Agent Systems 3(3), 285–312 (2000)
9. Vazquez-Salceda, J., Dignum, V., Dignum, F.: Organizing multiagent systems. Autonomous Agents and Multi-Agent Systems 11(3), 307–360 (2005)
10. Shoham, Y.: Agent-oriented programming. Artificial Intelligence 60(1), 51–92 (1993)
11. Rao, A.: AgentSpeak(L): BDI agents speak out in a logical computable language. In: Perram, J., Van de Velde, W. (eds.) MAAMAW 1996. LNCS, vol. 1038, pp. 42–55. Springer, Heidelberg (1996)
12. Dastani, M., van Riemsdijk, B., Dignum, F., Meyer, J.J.: A programming language for cognitive agents: Goal directed 3APL. In: Dastani, M., Dix, J., El Fallah-Seghrouchni, A. (eds.) PROMAS 2003. LNCS (LNAI), vol. 3067, pp. 111–130. Springer, Heidelberg (2004)
13. Collier, R., Ross, R., O'Hare, G.: Realising reusable agent behaviours with ALPHA. In: Eymann, T., Klügl, F., Lamersdorf, W., Klusch, M., Huhns, M.N. (eds.) MATES 2005. LNCS (LNAI), vol. 3550, pp. 210–215. Springer, Heidelberg (2005)

Subgoal Identification for Reinforcement Learning and Planning in Multiagent Problem Solving

Chung-Cheng Chiu[1] and Von-Wun Soo[1,2]

[1] Department of Computer Science, National Tsing Hua University
101, Section 2 Kuang Fu Road, Hsinchu, Taiwan, R.O.C.
g944345@oz.nthu.edu.tw
[2] Department of Computer Science and Information Engineering,
National Kaohsiung University
700, Kaohsiung University Rd, Nan Tzu Dist., 811. Kaohsiung, Taiwan, R.O.C.
soo@cs.nthu.edu.tw

Abstract. We provide a new probability flow analysis algorithm to automatically identify subgoals in a problem space. Our flow analysis, inspired by preflow-push algorithms, measures the topological structure of the problem space to identify states that connect different subset of state space as the subgoals within linear-time complexity. Then we apply a hybrid approach known as subgoal-based SMDP (semi-Markov Decision Process) that is composed of reinforcement learning and planning based on the identified subgoals to solve the problem in a multiagent environment. The effectiveness of this new method used in a multiagent system is demonstrated and evaluated using a capture-the-flag scenario. We showed also that the cooperative coordination emerged between two agents in the scenario through distributed policy learning.

1 Introduction

Traditional reinforcement learning and planning in multiagent problem solving have suffered the difficulty of scaling up the problem state space. One approach to reduce the multiagent problem solving complexity is to represent the problem state space of an agent in a hierarchical way in order to decompose a complicated problem into subproblems [2, 6, 15]. In conventional multiagent policy learning, the policy structure does not decompose the problem. Thus in problem solving, the tasks of each agent are overlapping, and learning to avoid redundant problem solving in an unstructured model is inefficient. This flaw can also be meliorated by decomposing problem into a hierarchical structure [11]. The hierarchical space is constructed as a collection of different levels of subtasks for problem solving, and each subtask at certain levels defines a subset of the state space in order to restrict the action search within a bounded action policy space. The decomposition not only avoids the overlap of each subtask, but also constructs the temporal abstraction on decision making [11].

However, defining a subtask and constructing the hierarchical state space often require domain knowledge to manually construct an optimal model with respect to a specific problem. For each subtask, the related state space and action space should

P. Petta et al. (Eds.): MATES 2007, LNAI 4687, pp. 37–48, 2007.
© Springer-Verlag Berlin Heidelberg 2007

also be specified in advance. To relieve such limitation, we propose a method of automatic subgoal identification for problem decomposition so that each subproblem can correspond to a subgoal. When the subgoals of a problem are identified, each subgoal becomes a subproblem that can be solved by a traditional planner. In hierarchical problem solving a problem can be decomposed into several subproblems and each subproblem can be solved by an abstract action to reach a specific subgoal. Furthermore, an abstract action for solving a subproblem can be realized by a set of primitive actions to reach a subgoal. Therefore, in hierarchal reinforcement learning, the corresponding action policy can be learned based on the abstract states of identified subgoals and the abstract actions.

A number of works had been proposed for automatic hierarchy construction both in reinforcement learning [4, 8, 9, 11, 12, 13] and planning [3, 7]. The common design philosophy in both fields is to find the abstract actions for the problem. The difference is that in planning, the automatic abstraction is performed based on a hierarchical action space while in reinforcement learning, the abstraction is based on a hierarchical state space. Our method performs decision making based on a learned action policy, and completes the selection of committed abstract actions via planning. The design of the abstract actions is in the state space, and is related to works for identifying subgoals in hierarchical reinforcement learning.

We propose a subgoal-based multiagent framework based on the subgoals that are identified by our algorithm. Each subgoal is solved by the planner, and the execution of resulting plan is an abstract action. The policy function of this framework is formulated by abstract actions. The execution time of an abstract action, or a plan, is variant, and we extend the semi-Markov Decision Process (SMDP) [15], a framework for decision making in which the execution time for an action is variant, to allow temporal abstraction in problem solving. With this extension, our framework reformulates the original problem into an abstract problem, and the complexity of problem solving on the abstract layer is greatly reduced. Our multiagent system is constructed with this abstract policy. The policy function is distributed that each agent is rational and maintains its own policy. For each agent, its policy function provides abstract actions according to the current self-state and the observation of other agents' behaviors. The multiagent abstract policy decomposes the problem into subtasks, and this decomposition provides coordination structure in multiagent problem solving. We apply our algorithm to identify subgoals of the problem and construct the policy structure automatically, thus the coordination structure is emerged without manual setting. The performance of this framework is demonstrated in our capture-the-flag scenario.

2   Subgoal Identification

In a hierarchical state space, the entire problem is decomposed into many subproblem spaces, and solving a subproblem is equivalent to achieving a subgoal. It allows the problem solver to choose another new subproblem to solve after achieving a subgoal. From this point of view, the subgoal can be viewed as a critical state for connecting two subproblem spaces. Each problem state can be represented as a node in the graph, and each problem solving action as an edge to transit from a state to another. This results in a state transition graph, in which a subproblem space can be regarded as a set of nodes, and subgoals can be viewed as the nodes that connect these sets of nodes. Therefore, the subgoal identification method can be viewed as a way of finding the cut points between two connected node sets in a graph. We propose a flow analysis algorithm for finding such features in a graph, which the underlying process is similar to a preflow-push algorithm in the network flow algorithms [1].

2.1 The Probability Flow Analysis Algorithm

The flooding process in the preflow-push algorithm determines the capacity of the network and finds bottleneck edges. We modify the flooding process to analyze the topological structure of the problem space and identify the states that connect different subsets of the state space as subgoals.

When an exploration iteration of an agent is terminated, a state transition graph can be constructed. A network is a directed graph with flow transition capacity labeled on all edges, and contains a source and a sink. The state transition graph can be treated as a network with infinite capacity on all edges, in which the source is the initial state and the sink is the terminal state. The flow on each node can represent the transition probability of transferring from the source to the sink. The higher transition probability of a node tends to indicate a higher density for the node to connect two set of nodes in the network and therefore these nodes can be identified as a subgoal. Suppose a flow of one unit is generated from the source to the sink at each iteration. Then after several iterations, a normalized flow value for each node represents a relative transition probability that is referred to as a *probability flow*. Generating flows in this manner and identifying a state with the highest flow value as a subgoal seems to be reasonable at first glance, but it is not always admissible. The state with the highest flow value is not guaranteed to be an ideal subgoal because while it might be the most frequently traversed state, reaching it does not necessarily by itself guarantee the ability to transit to the next subproblem easily. For example, imagine a room with two doors. For the problem of going outside, apparently the subgoal states should be the two doors. However, generating flows and selecting the most frequently traversed location might result in finding a location that is near the middle of two doors instead. Therefore, to find a subgoal, we should identify a critical transition state between subproblems, namely, a critical transition node between two subsets of connected nodes (two subspaces of states) in the graph.

Our probability flow analysis algorithm identifies subgoals by modeling the transition probabilities of the nodes in the network, and is described in Fig. 1. At the beginning of the algorithm, each node is supplied with one unit flow, and then it is flooded through the entire network. The accumulated flow value on each node represents the transition probability from the individual node to the sink. To account for the transition probability from the source to each individual node, the entire network is flooded backwards to the source in the same manner. After summing the two flow values on each node, the normalized accumulated flow value represents the transition probability of the node from the source to the sink. An example is illustrated in Fig. 2: the distance labels from the source S to the sink G in (a) are shown in (b) and (c)-(f) demonstrate the flooding process from the source to the sink step by step. The final accumulated flow value for each node is shown in (h) where the shaded nodes represent the identified subgoals.

```
algorithm probability flow analysis
begin
   obtain the distance labels d(i) from the sink
   fsink = flood process()
   relabel distance labels from the source
   fsource = flood process()
   ftotal = fsink + fsource
   for each node i
      if ftotal(i) ≥ ftotal(j) for all j where (i, j) is an
edge in
         the network then
         mark i as subgoal
   end

function flood process();
begin
   provide one unit flow to each node
   l = the highest label value
   while l > 0 do
      begin
      for each node i with d(i) equals l do
         for each child j of i do
            totalflow(j) += totalflow(i)/numchildren(i)
            l = l - 1
      end
   return totalflow
end
```

Fig. 1. Probability flow analysis

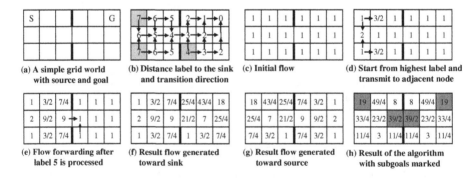

(a) A simple grid world with source and goal

(b) Distance label to the sink and transition direction

(c) Initial flow

(d) Start from highest label and transmit to adjacent node

(e) Flow forwarding after label 5 is processed

(f) Result flow generated toward sink

(g) Result flow generated toward source

(h) Result of the algorithm with subgoals marked

Fig. 2. A grid world example

In the probability flow analysis algorithm, the distance label of a node is the estimation of its minimum cost to the sink. The flood process floods probability flow based on distance labels as in a preflow-push algorithm, and the flow value of a node reflects its transition load in the network topology. To analyze the entire topological structure of the problem space, the algorithm must generate a flow that traverses all nodes evenly, instead of only generating a flow from the source to the sink. Without prior knowledge of the problem, a uniform distribution is applied, thus we give one unit flow to each node initially as in (c) that sends its accumulated flow evenly to all its outward edges as in (d). The resulting subgoals are identified as nodes whose flow values are higher than all their neighbors as in (h). Our subgoals identification process compares the flow value among neighbors within length of 2 to reduce the generation of noise. If two identified subgoals are connected with a single node, and then based on Markov property, the crucial bottleneck is the connection node, and the identified subgoals are replaced by their connection node.

2.2 Comparison to Previous Algorithms

In the works of [4] and [9], the subgoal is determined by randomly generating sufficient solutions and selecting the state with the highest visited frequency. Consider this method as a graph algorithm. It can be regarded as generating a *probability flow* from the source to the sink arbitrarily and accumulating the results as described above. However, in this way, the algorithm cannot find the subgoals that truly match our criterion.

In the works of [11] and [12], the subgoals were identified by finding a graph cut. In [11], the graph cut method is applied by min-cut algorithm with the capacity on each edge is defined. In [12], it applies normalized cut which was approximated by using a spectral clustering algorithm. The complexity of these algorithm is $O(n^3)$, where n is the number of nodes. The execution of the algorithm only finds one cut of the graph, which corresponds to certain subgoals. To find all the subgoals in the graph, [12] suggested that after each cut, the Q-Cut algorithm should take the divided components to perform the algorithm again to find additional subgoals. With this divide-and-conquer approach, more than one subgoal could be identified. However, how many cuts are sufficient to find all crucial subgoals without causing an over-cut problem becomes an important issue. The designer could define a threshold number of cuts, but the threshold can be problem-dependent and must be readjusted in different state spaces. In L-Cut [11], subgoals were found from observation graphs. But the observation graph can have noise that can be minimized by repeated sampling. If the algorithm samples m times, and observation graphs have h nodes, its total computation complexity becomes $O(mh^3)$. Our algorithm identifies subgoals from an observation graph with h nodes, then if it samples m times, the total computation complexity is $O(mh)$.

3 Subgoal-Based Multiagent Problem Solving

When subgoals are identified for each agent in the multi-agent problem solving environment, the designer could use them to implement the algorithm in many ways. One way is to design a hierarchical reinforcement learning algorithm for each agent. In the traditional hierarchical reinforcement learning, the hierarchy of a policy function must be predefined by a designer, and thus it requires the designer to understand the whole problem solving task before performing such modeling. With automatic subgoal identification method, the requirement can be relieved, and the entire algorithm becomes more flexible.

Another problem on designing the framework is how to construct the subtask. One approach is to apply the *option* framework [15]. The flaw of this framework is that it is limited to the originally constructed world states, and as the environment changes, incremental modification is required to adapt to the new world states. Planning is a more effective method for adapting to a new environment. As an action sequence is generated on-line by a planner, the alteration of the environment would in general not disturb the generation of a new sequence of actions to cope with the change by the planner. For this reason, we define planning according to a given subgoal as the subtask in the policy structure.

Our method constructs subgoals as abstract states, and the transition between abstract states are treated as abstract actions. The decision making for selecting proper abstract actions to perform can be learned as a subgoal-based policy, and the primitive actions for execution are derived via planning from available abstract actions. The actions are generated on-line, so that the policy can tolerate to the disturbance of possible environmental change. Thus the original global goal is decomposed into many subgoals. Which subgoal to achieve is decided by a policy and the planner only needs to solve the subproblem of transferring between the identified subgoals, and the planning complexity is thus reduced.

3.1 The Subgoal-Based Policy

In reinforcement learning, the expected utility in state s with discount factor γ is the cumulative discounted reward till the action terminates.

$$V(s) = E\left[\sum_{t=0}^{T} \gamma R(s_t)\right] \tag{1}$$

In our subgoal-based policy, if an abstract action a' which terminates after N steps is executed, the expected utility can be written as:

$$V(s) = E\left[\sum_{t=0}^{N-1} \gamma R(s_t) + \sum_{t=N}^{T} \gamma R(s_t)\right] \tag{2}$$

The first term of right hand side is the cumulative rewards of executing an abstract action a' at state s which terminates after N steps, and is represented as $R(a')$. The termination of a' results in state s', and the second term of right hand side is the expected utility at state s'. The transition probability of executing a' in state s results state s' is $P(s'|s,a')$, then we can rewrite equation 2 as:

$$V(s) = R(a') + P(s'\mid s,a')V(s') \tag{3}$$

In our framework, an abstract action is a plan, and the first term on the right hand side in equation (3) is the expected reward of the plan execution. Represent the reward of executing plan p as $R(p)$, equation (3) is rewritten as:

$$V(s) = R(p) + P(s'\mid s,a')V(s') \tag{4}$$

Equation (4) can be re-stated as the state-action value function, with π as the current policy function:

$$Q(s,a') = R(p) + P(s'\mid s,a')Q(s',\pi(s')) \tag{5}$$

This formula can be considered as the similar form of a decomposed value function defined in [5, 11]. The main feature of value function decomposition is its recursive form. In hierarchical reinforcement learning, the policy function can be constructed as a directed acyclic graph. The recursive invocations correspond to edges in the directed acyclic graph and represent the hierarchy structure for learning algorithm. But in the traditional design of MAXQ value function decomposition algorithm, to compute the completion function, corresponding to the second term on right hand side in equation (5), it requires a complete search among its successor nodes in the hierarchical graph, which is computationally expensive [5]. In our framework, a subtask is a plan resulted by the planner, which applies only primitive actions. In this design, the inner loop of each plan will not invoke another subtask, thus relieves the requirement of thorough search in the graph and reduce the high computation cost in the learning process of value function decomposition algorithm.

3.2 Subgoal-Based Multiagent SMDP Framework

In our multiagent systems, the policy function extends the semi-Markov Decision Process (SMDP) to provide temporal abstraction, and is similar to the multi-agent SMDP (MSMDP) defined in [11].

Definition 1. The multiagent subgoal-based SMDP is composed of six components (A, S, B, P, R, T).

A is a set of agents in the environment with each agent $i \in A$ has a set B^i of plans, where B^i is composed of abstract actions and subgoals of agent i. S is the state space of environment. B denotes the behaviors of all agents, which is the joint state space of B^i for $i \in A$. P is a multi-step transition probability function. R is the function that maps states to rewards. T is the terminal condition defined in the state space when the subgoal is achieved or no more plan is available. In the policy structure, the other agent's states are considered only at the higher abstract level, the lower level subtasks are not involved. In this way, the definition of a subtask is the same as an action, and the planning can be performed based only on environmental states by neglecting the possible behaviors and effects produced by others.

One major difference of our system is that we do not define coordination mechanism in advance. The system simulates a real world situation in which each agent is treated as a rational agent who does not share its knowledge or policy with others. In this setup, the decision process is distributed, and each agent carries out its own policy asynchronously to maximize its own expected utility. This kind of design is to provide the flexibility of application and relieve the requirement of manual design on coordination. In multiagent learning, the construction of coordination mechanism is achieved by decomposing the problem into subtasks and by reducing redundant subtasks for agents based on distributed problem solving. In our system, the subgoals of the problem are identified automatically, and the framework constructs the abstract layers on which agent decision process can be based. The structure of an abstract layer is a decomposition of a problem, thus the maximal policy learning based on this layer emerges the coordination behavior. In this way, the subgoal-based multiagent SMDP framework achieves the coordination automatically.

3.3 Multiagent Learning with Subgoal-Based Policies

In multiagent reinforcement learning environment, since the behaviors of other agents must be taken into consideration as some parameters for defining a current state for a multiagent policy function, a subgoal-based multiagent policy function is defined in definition 2.

Definition 2. The subgoal-based policy function of agent i in the multiagent framework with n agents is $\pi^i(s_i, p_1, p_2, \ldots, p_i, \ldots, p_n) \in B^i$, where $s_i \in S$ is the state of agent i, $p_j \in B^j$ is the plan executed by agent j for $1 \leq j \leq n$. S is the set of world states, B^j is a set of plans generated from identified subgoals. With the definition, the policy function defined in terms of a Q-value function is represented in equation (6).

$$\pi^i = \arg\max_{p_i} Q(s_i, p_1, p_2, \ldots, p_i, \ldots, p_n) \tag{6}$$

In state s_i, after executing a plan p_i which takes t steps to terminate and results in state s'_i, with learning rate α and discounting factor γ, we apply an update rule for the "Q-value function in equation (7).

$$Q(s_i, p_1, p_2, \ldots, p_i, \ldots, p_n) + = \alpha[R(p_i) +$$
$$\gamma^t \max_{p'_i} Q(s'_i, p'_1, p'_2, \ldots, p_i, \ldots, p'_n) - Q(s_i, p_1, p_2, \ldots, p_i, \ldots, p_n)] \tag{7}$$

4 Experimental Results

We set up a multi-agent capture-the-flag scenario to analyze the performance of learning subgoal identification method. In our experiment, without losing the main features in problem solving, we replaced the planner with a simple path finding algorithm with simple primitive action selection capability. The problem task could be solved by a single agent, and also could be solved with other agents together. The scenario is illustrated using a 21×21 grid world, which is divided into four rooms, and there are doors d1, d2, d3 and d4 connecting two neighbored rooms as shown in Fig. 3 (a). There are two flags A and B in the grid world, one is located at the left bottom corner, and the other is at the right bottom corner. The missions of the agents are to find and capture the flags at different places, and to plug these flags at the specific locations. Both agents start at S(0,0). The flag A at (0,20) should be plugged at the location of A'(9,9), and the flag B at (20,20) should be plugged at the location of B'(11,9). When both flags are plugged at the correct target location, the agent must go to the final goal G at the right upper corner (20,0), and the whole task is completed.

There are four primitive actions for the agents: go *west*, *north*, *east* and *south*, and each agent must move one grid at a time from one location to the other one. When an agent goes to the grid where a flag is located, the agent would capture that flag. Each agent could hold one flag at a time, and when it reaches the specified destination of a flag, the flag would be plugged onto that location. If an agent holds a flag and goes back to its origin location, then the flag will be dropped back to the ground. Either flag could be captured by both agents, and when a flag is held by an agent, the other agent could not snatch the flag back from it. The flag can be available only when it is

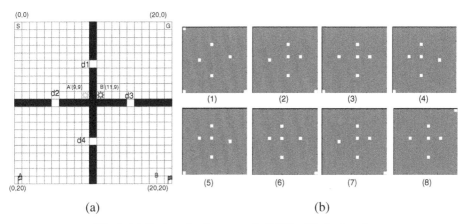

Fig. 3. (a) Capture-the-flag scenario (b) Identified subgoals

put back to the original location. When a flag is plugged onto its destination, it is fixed at that location and could no longer be unplugged.

Before the reinforcement learning process begins, subgoals in the state space are identified in advance, as explained in the Subfigures (1)-(8) in Fig. 3 (b). Each Subfigure in (1)-(8) shows subgoals identified at different subspaces in problem solving situations when:

(1) No flag is held or plugged by any agent. The subgoals identified are $d2$, one grid west from $d1$, one grid west from d4, one grid north from d3, and the others are A, B, and start state.

(2) Flag A is available, and flag B is held by the agent itself. The subgoals identified are d2, one grid East from $d1$ and $d4$, one grid north from d3, B' and B.

(3) Flag A is available, and flag B is not available. The subgoals are one grid East from $d1$ and $d4$, one grid North from $d2$ and $d3$, B' and A.

(4) Flag A is held by the agent itself, and flag B is available. The subgoals are d3, one grid East from d1 and d4, one grid North from d2, A and A'.

(5) Flag A is held by agent itself, and flag B is not available. The subgoals are the same as in (4).

(6) Flag A is not available, and flag B is available. The subgoals are one grid West from d1, d4 and one grid North from d2, d3, A' and B.

(7) Flag A is not available, and flag B is held by the agent itself. The subgoals are the same as in (2).

(8) Neither flag A nor flag B is available. The subgoals are B', one grid East from d1, d4 and one grid North from d2, d3 and the final goal.

After the subgoals are identified, the agent takes the achievement of these subgoals as its abstract actions and performs reinforcement learning to learn the action policy. To verify the performance, we setup three cases for comparison:

1. Single agent using conventional Q-learning.
2. Single agent using subgoal-based policy learning.
3. Two agents using subgoal based policy learning.

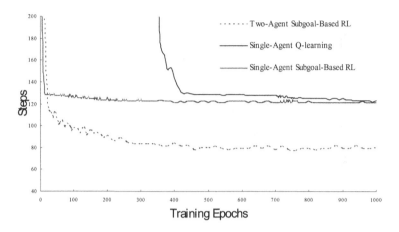

Fig. 4. Mean steps to reach the goal in capture-the-flag scenario

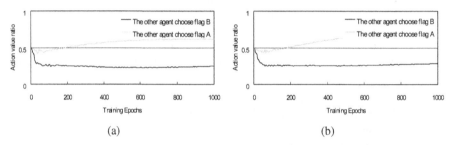

(a)   (b)

Fig. 5. The trend of coordination during distributed policy learning. The horizontal axis shows the training epochs. The vertical axis shows normalized action values for an agent to pick up flag B when the other agent decides to pick up flag A *(gray line)* and flag B *(black line)*, respectively.

For the case of two agents, we define a cooperative configuration so that rewards can be shared among cooperating agents. When one flag is plugged to its destination by the other agent, the flag can be regarded as having been plugged by the agent itself. In the result of the learning in this configuration, we found that the decision of an agent depends on another's behavior. When an agent observes that another agent has an intention to capture flag A, it will pick up flag B immediately. When an agent has plugged the flag and observes the other flag has been plugged or has been held by another agent who is on its way to the destination, then the agent would go toward the final goal directly.

The results of experiments were averaged over 1000 training cases in which each training case was measured up to 1000 epochs and the smoothed performance curves of the mean steps to reach the goal against the training epochs are shown in Fig. 4. The single agent Q-learning takes over 400 epochs to converge to a near optimal policy, while single agent subgoal-based reinforcement learning takes less than 10 epochs. And in the case of two agents, although there are additional efforts for an agent to model the other agent in the state space, it converges only a little bit slower than the single agent case. But it is still more efficient than the case of the single agent using conventional Q-learning.

The flow analysis algorithm identifies subgoals and decomposes the task in problem solving. Multiagent policy learning on this level emerges the cooperation and coordination behaviors. When an agent realizes the other agent is going to capture flag A, it would decide to capture flag B. This policy coordination is illustrated in Fig. 5. The policy value is normalized according to the formula: *Pick up B/(Pick up A + Pick up B)*. For example, the normalized policy value 0.51 means that the policy value ratio between picking up flag A and picking up flag B is 0.49:0.51. A point above 0.5 indicates the policy value for picking up flag B is higher than that of picking up flag A. Subfigure (a) illustrates the policy function of agent 1, and (b) illustrates the policy function of agent 2. This figure is the snapshot of policy values for both agents during learning. The most profitable decision in the starting state is to pick up flag A and let the other agent to pick up flag B, since the cost of handling the subgoal of picking up flag A is much smaller than handling the subgoal of picking up flag B. The policies are distributed, and each agent is rational, thus in the first 100 training epochs, they all compete to pick up flag A as shown in the downshoot below 0.5 of the gray line for about 200 epochs at the beginning. After 100 epochs, the agents started to realize to coordinate in order to get a higher utility value. Then, as Fig. 5 illustrates, after 200 epochs of learning, the cooperative coordination policies between the two agents emerged.

5   Conclusions

This work provides a probability flow analysis algorithm to identify subgoals in the problem space with linear-time complexity, and constructs a subgoal-based multiagent SMDP to perform efficient problem solving. The subgoals identified from the state space decompose the problem and reduce the entire state space drastically. As in the experiment, the original state space is the set of 404 locations and 8 flag states (2 flags and each with initial, held, plugged states), a total of 404×8 states, and after subgoal identification, the number of states is reduced to only 39. Therefore, the training efforts needed for the subgoal-based policy learning is greatly reduced in comparison to conventional Q-learning. This reduction is especially significant in the multi-agent case. As in the two-agent case in the grid world, to model the states of the other agent in conventional Q-learning, the state space grows up to 1,305,728, and the size of its Q table and its primitive actions becomes roughly 4 times of the size that is almost intractable. But in two-agent subgoal-based policy learning, the number of abstract states only grows to about less than 200 that can still be efficiently learned as shown in our experiments.

The improvement of our framework on multiagent problem solving comes from the same factors of hierarchical multiagent reinforcement learning, that is, the problem decomposition. The major different features of our system are the automatic subgoal identification and its combination with learning and planning. The subgoal-based problem decomposition provides a basis for further learning of coordination among agents, and by solving subtasks via planning, it not only reduces the complexity of learning but also causes a multiagent system to be more adaptive to alterations of environment.

Acknowledgements. This research is supported in part by National Science Council of ROC under grant number NSC 93-2213-E-007-061 and also by Ministry of Economic Affairs of ROC under grant number 93-EC-17-A-05-S1-030.

References

1. Ahuja, R.K., Magnanti, T.L., Orlin, J.B.: Network Flows: Theory, Algorithms, and Applications. Prentice-Hall, Englewood Cliffs (1993)
2. Barto, A.G., Mahadevan, S.: Recent Advances in Hierarchical Reinforcement Learning. Discrete Event Dynamic Systems 13(4), 341–379 (2003)
3. Botea, A., Müller, M., Schaeffer, J.: Using Component Abstraction for Automatic Generation of Macro-Actions. In: Proceedings of the Fourteenth International Conference on Automated Planning and Scheduling, pp. 181–190. AAAI Press, Stanford, California, USA (2004)
4. Digney, B.: Learning Hierarchical Control Structure for Multiple Tasks and Changing Environments. In: Proceedings of the Fifth Conference on the Simulation of Adaptive Behavior (1998)
5. Dietterich, T.: Hierarchical reinforcement learning with the MAXQ value function decomposition. Journal of Artificial Intelligence Research 13, 227–303 (2000)
6. Erol, K., Hendler, J., Nau, D.: Complexity results for HTN planning. Annals of Mathematics and Artificial Intelligence 18(1), 69–93 (1996)
7. Knoblock, C.A.: Automatically Generating Abstractions for Planning. Artificial Intelligence 68(2), 243–302 (1994)
8. Mannor, S., Menache, I., Hoze, A., Klein, U.: Dynamic abstraction in reinforcement learning via clustering. In: Proceedings of the Twenty-First International Conference on Machine Learning, pp. 560–567. ACM Press, New York (2004)
9. McGovern, A., Barto, A.G.: Automatic discovery of subgoals in reinforcement learning using diverse density. In: Proceedings of the Eighteenth International Conference on Machine Learning, pp. 361–368. Morgan Kaufmann, San Francisco (2001)
10. Menache, I., Mannor, S., Shimkin, N.: Q-Cut - Dynamic discovery of sub-goals in reinforcement learning. In: Elomaa, T., Mannila, H., Toivonen, H. (eds.) ECML 2002. LNCS (LNAI), vol. 2430, pp. 295–306. Springer, Heidelberg (2002)
11. Ghavamzadeh, M., Mahadevan, S., Makar, R.: Hierarchical multi-agent reinforcement learning. Journal of Autonomous Agents and Multiagent Systems 13(2), 197–229 (2006)
12. Şimşek, Ö., Wolfe, A.P., Barto, A.G.: Identifying Useful Subgoals in Reinforcement Learning by Local Graph Partitioning. In: Proceedings of the Twenty-Second International Conference on Machine Learning, pp. 816–823. ACM Press, New York (2005)
13. Şimşek, Ö., Barto, A.G.: Using relative novelty to identify useful temporal abstractions in reinforcement learning. In: Proceedings of the Twenty-First International Conference on Machine Learning, pp. 751–758. ACM Press, New York (2004)
14. Shi, J., Malik, J.: Normalized cuts and image segmentation. IEEE Transactions on Pattern Analysis and Machine Intelligence 22(8), 888–905 (2000)
15. Sutton, R.S., Precup, D., Singh, S.P.: Between MDPs and Semi-MDPs: A framework for temporal abstraction in reinforcement learning. Artificial Intelligence 112(1), 181–211 (1999)

Medical Image Segmentation by a Multi-Agent System Approach

Nacéra Benamrane and Samir Nassane

Vision and Medical Imaging GROUP, SIMPA Laboratory
Department of Computer Science, Faculty of Sciences,
University of Sciences and Technology of Oran "Mohamed BOUDIAF"
B.P 1505 El'Mnaouer 31000, Oran, Algeria
nabenamrane@yahoo.com,
nassan_samir@yahoo.fr

Abstract. In this paper, we propose an approach for medical Image segmentation based on a FIPA compliant multi-agent system. The idea consists in merging the regions following several criteria and with a massive population of situated agents which cooperate, negotiate with the help of interaction protocols and communicate by passing asynchronous messages. The efficiency of our approach is shown through some experimental results.

Keywords: medical image segmentation, region growing, multi-agent system, cooperation, negotiation, interaction protocol, JADE, FIPA.

1 Introduction

We are witnessing a continuing evolution of medical imaging techniques. However, produced images generally contain several artefacts that render its subsequent visual interpretation a very delicate task. Image processing, which is in progressive advance, offers efficient solutions for noise elimination and the detection of objects contained in the image, such as by filtering and segmentation methods, helping clinicians in their diagnosis aimed for example at detecting a tumor or studying its evolution. The segmentation phase is the most crucial step of a diagnosis aid system, because it strongly affects the quality of interpretation. Image segmentation consists of extracting symbolic entities which are the regions and the contours. Several segmentation algorithms are proposed in the literature, based on one of two principles; discontinuity and similarity [1]. The approach based on the first principle allows detection of contours. The other approach subdivides the image into regions determined by verifying homogeneity criteria. In addition, several methods based on neural networks [2] or Markov fields [3] have also proved their efficiency for medical images segmentation.

For several years, segmentation applications employed a monolithic, sequential system to perform complex tasks. Some of these operations can be done in parallel, or in a distributed fashion. Therefore, new approaches for tackling image segmentation from other angles are needed. One of these approaches, which is getting more and

P. Petta et al. (Eds.): MATES 2007, LNAI 4687, pp. 49–60, 2007.

more popular, is represented by multi-agent systems. These are distributed applications consisting of relatively independent modules, called agents, which cooperate for undertaking complex operations. Usually, agents are used in places where superior behaviours and complex interactions are needed, and where modularity, flexibility and scalability represent important issues [4].

In this paper, we propose a massive multi-agent system approach for the medical images segmentation. A multi-agent system no doubt allows a better exploitation of the local and heterogeneous information distributed in the image, with the help of very efficient services such as: communication, negotiation, cooperation, local adaptation, control distribution and parallelism.

The present paper is organized as follows: section 2 describes briefly the segmentation related works, recently proposed. In section 3, the multi-agent platform used for implementing is presented. In section 4, the proposed multi-agent system approach is described in detail. In section 5, some experimental results are presented. Finally, a conclusion and some prospects are given in the last section.

2 Related Work

Different multi-agent approaches have been proposed recently for the segmentation of medical images.

In the approach proposed by Liu et al. [5], several agents are anchored each one over one pixel of the image and collaborate in order to extract fine and homogeneous structures. They have different behaviours; such as perception, tagging, reproduction, diffusion and disappearance. The pixel tagging takes place according to an intensity criterion applied on the neighbouring pixels. Reproduction and diffusion behaviours are operated in preferential directions which depend on the agents previous displacements.

Duchesnay [6] proposes to organize agents population according to an irregular pyramid where region and contour agents cooperate to segment a mammography image. The region agents represent areas of the image whereas the contour agents are joined to contour chains. The region agents have different behaviours; neighbours identification, preparation of fusion with the neighbouring region agents, collaboration with the contour agents to decide on the fusion, and destruction / reproduction to create new region agents in higher levels of the pyramid.

Porquet et al. [7] propose a multi-agent platform for brain MRI (Magnetic Resonance Images) images segmentation, it permits to implement several contour-region cooperation strategies in order to achieve region fusion/division and contour extension/adjusting operations.

Haroun et al. [8] proposes a multi-agent approach permitting to segment brain MRI image in three tissue classes: White Matter (WM), Grey Matter (GM) and the Cerebral Spinal Fluid (CSF). The multi-agent system consists of one image agent and several region agents anchored each one initially over a germ pixel selected with the help of the FCM algorithm [9]. The image agent possesses the control behaviour (creation / destruction, activation / deactivation of region agents), whereas the region agent has the growing, negotiation and fusion behaviours.

In the approach by Richard et al. [10], situated and cooperative agents operate in an alternating manner to segment a 3D brain MRI image. Several types of agents are defined; global agent, local control agent and three other agents specialized for   brain tissue detection. The image is divided by the global agent in several 3D zones containing each one the three specialized agents (slaves) and one local control agent (master). The specialized agents collaborate with their neighbours situated in the adjacent partitions in order to serve their masters and to progress ultimately toward the global objective.

3   Multi-Agent Platform

Unlike the multi-agent approaches described above which are implemented within private and minimal platforms, our multi-agent system functions in an effective and promising execution environment: the free platform JADE which implements the basic specifications of the FIPA organization (Foundation for Intelligent Physical Agents) [11].

3.1   JADE (Java Agent DEvelopment Framework)

JADE is a free and open platform which is developed in Java and distributed by the Italian laboratory TILAB (Telecom Italian Laboratory) [12]. It aims to simplify the multi-agent systems development by offering a complete set of services and agents in accordance with the FIPA specifications.

JADE provides the three basic agents specified by FIPA: AMS (Agent Management System) which supervises the registration of the agents with a unique identifier, their authentification, their access and use of the system, ACC (Agent Communication Canal) which manages the messages routing between the agents, DF (Directory Facilitor) which provides a service of yellow pages to the platform. These agents are created and activated at every start of the platform, see Fig. 1.

JADE uses the Behaviour abstraction for modelling the tasks that an agent can execute, and the agents can instantiate dynamically their behaviours according to their needs and their capacities.

JADE is an agent development environment easy to manipulate and it is provided with a very interesting theoretical and technical documentation [13].

3.2   Agent Communication Language

JADE uses a high-level communication language based on the speech-act theory [14]; FIPA-ACL (Agent Communication language) [15].

A FIPA-ACL message is constituted of three layers: content, message, communication. The content is an information to communicate. This last is encapsulated in a message indicating the performative that the sender attaches to the content (such as affirmation, question or orders), the interaction protocol to respect and some features describing the information transported in the content. The message is also included in a communication packet which permits to specify some information necessary to the communication (such as sender and receiver).

A FIPA-ACL message has the following important fields:

- Sender: The emitter of the message.
- Receiver: The receiver of the message.
- Performative: type of the communicative act, such as: request, inform, and agree.
- Protocol of interaction: such as FIPA-Request, FIPA-contract-Net [17, 18].
- Content: Information to exchange.

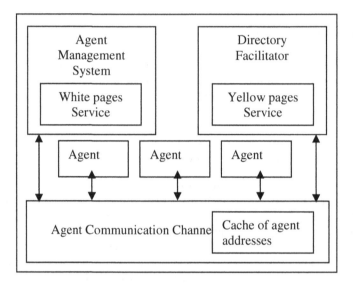

Fig. 1. The JADE Software Architecture

3.3 Interaction Protocols

An interaction protocol is a message sequence that two agents must exchange in order to converse in an optimal and efficient manner. The agents participating in dialogue session must therefore react to the received messages according to the interaction protocol adopted [16]. FIPA specifies a set of interaction protocols that the agents must adopt. Let's mention only those that we use in our segmentation approach: FIPA-request, FIPA-contract-net [17] [18]. These protocols are based on the FIPA-ACL communication language.

4 The Proposed Multi-Agent System Approach

4.1 Criteria Segmentation

The proposed segmentation method is based on three steps:

1. Initial segmentation of the image by region growing algorithm based on the following amplitude criterion:

$$C1 (R_i) = [Max_i - Min_i] < S1 \tag{1}$$

Max_i, Min_i are the maximal and minimal grey level of the region R_i, and S1 is a parameter.

2. Intermediate segmentation of the initial image by iterative merging of the initial regions using the following fusion criterion:

$$C2 (R_i,R_j) = [\mu_i - \mu_j] < S2 \tag{2}$$

μ_i, μ_j are the grey level averages of regions Ri and Rj, and S2 is a parameter.

3. Final segmentation of the intermediate image by iterative merging of the intermediate regions using the following fusion criterion:

$$C3 (R_i,R_j) = \alpha. Cont_{ij} + \beta.(1-Cr_{ij}) < S3 \tag{3}$$

α and β are coefficients, and S3 is parameter (α, β and $S3 \in [0, 1]$); Cr_{ij} is the normalized histograms interrelationship of regions R_i and R_j, ($Cr_{ij} \in [0, 1]$).

$$C_{rij} = \frac{h_i.h_j}{\|h_i\|.\|h_j\|} \tag{4}$$

h_i, h_j are the histograms of regions R_i and R_j; $Cont_{ij}$ is the normalized contrast between regions R_i and R_j.

$$Cont_{ij} = \frac{1}{L(F_{ij})} \sum_{p_i \in F_{ij}} \sum_{p_j \in V4(p_i)} |x_i - x_j| \tag{5}$$

$L(F_{ij})$ is the R_i frontier length with R_j, p_i are R_i frontier pixels with R_j, p_j are R_j frontier pixels with R_i, $V4(p_i)$ is the four-connected neighbouring pixels of p_i, x_i and x_j are respectively grey levels of pixels p_i and p_j.

4.2 Multi-Agent System

The proposed massive multi-agent system consists of one global agent and several region agents (see Fig. 2). They operate in cooperative, synchronous and parallel manner, and communicate with FIPA-ACL messages. The region agents interact between themselves according to the interaction protocols: FIPA-Request and FIPA-Contract-Net.

4.2.1 Global Agent

The global agent possesses two main behaviours:

- The system initialization: which permits to achieve sequentially the following operations:
  - **Initial segmentation** of the image to get a set of regions.

- **Creating and launching** the region agents which are going to function in a parallel manner and cooperate in order to do the required fusions. The initial region agents are anchored each one over an initial area whose label is the identifier of the owner agent.

  This behaviour is executed only once when the system starts.
- Coordination **of the region agents**: During this behaviour, the global agent reacts only to the task-end messages (reactive aspect) coming from the region agents in order to coordinate their actions. When a global agent perceives that all region agents have finished their current behaviour, it gives them the authorization to trigger other behaviours according to their plan. On the one hand, this centralized social control influences the autonomy of the agents, and on the other hand, it permits to guarantee the system consistency where all region agents share the same behaviour. The passage from the step 2 to the step 3 (see section 4.1) is also assured by this behaviour. If the segmentation is accomplished, an information message is sent to all current region agents.

The global agent needs the following information:

- The source image.
- The fusion criteria.
- List of all current region agents.

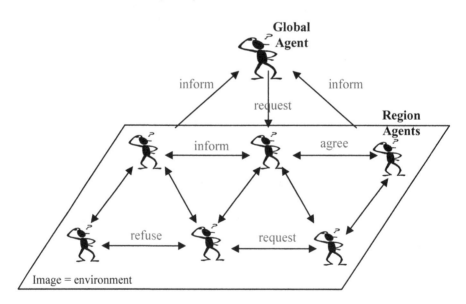

Fig. 2. The proposed multi-agent system

4.2.2 Region Agent
The region agent needs the following information:

- Unique identifier;
- List of neighbouring agents (L1) which includes their identifiers;
- List of neighbouring agents which verify the current fusion criterion (L2);
- List of pixels (LP);
- Lists of border pixels (spatial coordinates) with each neighbour (LF);
- Histogram of the region.

A region agent possesses two methods permitting to calculate respectively:

- Cr_{ij}: the normalized histograms interrelationship of the two region agents R_i and its neighbour R_j.
- $Cont_{ij}$: the normalized contrast between both region agents R_i and its neighbour R_j.

The region agent executes the following behaviours (see Fig. 3):

- Discovering the neighbour agents: During which time, the agent perceives its neighbourhood (at the border) and adapts its neighbour agents list L1, pixels list LP and LFs lists;
- Selection of the best neighbours verifying the current fusion criterion: during this behaviour, the agent must adapt its neighbours list L2;
- Search of the fusion neighbour with which the agent merges;
- Growing (fusion): during which time, the current agent aggregates to its pixels those of fusion neighbour whose surface is smallest, and labels them with its unique identifier;
- Disappearance: designate the death of the fusion neighbour agent or all agents in case of a segmentation end. This latter is only discovered by the global agent which sends to all agents a death message when it perceives that no fusion has taken place and all fusion criteria have been used.

At every behaviour end, the region agent sends an information message to the global agent in order to ensure a good control of the system.

In fact, the best neighbours selection behaviour and fusion neighbour search behaviour implement respectively the interaction protocols; FIPA-Request and FIPA-Contract-net (see section 3.3). Therefore, they are composed each one by two sub behaviours which are executed in a parallel manner; Initiator permitting to trigger the dialogue with the neighbours (proactive aspect) and Responder to react to the messages received from them (reactive aspect).

4.2.2.1 Best Neighbours Selection Behaviour (Step 2)

A region agent sends a REQUEST message containing its grey level average to its neighbour agents requesting them to verify C2.

- If C2 is verified, a neighbour agent returns an AGREE message, then a INFORM message containing the grey level difference value, otherwise it returns REFUSE message.

    – The agent receiving AGREE will wait the INFORM message to recover the grey level difference and the neighbour agent identifier, then it inserts this identifier, according to the corresponding difference, in its neighbours list (L2) sorted out in the ascending order of the grey level differences.

During the third step, the neighbour agents exchange their identifiers and histograms in order to be able to verify the C3 criterion.

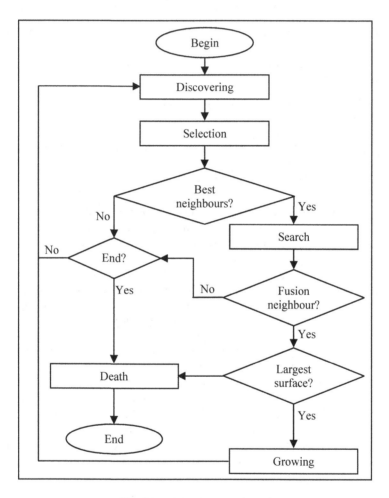

Fig. 3. Region agent behaviours

4.2.2.2 Fusion Neighbour Search Behaviour (Steps 2 and 3)

    – A region agent (called initiator agent) sends a CFP message (call for fusion proposal) to its neighbours previously selected.
    – Each neighbour returns a PROPOSE message containing initiator agent position in their corresponding neighbours list L2.

– The initiator agent chooses the offer which has the best position. If two offers have the same position, it chooses that whose owner agent has the best position in his list L2. Then, he sends an ACCEPT-PROPOSAL message to the corresponding agent called fusion neighbour and REJECT-PROPOSAL to the others.

– The neighbour agent receiving ACCEPT-PROPOSAL recovers the identifier of the agent initiator, compares it with the fusion neighbour selected by his initiator behaviour. If they are the same, it sends him an INFORM message containing its surface and pixels list, otherwise a FAILURE message is sent.

– The initiator agent recovers the surface and the associated pixels list from received INFORM, if it possesses the largest surface it goes to the growing state, otherwise it disappears. If it receives FAILURE message, it goes to the neighbours discovering state or it disappears if a segmentation end is reached (see Fig. 3).

5   Experimental Results and Discussion

The proposed multi-agent system approach has been tested on brain MRI images containing some types of brain tumours (see Fig. 4). These images have been obtained from medical school of Harvard University (USA) [19].

The parameters used are S1=25, S2=25, α=0.7, β=0.3 and S3=0.15.

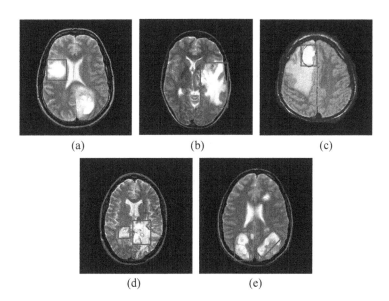

(a)   (b)   (c)

(d)   (e)

Fig. 4. Original images: brain MRI

In the following images, we present segmentation results obtained with Canny's algorithm [20] based on edge detection (see Fig. 5) and those obtained with our multi-agent system (see Fig. 6).

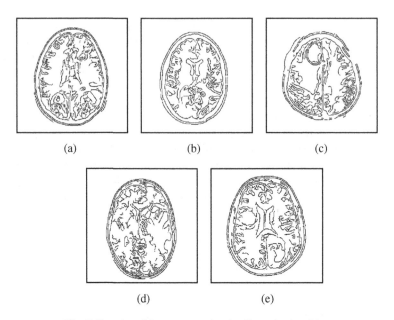

(a)   (b)   (c)

(d)   (e)

Fig. 5. Results of the segmentation by Canny's algorithm

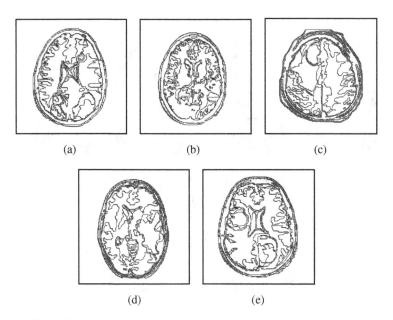

(a)   (b)   (c)

(d)   (e)

Fig. 6. Results of the segmentation by our multi-agent system approach

In the above images, we clearly notice that our multi-agent system approach has had acceptable results; each region presents clear cut limits, particularly the tumour regions which are correctly detected as opposed with Canny's algorithm which failed to completely locate the tumours borders and other wholesome regions. Indeed, such a right segmentation is plainly due to negotiations (interaction) done between region agents so as to select the best fusion neighbours and ultimately realize the necessary fusions.

6 Conclusion

In this paper, we have presented an approach of   medical image segmentation based on multi-agent system. A multi-agent system offers new services which are well adapted to this type of problem such as communication, cooperation, negotiation and treatments distribution, especially as the image includes heterogeneous, local and repartee information. Nevertheless, it is unfortunately achieved to the prejudice of the execution time which grows due to the communications and negotiations done between the agents.

The proposed system consists of one global agent and several region agents which are distributed on the image. The global agent permits to segment the original image in several initial regions to which it attaches the initial region agents, and also ensure a good control of the system. The region agent has the following behaviours; neighbour discovery, best neighbours selection, fusion neighbour search and growing. The agents communicate between them according to specific interaction protocols which permit a better negotiation and cooperation.

The multi-agent system goes through two segmentation phases, and each one has its own region fusion criterion. Besides, the agents work in JADE platform which is conforming to the FIPA norms.

To improve our approach, an optimization of the multi-agent system is feasible; it consists in returning the region agents capable of changing alone their states without calling the global agent which will have the system initialization as a unique role. Other agents can also be added such as the interpretation agents by artificial intelligence techniques for tumour detection. We propose also to implement this approach on multi-processor platform in order to decrease the execution time.

References

1. Coquerez, J.-P., Philipp, S.: Analyse d'images: filtrage et segmentation. Masson (1995)
2. Benamrane, N., Fekir, A.: Medical Images Segmentation by Neuro-Genetic Approach. International Journal of Pattern Recognition and Machine Intelligence 1(4), 95–102 (2005)
3. Held, K., Kops, E.R., Krause, B.J., Wells III, W.M., Kikinis, R., Müller-Gartner, H.-W.: Markov Random Field Segmentation of Brain MR Images. IEEE Transactions on Medical Imaging 16(6), 878–886 (1995)
4. Chaib-Draa, B., Jarras, I., Moulin, B.: Systèmes multi-agents: principes généraux et applications. Edition Hermès (2001)
5. Liu, J., Tang, Y.Y, Cao, Y.C.: An evolutionary autonomous agents approach to image feature extraction. IEEE Transactions on Evolutionary Computation 1(2), 141–158 (1997)
6. Duchesnay, E.: Agents situés dans l'image et organisés en pyramide irrégulière: contribution à la segmentation par une approche d'agrégation coopérative et adaptative. Ph.D. thesis. Université Rennes-1 (2001)

7. Porquet, C., Settache, H., Ruan, S., Revenu, M.: Une plate-forme multi-agent pour la segmentation d'images. Etude des stratégies de coopération contour-région. ORASIS Géradmer, 413–422 (2003)

8. Haroun, R., Hamami, L., Boumghar, F.: Segmentation d'images médicales IRM par un système hybride flou – croissance de régions, dans un système multi agents. Journées d'Etudes algéro-françaises en Imagerie Médicale, 21–30 (2004)

9. Bezdek, J.C.: Pattern Recognition with Fuzzy Objective Functions Algorithms. Plenum Press, New York (1981)

10. Richard, N., Dojat, M., Garbay, C.: Multi-Agent approach for image processing: A Case Study for MRI human brain scans interpretation. In: Dojat, M., Keravnou, E.T., Barahona, P. (eds.) AIME 2003. LNCS (LNAI), vol. 2780, pp. 91–100. Springer, Heidelberg (2003)

11. FIPA specifications website, http://www.fipa.org/specs

12. Bellifemine, F., Poggi, A., Rimassa, G.: JADE: A FIPA-compliant agent framework. In: PAAM'99. Proceedings of the 4th International Conference and Exhibition on The Practical Application of Intelligent Agents and Multi-Agent System, pp. 97–108 (1999)

13. Bellifemine, F., Caire, G., Trucco, T., Rimassa, G.: Jade Programmer's Guide. Jade version 3.3 (November 2005)

14. Austin, J.L.: How to do things with words. Clarendon Press, Oxford, UK (1962)

15. FIPA 97 Specification. Part 2, Agent Communication Language

16. FIPA Interaction Protocol Library Specification, http://www.fipa.org/specs/fipa00025

17. FIPA Request Interaction Protocol Library Specification, http://www.fipa.org/specs/fipa00026

18. FIPA Contract Net Interaction Protocol Library Specification, http://www.fipa.org/specs/fipa00029

19. Harvard University Medical School, http://www.med.harvard.edu/AANLIB/home.html

20. Canny, J.: A Computational Approach To Edge Detection. IEEE Transactions on Pattern Analysis and Machine Intelligence 8(6), 679–689 (1986)

Using DESs for Temporal Diagnosis of Multi-agent Plan Execution*

Femke de Jonge, Nico Roos, and Huib Aldewereld

Dept. of Computer Science, Universiteit Maastricht
P.O. Box 616, NL-6200 MD Maastricht
{f.dejonge,roos,h.aldewereld}@micc.unimaas.nl

Abstract. The most common reason for plan repair are the violation of a plan's temporal constraints. Air Traffic Control is an example of an area in which violations of the plan's temporal constraints is rather a rule than an exception. In such domains there is a need for identifying the underlying causes of the constraint violations in order to improve plan repairs and to anticipate future constraint violations. This paper presents a model for identifying the causes of the temporal constraint violations.

1 Introduction

Violation of a plan's temporal constraints is one of the most common problems during plan execution. In air traffic control, for instance, violation of a plan's temporal constraints is rather a rule than an exception requiring constant adaptions of aircraft's plans. Common causes are problems in luggage handling, security issues, no-shows of passengers, unforseen changes in the weather conditions, and so on and so forth. In order to repair plans, accurate information about the cause of the problem is important. It enables planners to come up with better plan repairs, thereby avoiding fire fighting tactics. This requires that we not only identify *primary* cause, that is, failing plan step(s) causing constraint violations, but also the *secondary* cause, that is, failing equipment, unforseen changes in the environment and malfunctioning agents that are responsible for plan step failures.

In order to make a diagnosis of temporal constraint violations, we need a model of a plan's temporal execution. In this paper we will investigate the use of discrete event systems (DES) [1] for this purpose. Section 3 discusses how discrete event systems can be adapted for this purpose, and Sect. 4 discusses how the resulting model of a plan can be used to make predictions. Section 5 defines plan-execution diagnosis for temporal constraint violations. We will argue that diagnosis of temporal constraint violations differs from standard diagnosis using DESs [2,3,4]. Section 6 presents a small example and Sect. 7 concludes the paper. First, to place our approach into perspective, we discuss some some related work.

---

* This research is supported by the Technology Foundation STW, applied science division of NWO and the technology programme of the Ministry of Economic Affairs (the Netherlands). Project DIT5780: Distributed Model Based Diagnosis and Repair.

P. Petta et al. (Eds.): MATES 2007, LNAI 4687, pp. 61–72, 2007.

2 Related Work

In this section we briefly discuss some other approaches to plan diagnosis and subsequently some approaches to diagnosis using discrete event systems.

Plan Diagnosis. There are several papers addressing different aspects of plan diagnosis. These papers discuss diagnosis of the planning agent [5], diagnosis of a plan consisting of a hierarchy of behaviors [6,7], diagnosis of the execution of a single task of a plan [8,9], and diagnosis of plans consisting of several plan steps (task) [10,11,12,13,14]. None of the papers, however, address the violation of a plan's temporal constraints. This also holds for the approach of de Jonge et al. [15,16], which is closely related to the approach proposed in this paper. de Jonge et al. apply discrete event systems to describe linear plans of individual agents. However, temporal aspects of the agents' plan cannot be modeled. The agents' plans may interact through constraints over the states of plan steps (representing for instance resource constraints). Diagnosis is subsequently applied to identify disruption events causing constraint violations. If disruption events are observable future constraint violations can be predicted and diagnosis is used to propose repair events to avoid these future constraint violations. This paper extends the approach of de Jonge et al. by enabling diagnosis of temporal constraint violations.

Discrete Event Systems. Discrete Event Systems (DES) are a modeling method of real world systems based on finite state machines (FSM) [1]. In a DES a finite set of states describes at some abstraction level the state of a real world system. State changes are caused by events and a transition function specifies the changes triggered by the events. The events are usually observable control events. However, unobservable failure events mays also cause state changes. Diagnosis of a DES aims at identifying the unobserved failure events based on a trace of observable events [2]. Essentially, this is a form of abductive diagnosis. Note that the trace of observable events depends on the state of the system and the transition function. Therefore, a DES is sometimes viewed as a machine accepting a language of observable and unobservable events.

To model a system, usually one starts modeling individual components using Discrete Event Systems. Interactions between the components are described by exchanging events between the components. For diagnosis, these DESs may be combined into a global DES [17]. More recently, methods for diagnosing coupled DESs without first creating a global DES have been proposed [3,4].

3 Modeling Plan Execution

This section formalizes the description of the plan execution to be diagnosed.

The Environment. In a domain such as air traffic control, the environment has an important influence on the intended execution of a plan. Unforeseen changes in the state of the environment such as snow on runways or strong headwinds, may influence the temporal execution of a plan. In order to identify this type of influences using diagnosis, we first need to model them.

The deviations in the strength of the aircraft's headwind is a continuous function over time. Obviously, we will never have enough information to identify this function in our diagnostic process. Therefore, we should abstract from the continuous function and use abstract values such as *strong-tailwind*, *tailwind*, *no-wind*, *headwind* and *strong-headwind* instead. These values hold for certain time intervals. Hence, we define the environment by a set of objects $\mathcal{O}^{env}$ where with each object $o \in \mathcal{O}^{env}$ a finite set of possible states S_o is associated.

A state change of one object may cause a state change in another object. For instance heavy snowfall may influence the state of the runway on an airport. If a state change of, for instance, the weather immediately influences the state of the runway, Discrete Event Systems (DES) [1] would be an obvious choice to describe the causal dependencies between objects. However, heavy snow fall does not immediately causes the closure of a runway. Therefore, we introduce Discrete Event Systems that can generate an event after an object has been in a certain state for some period of time. Using such a time delayed event we may change the state of the runway after it has been snowing for a specified period of time. Unfortunately, this does not solve the problem completely. How long it will have to snow before snowfall changes the state of the runway, may depend on the condition of the runway such as the presence of salt, and on other events such as snow removal activities. Therefore, in this example the time delayed event must be generated by runway and not by the weather. Figure 1 gives an illustration.

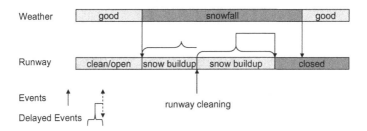

Fig. 1. An application of delayed events

Note that the event generated by the weather causes the state change of the runway from 'clean/open' to 'snow buildup'. The event 'runway cleaning' indicating the removal of snow from the runway, causes a state change from 'snow buildup' to 'snow buildup'. The latter event may seem odd. The effect of a reflexive state transition is that all timers of the time delayed events are reset. Also note that in a more refined model one may also distinguish levels of snow that have been buildup on the runway.

Summarizing the above, an environment object $o \in \mathcal{O}^{env}$ is modeled as a Discrete Event System in which output events can be generated after the object o has been in some state for some specified period of time. This is described by rules of the form:

$$(S_o \times (\mathbb{R} \times \mathbb{R}) \Rightarrow E_o^{out} \times 2^{\mathcal{O}})$$

These rules specify the state to which the rule applies and the time the object must be in this state. Note that for the latter we use an interval $[t_{\min}, t_{\max}] \subseteq (\mathbb{R} \times \mathbb{R})$. The reason for using a time interval is the following. Since an object's state in the model is an abstract representation of the actual state, we cannot know exactly how long the object must be in a state before the event will occur. We can model this uncertainty using intervals.

Also note that these rules specify the output event that is generated and a set of objects $O^{des} \subseteq O$ to which the event is sent. The set of objects O contains the environment objects as well as objects for describing plan steps, equipment and agents.

Plans. Since the execution of a step (action) of a plan may depend on the state of the environment objects and since the state of environment objects may change during the execution, we cannot use a representation in which plan steps are treated as atoms. Therefore, most representations are not suited for our purpose. What we need is a representation that enables us to state that a plan step finishes too late because it started too late or because a delay occurred during execution as a result of unforseen changes in the environment. Hence, we should be able to assign states to plan steps and these states may change during the execution of a plan step. This suggests that we should also use Discrete Event Systems to model plan steps [16]. We therefore introduce a special set of objects O^{plan} to represent plan steps. Figure 2 gives an illustration.

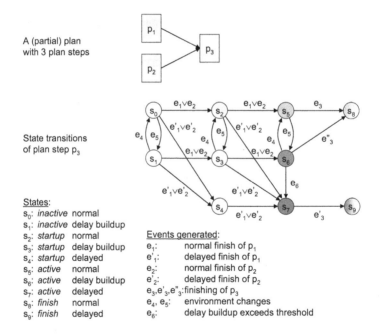

Fig. 2. Modeling a plan step

Summarizing the above, a plan step p is modeled as a Discrete Event System in which the set of state S_p contains:

– a special *initial* state representing the expected initial situation before the start of executing the plan step,

- A set of inactive states representing environment changes that may influence the execution of the plan step,
- a set of startup states representing (*i*) that some but not all preceding plan steps have finished as well as how they have finished, and (*ii*) environment changes that may influence the execution of the plan step,
- a set of active state representing how the plan step is executed, and
- a set of finish states of the plan step.

These special states are all disjunct. Note that no startup states are needed in a linear plan.

Based on the state of a plan step p, at a certain time point an event must be generated that brings the plan step into a finishing state. (One of the events e_3, e'_3, e''_3 in the example of Fig. 2.) We therefore need rules for generating events based on the scheduled finishing times and the current state of plan steps.

$$(S \times (\mathbb{R} \times \mathbb{R}) \to E^{out} \times 2^{\mathcal{O}})$$

So, somewhere in the interval $[t_{\min}, t_{\max}] \subseteq (\mathbb{R} \times \mathbb{R})$ an output event $e \in E^{out}$ is generated and is sent to the objects $O \subseteq \mathcal{O}$. If the object is not in the state specified by the rule during the interval $[t_{\min}, t_{\max}]$, the rule will not generate an event. In this way we can, for instance, specify the finish events of an plan step, as illustrated in Fig. 3. Finally, if the object is in the state specified by a rule and subsequently changes to another state during the interval specified by the rule, then the event is either generated by this rule or is generated by another object or is an external event. In the latter two cases the rule will not generate an event because the state of the object has changed.

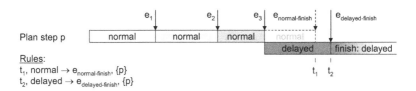

Fig. 3. An application of time generated events

The Discrete Event System. Based on the above described requirements we can give a specification of the objects we will use to describe plan executions by a group of agents in some environment. We assume that the set of objects $\mathcal{O}$ can be partitions into plan steps $\mathcal{O}^{plan}$, agents $\mathcal{O}^{ag}$, equipment $\mathcal{O}^{eq}$ and environment objects $\mathcal{O}^{env}$. Each object $o \in \mathcal{O}$ is described by a Discrete Event System [1].

Definition 1. *An object $o \in \mathcal{O}$ is a Discrete Event System $(S_o, s_o, E_o^{in}, E_o^{out}, \tau_o, \rho_o)$ where*

- *S_o is a set of states,*
- *$s_o \in S_o$ is the initial state at time point 0,*
- *E_o^{in} is the set of events the object may react to,*

- E_o^{out} is the set of events the object may generate,
- τ_o is a set of state transition rules of the form $(S_o \times E_o^{in} \to S_o)$, and
- ρ_o is a set consisting of duration generated event rules of the form:

$$((S_o \times (\mathbb{R} \times \mathbb{R})) \Rightarrow E_o^{out} \times 2^O))$$

and time generated event rules of the form:

$$(S_o \times (\mathbb{R} \times \mathbb{R})) \to E_o^{out} \times 2^O).$$

Above we did not discuss agent and equipment objects explicitly. Equipment objects do not differ much from environment objects. For equipment we distinguish a special state 'normal' and possibly several states for describing malfunctions. Also for agents we distinguish a state 'normal'. Agents may also have several other health state as well as states indicate beliefs about the environment, which might be incorrect.

Timed Events. To describe the (expected) occurrence of events, we introduce so called *timed events*. A *timed event* is a couple $(e, [t, t'])$ where $e \in E$ is an event and $[t, t'] \subseteq (\mathbb{R} \times \mathbb{R})$ is a time interval in which e occurs. A set of timed events will be denoted by: Π.

Constraints. A plan description normally consists of a set of plan steps with precedence relations between the plan steps. We can distinguish two types of precedence relation, namely those that describe the order of plan steps needed to guarantee the desired effect of a plan and precedence relations that have been added to avoid resource conflicts. Although all precedence relations can be modeled using the above described events, we will use a different description for precedence relations that are added for avoiding resource conflicts. When, for instance, an aircraft is delayed, it may be better to change the planned landing sequence of aircraft so that other aircraft can still arrive as scheduled. Therefore, we will model resource constraints separately as constraints over the states of plan steps requiring the same resource. These constraints can be used to specify for instance that a combination of plane a being delayed and plane b being early is not allowed because both planes are scheduled on the same gate.

Definition 2. *A constraint ctr over n objects $(S_{o_i}, s_{o_i}, E_{o_i}^{in}, E_{o_i}^{out}, \tau_{o_i}, \rho_{o_i})$ is a tuple:*

$$\langle o_1, ..., o_n, AS \rangle$$

with $AS \subseteq S_{o_1} \times ... \times S_{o_n}$, describing states of objects that are allowed at the same time.

A set of constraints will be denoted by C.

Constraints can be observed to hold or to be violated during the execution of a plan. *Timed constraints* are used to denote the time interval in which the constraint is observed *to hold* or *to be violated*: $(ctr, [t, t'])$ and $(\neg ctr, [t, t'])$, respectively, where $ctr \in C$ is a constraint and $[t, t'] \subseteq (\mathbb{R} \times \mathbb{R})$ is a time interval in which ctr is observed to hold or to be violated. A set of timed constraints will be denoted by $\mathcal{C}$.

The Model. Using the discrete event systems introduced in this section and applying the modeling method discussed, we can now build a model of possible ways of executing a plan. To summarize, we have to:

- describe the environment objects $\mathcal{O}^{env}$, their state transitions, their states at time point 0, and the rules generating events;
- describe the states of each plan step $\mathcal{O}^{plan}$, their state transitions, states of the plan steps at time point 0, and, using information about the schedule of each plan step, the rules generating (finishing) events;
- if necessary, also describe the equipment $\mathcal{O}^{eq}$ and the agents $\mathcal{O}^{ag}$; and
- describe the constraints C that must hold between states of different agents' plan steps.

Any model has a boundary of what is and what is not modeled. For instance, we may model the state of the weather but not the processes that determine the changes of the weather. Still, based on the weather forecasts we wish to be able to adapt state of the weather object. External events can be used for this purpose. An external event is an input event of an object that is not generated by some object; i.e., it is not an output event of some object and there is no rule generating it. So, $E^{ext} = \bigcup_{o \in \mathcal{O}} E_o^{in} - \bigcup_{o \in \mathcal{O}} E_o^{out}$. The *expected* external timed-events are external events occurring within specific time intervals. We use the set Π^{exp} to denote expected external timed-event.

The objects $\mathcal{O}$, the expected external timed-events Π^{exp} and the constraints C gives us the execution model $M = (\mathcal{O}, \Pi^{exp}, C)$ with $\mathcal{O} = \mathcal{O}^{env} \cup \mathcal{O}^{plan} \cup \mathcal{O}^{eq} \cup \mathcal{O}^{ag}$.

4 Making Predictions

The model proposed in the previous section enables us to simulate, at an abstract level, the normal and the abnormal execution of a plan. Deviations with observations made enables us to formulate the diagnostic problem.

Simulation. An execution model $(\mathcal{O}, \Pi)$ consisting of objects $\mathcal{O}$ and external timed events Π can be used to simulate a multi-agent plan execution starting from the initial state of the plan at time point 0. The history of an object $o \in \mathcal{O}$ describes for each object a sequence of timed events that generate state changes in the object o. Together with each state change of o, the history also describes the timed events generated by the rules of the object o during the current state of o.

Definition 3. *Let $o \in \mathcal{O}$ be an object with DES $(S_o, s_o, E_o^{in}, E_o^{out}, \tau_o, \rho_o)$.*
A history H_o of the object $o \in \mathcal{O}$ is a sequence of the form:

$$H_o = \langle\ (e_0, t_0, s_0, \langle(e_{0,0}, t_{0,0}, O_{0,0}^{des}), ..., (e_{0,m}, t_{0,m_0}, O_{0,m_0}^{des})\rangle), \ ... \ ,$$
$$(e_n, t_n, s_n, \langle(e_{n,0}, t_{n,0}, O_{n,0}^{des}), ..., (e_{n,m_n}, t_{n,m_n}, O_{n,m_n}^{des})\rangle)\ \rangle$$

where

- $e_0 = nill$, $t_0 = 0$ and $s_0 = s_o$;
- $t_{i-1} < t_i$ and $(s_{i-1}, e_i \rightarrow s_i) \in \tau_o$ for each $0 < i \leq n$;
- *for each timed event $(e_{i,j}, t_{i,j})$ there is either a rule:*
    - $(s_i, [t, t'] \rightarrow e_{i,j}, O_{i,j}^{des}) \in \rho_o$ such that $t_{i,j} \in [t, t'] \cap [t_i, t_{i+1}] \neq \emptyset$, or
    - $(s_i, [t, t'] \Rightarrow e_{i,j}, O_{i,j}^{des}) \in \rho_o$ such that $t_{i,j} \in [t_i + t, t_i + t'] \cap [t_i, t_{i+1}] \neq \emptyset$
    generating this timed event.

The history of the whole model consists of the history of all the objects. Of course, the history of the objects are not independent of each other. Every event that causes a state transition of an object is an external event, or an event that is *generated* by a rule of a possibly different object. Moreover, an event generated by a rule of an object must be *sent* to every object in the corresponding set O^{des}.

Definition 4. *A history H is the set of histories of all objects in $\mathcal{O}$:*

$$H = \{H_o \mid o \in \mathcal{O}\}$$

where for each object $o \in \mathcal{O}$ and for each element

$$(e_i, t_i, s_i, \langle (e_{i,0}, t_{i,0}, O_{i,0}^{des}), ..., (e_{i,m_i}, t_{i,m_i}, O_{i,m_i}^{des}) \rangle) \in H_o,$$

(e_i **is generated**) $e_i \in E^{ext}$, *or there is a* $(e_j, t_j, s_j, \langle ..., (e_{j,k}, t_{j,k}, O_{j,k}^{des}), ... \rangle) \in H_{o'}$
such that $e_i = e_{j,k}$, $t_i = t_{j,k}$ and $o \in O_{j,k}^{des}$, and

($e_{i,j}$ **is sent**) *for each $(e_{i,j}, t_{i,j}, O_{i,j}^{des})$ and for each object $o' \in O_{i,j}^{des}$, either $e_{i,j}$ is not applicable in the state of o' at $t_{i,j}$, or there is a $(e_k, t_k, s_k, \langle ... \rangle) \in H_{o'}$ such that $e_{i,j} = e_k$ and $t_{i,j} = t_k$.*

An event e is applicable *in the state s of an object o iff $(s, e \rightarrow s') \in \tau_o$.*

Satisfiability and Consistency of Timed Constraints and Events. Since a history H of the objects $\mathcal{O}$ specifies all the occurring events, we can check whether an (observed) timed event $(e, [t, t'])$ is satisfied by the history H. That is, whether there exists an object $o \in \mathcal{O}$ and a history of that object H_o such that $(e_j, t_j, s_j, \langle ... \rangle) \in H_o$, $e = e_j$ and $t_j \in [t, t']$. Since we can view a history H as a possible description of the world and since we can view a timed event $(e, [t, t'])$ as a *proposition*, we say that the history *satisfies* the timed event: $H \models (e, [t, t'])$.

Similarly we can check whether the timed constraints $(ctr, [t, t'])$ and $(\neg ctr, [t, t'])$ with $ctr = \langle o_1, ..., o_n, AS \rangle \in C$ are *satisfied* by a history H, denoted by $H \models (ctr, [t, t'])$ and $H \models (\neg ctr, [t, t'])$, respectively. So, also the timed constraints are viewed as *propositions*.

An execution model $(\mathcal{O}, \Pi)$ specifies a set of histories because of the uncertainty that results from the use of time intervals. Some of the histories may satisfy a proposition φ; i.e. a timed constraint or a timed event, while others do not. If the propositions describe observations, then as long as there is one history H satisfying the propositions, there is no conflict between the observations and the execution model $(\mathcal{O}, \Pi)$. In other words, the observations are *consistent* with the execution model. If one or more observations are *inconsistent* with the execution model $(\mathcal{O}, \Pi)$, we know that the current set of external timed events Π needs revision. Diagnosis will give us a revised set of external events.

5   Diagnosis and Explanation

Some of the observed timed constraints C and some of the observed timed events Π^{obs} may not be consistent with the execution model $M = (\mathcal{O}, \Pi^{exp}, C)$. These inconsistencies indicate that the expected external events did not occur as specified by Π^{exp}.[1]

---

[1] We assume the absence of errors in the description of the objects $\mathcal{O}$.

Hence, we can formulate a *plan execution diagnosis problem*: $(M, \Pi^{obs}, \mathcal{C}^{obs})$. This section defines a diagnosis and an explanation given a plan execution diagnosis problem.

Diagnosis. Diagnosis of plan execution differs from traditional diagnosis of discrete event systems [2,3,4]. Traditional diagnosis of discrete event systems is *abductive diagnosis*. In abductive diagnosis, the model of the plan execution extended with a diagnosis must *satisfy* all observed events and all constraints. As we saw in the previous section, because of the uncertainty in the model of the plan execution, this requirement is too strong. What we need is *consistency-based diagnosis*. Consistency-based diagnosis enables us to identify the set of external timed events that resolve the inconsistencies between the execution model M, the observed timed events Π^{obs} and the observed timed constraints $\mathcal{C}^{obs}$.

Definition 5. *Let* $(M, \Pi^{obs}, \mathcal{C}^{obs})$ *be a plan execution diagnosis problem where* $M = (\mathcal{O}, \Pi^{exp}, C)$ *is a model of the intended plan execution. Moreover, let* Δ *with* $\Delta \subseteq \{(e, [t, t']) \mid e \in E^{ext}, 0 \le t \le t'\}$ *be a* candidate diagnosis.
   Δ *is a* diagnosis *of a plan execution iff* $((\mathcal{O}, \Delta), \Pi^{obs}, \mathcal{C}^{obs})$ *is consistent; i.e., there is a history* H *for* $(\mathcal{O}, \Delta)$ *such that* $H \models \Pi^{obs} \cup \mathcal{C}^{obs}$.

Preference Criteria. There may be several diagnoses Δ according to Definition 5. The quality of these diagnoses need not be the same. Preference criteria are used to select the subset of the diagnoses. Usually, the preference criteria select the most probable diagnoses. A criterium that is often used for diagnoses is preferring diagnoses that minimize the difference with the normal state of affairs. In plan diagnosis this would be the external timed events Π^{exp}.

A difficulty in comparing Π^{exp} and Δ is that there are transitions to the same state s starting from different states that are triggered by different events. For instance, two events causing a transition to a state representing strong winds, one from a state representing no wind and one from the state representing a light breeze. If the expected light breeze did not occur, we should still be able to infer that the change to strong winds did occur. Therefore we will restrict the external events to so called *absolute* events. An absolute event causes a transition to a new state independent of the previous state thereby simplifying comparison of external events.

Definition 6. *An external event* $e \in E^{ext}$ *of an object* $o \in \mathcal{O}$ *is an* absolute *event iff for every* $s, s' \in S_o$: $\tau_o(s, e) = \tau_o(s', e)$.

The use of absolute events enables us to determine the difference between the expected timed events Π^{exp} and a diagnosis Δ. The difference consists of two aspects, (i) the unexpected timed events that occurred according to the diagnosis: $\Delta \ominus \Pi^{exp}$, and (ii) the expected timed events that did not occur according to the diagnosis: $\Pi^{exp} \ominus \Delta$. Here, the function $\ominus$ is defined as:

$$(X \ominus Y) = \{(e, [t, t']) \in X \mid \forall (e, [t'', t''']) \in Y : [t, t'] \cap [t'', t'''] = \varnothing\}.$$

We prefer diagnoses Δ that *minimize* the differences with Π^{exp} if the probability that differences with Π^{exp} occur is sufficiently small.

Explanation. In our application domain of air traffic control one often claims that during normal daily operation all relevant events, including the external events, are observable. This does not imply that no constraint violation will occur when agents execute their plans. On the contrary, air traffic controllers are working around the clock to avoid incidents. Clearly, if all external events that have occurred, are observed, then $\{(e, [t, t']) \mid (e, [t, t']) \in \Pi^{obs}, e \in E^{ext}\}$ is a diagnosis. However, such a diagnosis does not give an adequate explanation of an observed constraint violation.

For the purpose of plan repair, distributing cost of a plan repair, improvements of future plans, and so on and so forth, we would like to know which external events are accountable of the observed constrain violation during some time interval. A diagnosis does not provide this information. It only specifies the expected and unexpected external events that occurred without linking them to a specific observed constraint violation. So, given a diagnosis, an *explanation* of an observed constraint violation must specify the presence of unexpected external timed events and the absence of expected timed events causing the constraint violation.[2]

Determining an explanation for a constraint violation is not straight forward. To illustrate this, consider the following example. An aircraft that has a delayed departure may still arrive on time at its destination because of the absence of strong headwinds. However, because no gate is available after landing, the aircraft has a delayed arrival resulting in a constraint violation. The constraint violation could be explained by considering the external event causing the delayed departure while ignoring in the explanation the absence of strong headwinds and the unavailability of a gate after landing. Clearly, this is not a proper explanation of the delayed arrival because the plane landed on time.

How do we determine the external events that explain a proposition (an observed timed event or an observed timed constraint)? First, observe that for every proposition, there is a non-empty set of objects the history of which determine the satisfiability of the proposition. Second, the use of absolute external events implies that we do not have to consider any event changing the state of an object o that occurs before an absolute external event e changing the state of o. We do have to consider every event e' generated by and event rule of an object o' changing the state of o after e. We also have to consider the absent absolute events that where expected to occur after e.

Definition 7. *Let* (M, Π^{obs}, C^{obs}) *be a plan diagnosis problem and let* Δ *be a diagnosis. Moreover, let* $\varphi = (\epsilon, [t_\epsilon, t'_\epsilon])$ *be a proposition for which we seek an explanation. Finally, let us view an observation of a timed constraint as a timed event to which we can extend precedence relation* $\prec_H$ *induced by a history* H.

$(\mathcal{X}^a, \mathcal{X}^p)$ *with* $\mathcal{X}^p \subseteq (\Delta \ominus \Pi^{exp})$ *and* $\mathcal{X}^a \subseteq (\Pi^{exp} \ominus \Delta)$ *is an explanation of* φ *iff*

1. $\mathcal{X}^p \cup (\Pi^{exp} \ominus \mathcal{X}^a)$ *is a preferred diagnosis of the plan execution diagnosis problem* $(M, \{\varphi\})$,
2. *for no* $(\mathcal{Y}^p, \mathcal{Y}^a)$ *with* $\mathcal{Y}^p \subseteq (\Delta \ominus \Pi^{exp})$ *and* $\mathcal{Y}^a \subseteq (\Pi^{exp} \ominus \Delta)$:
   $\mathcal{X}^p \cup \mathcal{Y}^p \cup (\Pi^{exp} - \mathcal{X}^a - \mathcal{Y}^a)$ *is not a diagnosis of the plan execution diagnosis problem* $(M, \{\varphi\})$.

Note that $\mathcal{X}^p$ denotes the unexpected external events are present in the diagnosis Δ, and $\mathcal{X}^a$ denotes the expected external events that absent in the diagnosis Δ. Also note that

---

[2] Here, we use a pragmatic interpretation of the concept 'causes'.

the second requirement in the above definition is needed because of *non-monotonicity* of explanations.

6   Example

This section illustrates the relevance of the model in our application domain, the field of air traffic control, using a small example.

Flight KL1243 to DeGaulle Paris, which is docked at gate E11, is delayed because it has to wait for passengers (the expected off-block event after which the aircraft is to taxi to the runway does not occur at the planned time, but occurs 15 minutes later). After further investigation it becomes apparent that the passengers that KL1243 is waiting for are transfers from flight D845. Flight D845, from Heathrow London, was delayed due to strong headwinds, and only just began de-boarding at gate D21.

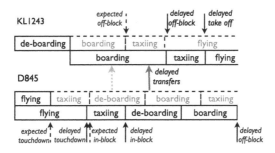

Fig. 4. Example diagnosis

Figure 4 shows the model of the schedule for flights KL1243 and D845. As can be seen, the expected in-block time of D845, which is the start of the de-boarding, was expected before the off-block time of KL1243, but due to (unexpected) weather changes has been delayed. This delay causes a delay in the boarding of KL1243, which is noted by the delay in the occurrence of it's off-block event.

Clearly, diagnosis identifies the explanation: 'strong headwinds: London to Amsterdam'. Note that this diagnosis can be used to predict that other flights from the same direction will probably be delayed as well (until the weather changes).

7   Conclusion

Identifying causes of temporal constraint violations during plan execution is an important issue in many domains, especially in our application domain of air traffic control. Identifying causes of these constraint violations support plan repair and can help improving new plans. In this paper we have investigated whether a plan can be modeled using Discrete Event Systems for the purpose of diagnosing cause of temporal constraint violations. We have shown that plan execution can be modeled using DESs and that a diagnosis can be defined in terms of the presence or absence of external events. Such a diagnosis describes the unforseen state changes in agents executing the plan, equipment used to execute the plan and the environment in which the plan is executed. Finally, we have shown that explanations for individual constraint violations can be determined.

In future work we will investigate whether we can abstract from time information of events and of event generation rules. Moreover, we will investigate efficient distributed implementations of the model based on approaches proposed in [16] and [4].

References

1. Cassandras, C.G., Lafortune, S.: Introduction to Discrete Event Systems. Kluwer Academic Publishers, Boston, MA (1999)
2. Sampath, M., Sengupta, R., Lafortune, S., Sinnamohideen, K., Teneketzis, D.: Diagnosibility of discrete event systems. IEEE Transactions on Automatic Control 40, 1555–1575 (1995)
3. Baroni, P., Lamperti, G., Pogliano, P., Zanella, M.: Diagnosis of large active systems. Artificial Intelligence 110(1), 135–183 (1999)
4. Pencolé, Y., Cordier, M.: A formal framework for the decentralised diagnosis of large scale discrete event systems and its application to telecommunication networks. Artificial Intelligence 164(1–2), 121–170 (2005)
5. Birnbaum, L., Collins, G., Freed, M., Krulwich, B.: Model-based diagnosis of planning failures. In: AAAI 90, pp. 318–323 (1990)
6. Kalech, M., Kaminka, G.A.: On the design of social diagnosis algorithms for multi-agent teams. In: IJCAI-03, pp. 370–375 (2003)
7. Kalech, M., Kaminka, G.A.: Diagnosing a team of agents: Scaling-up. In: AAMAS 2005, pp. 249–255 (2005)
8. Carver, N., Lesser, V.: Domain monotonicity and the performance of local solutions strategies for CDPS-based distributed sensor interpretation and distributed diagnosis. Autonomous Agents and Multi-Agent Systems 6(1), 35–76 (2003)
9. Horling, B., Benyo, B., Lesser, V.: Using self-diagnosis to adapt organizational structures. In: Proc. 5th Int'l Conf. on Autonomous Agents, pp. 529–536. ACM Press, New York (2001)
10. de Jonge, F., Roos, N., Witteveen, C.: Primary and secondary plan diagnosis. In: DX'06. 17th International Workshop on Principles of Diagnosis, pp. 133–140. Universidad de Valladolid (2006)
11. Jonge, F., Roos, N., Witteveen, C.: Diagnosis of multi-agent plan execution. In: Fischer, K., Timm, I.J., André, E., Zhong, N. (eds.) MATES 2006. LNCS (LNAI), vol. 4196, pp. 86–97. Springer, Heidelberg (2006)
12. Roos, N., Witteveen, C.: Diagnosis of plans and agents. In: Pěchouček, M., Petta, P., Varga, L.Z. (eds.) CEEMAS 2005. LNCS (LNAI), vol. 3690, pp. 357–366. Springer, Heidelberg (2005)
13. Roos, N., Witteveen, C.: Models and methods for plan diagnosis. In: Formal Approaches to Multi-Agent Systems (FAMAS'06), ECAI 2006, Workshop Notes (2006)
14. Witteveen, C., Roos, N., van der Krogt, R., de Weerdt, M.: Diagnosis of single and multi-agent plans. In: AAMAS 2005, pp. 805–812 (2005)
15. de Jonge, F., Roos, N.: Plan-execution health repair in a multi-agent system. In: PlanSIG 2004. Proc. 23rd Annual Workshop of the UK Planning and Scheduling SIG (2004)
16. de Jonge, F., Roos, N., van den Herik, H.: Keeping plan execution healthy. In: Pěchouček, M., Petta, P., Varga, L.Z. (eds.) CEEMAS 2005. LNCS (LNAI), vol. 3690, pp. 377–387. Springer, Heidelberg (2005)
17. Sampath, M., Sengupta, R., Lafortune, S., Sinnamohideen, K., Teneketzis, D.: Failure diagnosis using discrete event models. IEEE Transactions on Control Systems Technology 4, 105–124 (1996)

Agent Communication Using Web Services, a New FIPA Message Transport Service for Jade

Esteban León Soto

German Research Center for Artificial Intelligence (DFKI)
Multiagents Systems Group
Esteban.Leon@dfki.de

Abstract. Integration of agents and Web Services has been target of much interest and significant work in the last few years. In this paper an openly available implementation of a FIPA compliant Jade Message Transport System for Web Services is presented and evaluated. It provides a mechanism to integrate Jade agents transparently with Web Services, The proposed message representation is compliant with FIPA and modern Web Services standards and is part of FIPA's initiative to create specifications for Web Services integration. Agent implementations do not require to be changed to interact with Web Services or to provide services using this tool. It also can be used to implement complex conversations as choreographies of Web Services.

1 Introduction

For a long time there has been interest by the agent community to integrate agent technologies with Web Services. The main reason being that Web Services became one of the preferred ways for integrating distributed systems. The integration of Web Services and agents provides agents the accessibility to services they can use and at the same time, agents can provide their services to other interested parties that are not necessarily agents. Initial work in this area started a few years ago in the form of gateways [1] [2]. Their features have improved over time, but in general they base their concept on simple request-response interactions.

The intention in the Web Services community has always been to produce architectures that are service-oriented and that enable the interaction of multiple systems in a business process. There is a strong interest for Web Services platforms to be capable of performing complex interactions between autonomous entities. These processes normally are more complex than the a request-respond interaction between only two parties. Web Services standards covering this area, like Web Services Addressing (WS-Addressing), are making Web Services to be more agent-like. At the same time the main task of multiagent systems' middleware, particularly those based on FIPA standards, has always been to support complex interactions [3]. Therefore to perform complex interactions between FIPA compliant agents using Web Service standards would provide a very solid framework for creating Web Services complex conversations.

P. Petta et al. (Eds.): MATES 2007, LNAI 4687, pp. 73–84, 2007.

The present work is about a Message Transport Service (MTS) implementation for Jade agent platform called Jade WSMTS. The implementation provides a middle-ware grounded on Web Services. The next section describes briefly Jade and Web Services. In Sect. 3 the objectives of Jade WSMTS are stated. After that, in Sect. 4 the implementation is described. A brief example of a message is provided in Sect. 5. Following up is Sect. 6 where the results are discussed and analysed against related work. Also several new tasks which are enabled by this implementation are discussed in this section, before the conclusion.

2   Underlying Technologies

2.1   Jade

Jade[4] is a FIPA [5] compliant multiagent system middle-ware which also serves as agent platform and provides basic services like directories and messaging. Its framework supports the implementation of ontologies for the contents of messages and knowledge of agents. Its http Message Transport Protocol (MTP) and XML encoding specifications do not suffice for true Web Services interoperability: the http MTP and the XML schema for the codec do not follow widely used Web Services standards like Simple Object Access Protocol (SOAP), WS-Addressing, etc. The majority of agent developers have used FIPA's string representation, mainly because it is ready to use and set as default in Jade. Jade is also one of the preferred platforms to implement complex conversations between autonomous agents, because it provides a library of behaviours for performing FIPA interaction protocols. New complex conversations and their corresponding behaviours can be produced from scratch or by combining protocols. This makes Jade a very suitable tool for implementing business processes using agent systems.

2.2   Web Services

Web Services, as defined by the World Wide Web Consortium (W3C)[6], are one of the most accepted mechanisms used for integration of distributed systems and interoperability. They are intended to be used through search, discovery and usage, promoting decoupling of system modules. Web Services are one of the development techniques that have been moving faster towards [7] a level closer to a Service Oriented Architecture (SOA). It provides standards for different aspects, one of them being dynamic messaging: WS-Addressing [8] states the basic properties a Message Envelope must have. This is part of the emerging effort in the Web Services community to perform complex conversations in business processes, which go beyond simple request-response interactions.

3   Objectives

The main objective is to produce a *Web Services based MTS* that enables agents to interact through the web with other Web Services and agents. The FIPA compliant communication framework must remain the same, with the only difference that the grounding of the messages must use Web Services standards. Agents that can communicate using the infrastructure provided by Jade without using the add-on, should be able to communicate using the add-on on Jade, it should not require changes in their implementation.

Other objectives are:

Accessibility. Agents must be capable of connecting to Web Services using the same mechanisms for communicating with other agents. Agents must also be accessible by conventional Web Services. Accessibility must be possible not only with WS-Addressing compliant Web Services, but also with simple or REST services.

Web Services Compliance. Jade should, with this add-on, use conventional Web Services standards, particularly SOAP and WS-Addressing. This is important to ensure that any contribution achieved with this tool works appropriately in any Web Services scenario.

Enable Complex Interaction Patterns for Web Services. Web Services are used dominantly in interaction patterns similar to RPC. An increasing interest exists on supporting more complex interaction patterns, specially in areas like Business Process or Workflows enactment. This tool should enable the implementation of such conversations: using Jade to implement FIPA interaction patterns but grounding them using Web Services standards.

Integrate Jade in a Web Services Infrastructure. Jade should not be used for development only, but also for performing as any other system in a Web Services environment. Therefore it must be integrated as any other conventional java Web application.

XML Content Description. Jade provides mechanisms for creating ontologies, that can be used in the contents of agents' knowledge and also for the contents of messages. Jade will be extended with a XML grammar for the SL language (a XML schema).

4   Jade WSMTS Implementation

For the implementation of the proposed system, the framework chosen for creating the Web Services interface is Axis2 [9] as it is one of the most updated implementations of the aforementioned Web Services standards. This way, it delegates the following up of Web Services standards, isolating the implementation of Jade WSMTS from these constant changes, unburdening the maintenance of Jade WSMTS. Architecturally an Axis2 message Receiver that implements the transformation is registered in Jade as any other MTS, together with Jade and the agent implementations, it constitutes the Axis2 Web Application. Agents can instruct this MTS to *transform*, where applicable, the asynchronous communication of agents in Jade to synchronous communication in Web Services. Apart

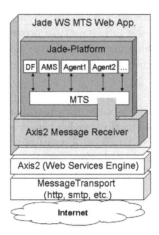

Fig. 1. Jade WSMTS Architectural stack

of that, there is a feature available for agents to register addresses specific for them, in case agents are to be published as REST services instead of the normal mechanism of this tool: a single address for the platform and header annotations with the agent ID of the targeted agent. Figure 1 shows how Jade is integrated into a Web Services environment the same way any other application of this kind is integrated, ready to run over any standard message transport infrastructure.

4.1   Endpoint References (EPR)

The first data information type defined in this implementation, shown in Fig. 2, is the merge of an Endpoint Reference (EPR) [8] and a Agent ID (AID) [10]. EPRs, as its name states, are intended to *refer to endpoints*. This is not sufficient to *identify entities* lying behind the endpoints, the normal practice with agents. This resembles the difference between agents (sateful) and services (stateless). To solve this, EPRs are enriched with the information items that compose an AID in such a way that properties with matching semantics stay as specified for EPRs, making EPRs a subset of the properties defined by an AID. On one hand, FIPA properties are transparent for entities that cannot process them, like conventional Web Service consumers which need only to know how to reach the service. On the other hand EPRs from conventional Web Services are treated as AIDs of agents that prefer to stay *anonymous*.

4.2   Messaging

The primary contribution of this implementation is the specification of a message envelope for SOAP that merges both properties from FIPA and WS-Addressing standards [11]. The envelope follows a structure defined in [12] which is described in Fig. 3. The structure of the envelope shows how the envelope specification of WS-Addressing is augmented with FIPA specific properties [13] to

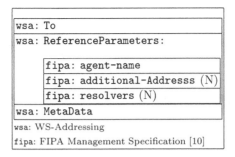

Fig. 2. FIPA AID–WS-Addressing Endpoint Reference

support FIPA standardized communication. The four messaging properties written in *slanted* letters are containers for extra Endpoint References, since the FIPA envelope specification gives these properties plural cardinality in opposite to WS-Addressing which gives them singular cardinality. The value in `wsa:To` will be used as default target address for the message, the extra headers are expected to be processed only by FIPA entities. Some properties belonging to WS-Addressing have taken the roles of analogous properties in FIPA: action, messageID, inReplyTo and message body. Apart of these, other FIPA messaging properties were added, related to the description of the message contents: encoding, language, ontology, protocol, date and details about payload. Agents are free to decide which mechanism to use for a message: to send a message through Jade WSMTS the value identifying SOAP representation is to be set in the *aclRepresentation* envelope property, Jade will automatically choose the corresponding mechanism for delivering the message.

Transport. Message transportation is delegated to Axis2 whenever SOAP messages go outside the agent platform. Axis2 allows also to use other transport protocols, implementations for http and smtp are already provided, others can be implemented which is very useful, because there is interest also in using communication based on other transport mechanisms [14].

Contents. Web Services and FIPA standards leave content metamodel definition open. Even so, it is important to remark the dominance of XML as content representation mechanism, a tendency well supported by Web Services and partially adopted by FIPA standards. FIPA provides also a *Semantic Language (SL)* [15] for the representation of contents. Being this the representation most frequently used for messages that refer to FIPA ontologies, it was also convenient to provide SL representation in XML, to allow other participants that do not share the capability of processing traditional FIPA String representation, to interact with agents that use SL as a grounding for their contents. For that reason, an XML-based codec is provided. It produces contents based on the schema specification provided in [16]. This schema can be used for content type definition in a WSDL description.

wsa: **Action** (fipa performative)	
wsa: **To**	*fipaEnv: IntendedReceivers* *fipaACL: ExtraReceivers*
wsa: **From**	*fipaEnv: From*
wsa: **ReplyTo**	*fipaACL: ReplyTo*
wsa: **MessageID** (fipa ReplyWith)	
fipaACL: **ConversationID**	
wsa: **Relationships** (includes fipaACL:InReplyTo)	
fipaACL: Encoding	fipaACL: Language
fipaACL: Ontology	fipaACL: Protocol
fipaEnv: Date	**fipaEnv: aclRepresentation**
fipaEnv: payloadLength	fipaEnv: payloadEncoding
soap: **Body** (Message content)	
wsa: WS-Addressing	
fipaEnv: FIPA Envelope	
fipaACL: FIPA ACL specification	

Fig. 3. FIPA–WS-Addressing message envelope

4.3 Publication and Discovery

From the perspective of message transportation, the concepts of publication and discovery are a specific kind of content specification [11].

FIPA architectures provide two registry services [10], the *Agent Management Service (AMS)*, and the *Directory facilitator (DF)*. Publication and discovery, are performed using FIPA SL language. Web Services interaction with these services is enabled using the FIPA-XML-SL codec presented previously, to enable an easier integration with other entities and not only agents.

Agents in the Jade platform are as well capable of using registries outside the agent platform, for instance: UDDI. The contents for both registries is represented differently but the interaction is in principle the same. An integration of the DF and UDDI concepts will not be approached in this implementation since these are considered different solutions for similar problems. Both possibilities are enabled as well as any other facility accessible through Web Services, like semantic matchmakers.

5 Example

The example in Listing 1 shows a message sent using Jade WSMTS. This message is sent by agent *TestAgent1* of *Jade-WebServices-Platform1* (lines 4-13) to agent *df* (the directory facilitator) of *Jade-WebServices-Platform2* (lines 14-19). Some message annotations are added (lines 20 - 30). Note the value for the *acl-representation* (line 26) which identifies the codec used by Jade for processing the envelope. The last header for the message is the action identifying

Listing 1. WS-FIPA message example

```
1   <soapenv:Envelope xmlsl:soapenv="..." xmlsl:wsa="..."
2       xmlsl:fipaEnv="..." xmlsl:am="..." xmlsl:acl="...">
3   <soapenv:Header>
4       <wsa:From>
5           <wsa:Address>
6               http://localhost:8085/axis2/services/MTS
7           </wsa:Address>
8           <wsa:ReferenceParameters>
9               <axis2ns4:agent-name>
10                  TestAgent1@Jade-WebServices-Platform1
11              </axis2ns4:agent-name>
12          </wsa:ReferenceParameters>
13      </wsa:From>
14      <wsa:To>
15          http://localhost:8195/axis2/services/MTS
16      </wsa:To>
17      <axis2ns3:agent-name wsa:IsReferenceParameter="true">
18          df@Jade-WebServices-Platform2
19      </axis2ns3:agent-name>
20      <wsa:MessageID>12356671570200906-0</wsa:MessageID>
21      <acl:conversationID>11176570200906</acl:conversationID>
22      <acl:language>fipa-xml-sl</acl:language>
23      <acl:ontology>FIPA-Agent-Management</acl:ontology>
24      <acl:protocol>fipa-request</acl:protocol>
25      <fipaEnv:acl-representation>
26          fipa.acl.rep.soap.dfki.v.0.1
27      </fipaEnv:acl-representation>
28      <wsa:Action>
29          http://dfki.de/fipa/speechacts/request
30      </wsa:Action>
31  </soapenv:Header>
32  <soapenv:Body>
33  <sl:action-expression xmlsl:ns="...">
34      <sl:actor functionSymbol="agent-identifier">
35          <sl:parameter name="name">
36              <sl:value> <sl:stringValue>
37                  df@Jade-WebServices-Platform2
38              </sl:stringValue> </sl:value>
39          </sl:parameter>
40          <sl:parameter name="addresses">
41              <sl:value>. . .
42                  http://localhost:8085/axis2/services/MTS
43                  . . .</sl:value>
44          </sl:parameter>
45      </sl:actor>
46      <sl:action functionSymbol="register">
47          <sl:operand functionSymbol="df-agent-description">
48              <sl:parameter name="name">
49                  <sl:value functionSymbol="agent-identifier">
50                      . . .
51                  </sl:value>
52              </sl:parameter>
53              <sl:parameter name="protocol">
54                  <sl:value> <sl:element>
55                      <sl:stringValue>fipa-request</sl:stringValue>
56                  </sl:element> </sl:value>
57              </sl:parameter>
58          </sl:operand>
59      </sl:action>
60  </sl:action-expression>
61  </soapenv:Body>
62  </soapenv:Envelope>
```

which speech act is being performed (lines 28-30). Then comes the message contents, as mentioned in line 22, it is represented using FIPA-XML-SL language presented in Sect. 4.2. As stated in line 29, it is a *request* described using

FIPA-Agent-Management ontology (line 23) for the *actor* (lines 34-45) to perform the action (lines 46-60) of *register*ing (line 46) the agent description of the agent sending the message (lines 47-58).

6   Discussion

The most important advantage of this proposal is that it merges, as it can be seen in Fig. 3 and in the example provided, information items from WS-Addressing as well as from FIPA Envelope Specification in a single level. This at the same time enables both technologies to connect transparently and their messages to be processed appropriately by endpoints of any of both technologies. The usage of message addressing properties make it possible to perform complex conversations as proposed by FIPA. Agents not only take advantage of the accessibility to Web Services, as it happens with other proposals, but this implementation provides the possibility to perform complex interaction patterns using SOAP between agents and other agents or Web Services.

For achieving integration, some gaps had to be covered like the sateful nature of agents vs. stateless nature of services or the possible difference in reasoning power between participants. The first one manifests clearly in the definition of the augmented EPR, service-implementing instances are not required to be identifiable. In this implementation Web Services are presented to agents as other agents which are or desire to be anonymous. Agents should therefore be prepared to interact with anonymous agents and to distinguish between them by means other than its name, normally its address. This at least covers the first and most urgent issue, still some others stay open for future study, as discussed in Sect. 6.2 .

6.1   Related Work

The FIPA Agents and Web Services Integration (AWSI) group, dedicated to the creation of new specifications in this area, gathers different approaches for integrating agents and Web Services [17] including the one presented here. The different strategies share in principle the same idea of a wrapper or adapter module. This is the recommended way to integrate heterogeneous systems to a Web Services architecture [18]. Web Services used to lack support for complex conversations and accordingly, integration with agents was done using wrappers[19]. The experience gained in the Agentcities project [20] proposed to enable interoperability using a gateway [21] for the interaction of services and agents. Several solutions have adopted the Gateway approach [22], [7], [23]. Most of them focused on simple Web services request-responses conversations not enabling more complex interactions. Even so, significant results were achieved in the mapping of description [22] and the complex semantics [2], [1] which are areas where approaches tend to be different to those proposed by FIPA.

Jade WSMTS is similar to most of these gateways in the sense that it translates messages, even so, the implementation provides some advantages like the delegation of message transport to Axis2, allowing Jade WSMTS to stay up-to-date with less effort and simplifying Web Services compliance. In fact, Jade WSMTS provides at the moment the most modern FIPA ACL message representation using Web Services standards, which allows to take better advantage of Web Services messaging infrastructure, something useful when implementing agents that should work in a SOA like, for instance: in [24] specific SOAP headers were created to implement a service mediator in charge of forwarding requests to agents performing the actual task, Jade WSMTS would have simplified this significantly: WS-Addressing already provides the headers required which are used accordingly, based on the information in the FIPA ACLMessages.

Jade WSMTS is implemented as any other MTS inside Jade, which is a cleaner integration technique than using an agent for providing such a service. Having such a natural integration in the platform allows a very straightforward and little intrusive integration of agents not originally implemented to use Web Services. The transparent communicational integration in this tool allows agents to use UDDI or services outside of the platform to use the DF, which avoids the overhead of replications and extra translations used in some of the gateways. Even though the DF can provide a Web Service interface to the outside, this feature is not expected to be used frequently by conventional Web Services. The opposite alternative, usage of UDDI by agents, requires additional development, since agent implementations using Jade WSMTS need to process UDDI message contents directly, a codec for this content type is not provided. Most of the gateways provide a translation of WSDL descriptions and UDDI entries to and from their FIPA.

One approach for supporting complex conversations with partners that possess little reasoning power was proposed in [25], an orchestrator services that performs the reasoning about the dialog and guides the participants with the speech acts available to proceed in the dialog, hindering the autonomy of agents. EPRs allow inside their *Metamodel* field to describe the service interface of an Endpoint. This is a feature an agent can use to provide a detailed description of how an answer is expected, an alternative that lets agents interact with entities of less reasoning power, but without compromising autonomy.

Agents can enact complex conversations using Jade .This does not change when using Jade WSMTS: the execution of complex conversations works the same way agents perform in FIPA interaction protocols.

6.2   Future Work

Jade WSMTS clears barriers at the levels of message transportation and representation. Still the difference between natures of both technologies remains, opening new questions and problems. Agents in a multiagent system interact with the assumption that the other agents can understand the meaning of their messages and are capable of reasoning about it. Interaction between parties with different reasoning capabilities tend to reduce the overall communication capacity to levels that can be as low as that of the lowest capable participant, as it happens in some gateways. There can be different scenarios and decisions concerning this aspect: in the case of P2P, the notion of peer implies that all participants share the same level, in some multiagent systems with agents of heterogeneous complexity, the description of agents and the ACLMessage annotations allow to be aware of the communicative capabilities of the agent, like what protocols or ontologies it can process. Another option to cope with this is to provide a taxonomy for participants of a conversation, which takes into account special features the other parties should know about and define the kind of participant and the assumptions that can be made about them to facilitate interaction, after all, the pure communicative capabilities do not define the reasoning power of a participant.

Other open issues are those related to the stateful nature of agents and also the identification mechanisms. The concept of anonymity can be a challenge for agent implementations, because agents will require other mechanisms to differentiate the anonymous parties in a conversation. The traditional stateless nature of services can have bigger repercussions at the time of performing complex conversations, since it relies some times on the concept of commitments which normally implies that parties manage different states during the conversation. Some Web Services support this, at least in certain sense, by using sessions or similar concepts. It is relevant to study the relationship between stateful entities, commitments and complex conversations, also to compare messaging mechanisms like REST and robust messaging like in FIPA or WS-Addressing.

7   Conclusion

Jade WSMTS, a message transport system for Jade agent platform, has been presented. It transports messages using Web Services messaging based on WS-Addressing using Axis2. Agents using Jade WSMTS interact with Web Services using the same mechanism used to interact with other agents. Web Services can interact with agents, they are presented as anonymous agents that provide only an address to reach them. Some considerations have to be taken into account when interacting with Web Services counter-parts, like their reasoning capabilities and communicative flexibility. Entries in the ACLMessage like protocols, language and ontologies give agents an idea of the capabilities of the entities participating in the conversation. At the same time, this tool enables the enactment of complex conversations based on, but not limited to, the FIPA interaction protocols specifications.

The implementation is available as a Jade add-on [26], it provides more comprenhensive examples of synchronous and asynchronous communication, complex conversations and interaction with simple services, also how agents can be reached as REST Service. Apart of that it provides a codec for representing FIPA ontology contents using XML. This proposal is part of the initiative to create a new FIPA specifications for Web Services integration [17].

This implementation opens new doors for experimenting with agent technologies and theories in areas of Web Services like interoperability [27], Web Services, interaction patterns, business processes [28], service composition, etc. One of the main subjects will be to compare REST services vs. robust messaging, stateful vs. stateless peers in a conversation, the necessity or advantages of commitments and also the interaction of entities with different processing power. Ontology contents represented using XML allows for better integration and to compare and study better the effects of ontologies in scenarios of heterogeneous participants, in context, commitments and collective knowledge in a complex conversation.

References

1. Greenwood, D., Nagy, J., Calisti, M.: Semantic Enhancement of a Web Service Integration Gateway. In: Workshop on Services-Oriented Computing and Agent-Based Engineering at AAMAS 05 (2005)
2. Nguyen, X.T., Kowalczyk, R.: WS2JADE: Integrating Web Services with Jade Agents. In: Workshop on Services-Oriented Computing and Agent-Based Engineering at AAMAS 05 (2005)
3. León Soto, E., Fischer, K.: FIPA Agents Platform Integration in an Architecture based on Web Services. In: Agent-based Technologies and applications for Enterprise Interoperability, ATOP Workshop at AAMAS 05 (2005)
4. JADE: Java Agent Development Framework (2001), On line `http://jade.tilab.com`
5. FIPA: Foundation for Intelligent Physical Agents (2002), On line `http://www.fipa.org`
6. W3C: World Wide Web Consortium, `http://www.w3.org`
7. Curbera, F., Khalaf, R., Mukhi, N., Tai, S., Weerawarana, S.: The next step in web services. Communications of the ACM 46(10), 29–34 (2003)
8. W3C: Web services addressing (2006), `http://www.w3.org/2002/ws/addr/`
9. AXIS2: Axis2 SOAP Stack implementation (2006), `http://ws.apache.org/axis2/`
10. FIPA: FIPA Agent Management Specification (2002)
11. León Soto, E.: FIPA Agents Messaging grounded on Web Services. In: Grid Services Engineering and Management (GSEM) P-88 of LNI (2006)
12. DFKI: FIPA Message Envelope representation for Web Services (2007), `http://www.dfki.de/~estebanl/JadeWSMTS/fipaEnvSchema.xsd`
13. FIPA: FIPA Agent Message Transport Envelope Representation in XML Specification. Technical report, Foundation For Intelligent Physical Agents (FIPA) (2002), `http://www.fipa.org/specs/fipa00071/`
14. Palanca, J., Escrivá, M., Aranda, G., García-Fornes, A., Julian, V., Botti, V.: Adding New Communication Services to the FIPA Message Transport System. In: Fischer, K., Timm, I.J., André, E., Zhong, N. (eds.) MATES 2006. LNCS (LNAI), vol. 4196, pp. 1–11. Springer, Heidelberg (2006)
15. FIPA: FIPA SL Content Language Specification (2002)
16. DFKI: FIPA SL representation in XML (2007), `http://www.dfki.de/~estebanl/JadeWSMTS/FIPA-XML-SL.xsd`
17. Greenwood, D., Lyell, M., Mallya, A., Suguri, H.: The IEEE FIPA Approach to Integrating Software Agents and Web Services. In: Sixth International Conference on Autonomous Agents and Multiagent Systems, Industrial Track (2007)
18. Barry, D.K.: Web Services and Service-Oriented Architectures. Morgan Kaufmann, San Francisco (2003)

19. Jennings, N.R.: An agent-based approach for building complex software systems. Commun. ACM 44(4), 35–41 (2001)
20. Agentcities: Agentcities (2002), http://www.agentcities.org
21. Agentcities Web Services Working Group: Integrating Web Services into Agentcities (2002), http://www.agentcities.org/Activities/WG/WebServices/
22. Greenwood, D., Calisti, M.: Engineering web service - agent integration. In: Proceedings of the IEEE International Conference on Systems, Man & Conference, Whitestein, vol. 2, pp. 1918–1925. IEEE, Los Alamitos (2004)
23. Singh, M.P., Huns, M.N.: Service-Oriented Computing Semantics, Processes and Agents. Wiley, Chichester (2005)
24. Sonntag, M.: Agents as Web Service providers: Single agents or MAS? Applied Artificial Intelligence 20, 203–227 (2006)
25. Ardissono, L., Goy, A., Petrone, G.: Enabling conversations with web services. In: AAMAS '03: Proceedings of the second international joint conference on Autonomous agents and multiagent systems, pp. 819–826. ACM Press, New York (2003)
26. León Soto, E.: Jade WS-MTS Add-on, http://jade.tilab.com/community-addons.php
27. Hahn, C., Madrigal-Mora, C., Fischer, K., Elvesæter, B., Berre, A.J., Zinnikus, I.: Meta-models, Models, and Model Transformations: Towards Interoperable Agents. In: Fischer, K., Timm, I.J., André, E., Zhong, N. (eds.) MATES 2006. LNCS (LNAI), vol. 4196, pp. 123–134. Springer, Heidelberg (2006)
28. Zinnikus, I., Elguezabal, G.B., Elvesæter, B., Fischer, K., Vayssière, J.: A model driven approach to agent-based service-oriented architectures. In: Fischer, K., Timm, I.J., André, E., Zhong, N. (eds.) MATES 2006. LNCS (LNAI), vol. 4196, pp. 110–122. Springer, Heidelberg (2006)

Goal-Oriented Interaction Protocols

Lars Braubach and Alexander Pokahr

Distributed Systems and Information Systems
Computer Science Department, University of Hamburg
{braubach, pokahr}@informatik.uni-hamburg.de

Abstract. Developing agent applications is a complex and difficult task due to a variety of reasons. One key aspect making multi-agent systems more complicated than traditional applications is that interaction behavior is based on elaborate communication forms such as negotiations instead of simple method calls. Aimed at facilitating the specification and usage of agent communication, agent research resulted e.g. in the definition and standardization of several general purpose interaction protocols such as contract-net or English auction. Nevertheless, the usage of these valuable interaction patterns currently forces developers to concentrate on the details of message passing instead of thinking in terms of the application domain. To alleviate this problem in this paper a goal-oriented approach is proposed, which hides message passing details allowing developers to concentrate on the domain aspects of protocols. The new approach is based on the BDI agent model and is implemented within the Jadex agent framework. The advantages of the goal-based interaction handling are further illustrated by an example application.

1   Introduction

The ability to interact with each other is generally accepted as one of the important properties of software agents [1]. Interaction is required as a means to coordinate the actions of the individual agents of a multi-agent system (MAS) in order to achieve overall system goals and to improve the effectiveness of the system [2]. Despite the importance of interacting agents, realizing the necessary interactions is one main source of difficulties during the development of a multi-agent system. These difficulties stem from the fact that, unlike traditional systems, multi-agent systems are usually inherently distributed and asynchronous without any central control. Regarding the design and implementation of interactions in a multi-agent system, developers are therefore confronted with a multitude of conceptual and implementation related questions such as:

	1. What are the objectives behind the interaction?
Macro Level	2. What are the characteristic properties of the interaction?
	3. How can the interaction be described and analyzed?

	4. What are the objectives of the interacting agents?
Micro Level	5. How is the interaction related to the agent architecture?
	6. How is the interaction related to domain-specific behavior?

P. Petta et al. (Eds.): MATES 2007, LNAI 4687, pp. 85–97, 2007.
© Springer-Verlag Berlin Heidelberg 2007

According to Ferber [2], interaction can be viewed from a macro level perspective (i.e., for the MAS as a whole) as well as on the micro level (i.e., considering the individual agents). In the macro level perspective, the objectives of the system as a whole (question 1) need to be considered that aim at coordinating the behavior of individual agents towards establishing some global properties of the system (e.g. using market-based coordination mechanisms to achieve fair pricing of traded goods). Properties of interactions (question 2) can be classified according to different criteria related to the dialog structure, which can be defined in advance as a fixed sequence of messages with only a limited number of alternatives (called interaction protocols) or evolve dynamically according to loose regulations allowing flexible reactions of the participants. To support a systematic construction of interactions adequate macro level description means are necessary (question 3) that contain information about the interaction objective as well as the specific properties. Restricting the topic to interaction protocols a variety of techniques has been proposed in the field of multi-agent systems, such as the well known AUML sequence diagrams [3]. Besides the description also the analysis is important for the validation of the system, where approaches range from formal verification to runtime monitoring of agent behavior.

The micro level perspective deals with questions regarding the implementation of the individual agents. To implement the local decision processes of the individual agents, the developer has to lay down the individual objectives (question 4) that apply to the steps of the interaction. After deciding on the agents objectives, the developer is confronted with numerous implementation choices. Nowadays, there exists a vast number of more or less mature software frameworks supporting developers in building complex multi-agent systems [4]. These frameworks employ different agent architectures used to define the behavior of the agents, which are commonly based on abstract mentalistic notions (e.g. the BDI model [5]) or on simple task-centric concepts derived from software engineering needs. Therefore, the question arises, how these internal agent architectures relate to separately designed interactions (question 5). Finally, the developer has to solve the problem of how to integrate the domain-specific application logic with the previously designed interaction flow (question 6).

Despite the importance of all these questions and also of the link between both levels this paper focuses on micro level questions (4-6) and is organized as follows: In Sect. 2, related work regarding the support for interactions in multi-agent systems is presented. Section 3 describes a new approach to the implementation of protocols for BDI-style agents, employing goals as a central concept for establishing the connection between (external) interactions and (internal) reasoning. In Sect. 4, the realization of this approach within the Jadex agent framework is explained and demonstrated with an illustrative example in Sect. 5. The paper concludes with a summary and an outlook in Sect. 6.

2   Related Work

Research that aims at improving the agent interaction realization can be coarsely divided in *protocol-based interactions* and *flexible interactions*, whereby *protocol-based interactions* can be subdivided in *generator-* and *interpreter-oriented approaches*. Generally, *generator approaches* allow transforming protocol descriptions into executable code specifications. E.g. in [6] a tool is presented for the automatic transition of AUML protocol descriptions into JADE behaviors. Further work supports other agent platforms such as Mulan or AgentFactory as well [7,8]. Most generator approaches produce initial code skeletons and leave the connection with the domain logic to the developer (question 6), leading to code maintenance problems as generic protocol code and domain-specific code are highly intertwined. As those approaches are mostly targeted towards simple task-centric agent platforms, the connection of protocols with the target agent architecture is currently also neglected (question 5). The alternative are *interpreter-oriented approaches* that process protocol descriptions at runtime, requiring a mechanism for integrating protocol execution with domain-specific behavior (question 6). E.g. in [9] and [10] interpreters based on (different) formalizations of AUML are proposed, whereby the domain-dependent parts are connected via method invocations whenever a message is received or has to be sent. These approaches still focus on message sequences and do not provide domain level abstractions. Interpreter approaches are also architecture-independent and do not exploit the full potential of a specific agent architecture (question 5).

Flexibility of interactions is achieved by relaxing the constraints that exist in using predefined protocols, leading to more fault-tolerant and hence robust communications, which are driven by the interests of the communication participants and not by predefined sequences of message patterns. E.g. in Hermes [11] a goal-oriented approach is proposed that focuses on the macro level questions (1-3) and aims at decomposing interactions into a hierarchy of interaction goals, where each leaf goal represents a partial interaction. These goals enable failure recovery and rollbacks in case of unexpected communication outcomes. Other approaches exploit the message semantics, i.e., performative and content, to determine how to react to a message (see e.g. the JADE semantic agent [12] and the LS/TS SemCom architecture [13]) or use separate artifacts for mediated interactions between agents (e.g. CArtAgO [14]). These approaches focus on the openness of interactions, targeting question 5 and to some extend also 4 and 6, but usually employ custom control structures instead of established agent architectures such as BDI. As standardized interaction protocols have proven their value also for design and implementation of open systems, flexible interaction approaches should be regarded as augmentation and not as a replacement for protocol-based interaction. While Hermes does not focus on how the partial interactions represented by leaf interaction goals should be implemented, the semantic communication approaches currently do not allow the use of protocols.

An ideal approach should address all the questions posed in the introduction. Specifically, we think that a unified perspective is required that considers protocols with respect to their objectives, agent architecture and domain connection. Only such a holistic view, that is achieved by none of the presented research efforts, will enable an abstract domain-centered perception of interaction protocols. The approach presented in this paper can be regarded as one step in this direction and is motivated by the interpreter-based perspective.

3   Goal-Oriented Protocols Approach

Interaction protocols have gained high attention in the context of multi-agent communication, as they capture established best-practices that facilitate the realization of interaction-based application scenarios. Standardized protocols concretize abstract mechanisms specifically designed for generic domain-independent use-cases. Mechanism-dependent properties help deciding which protocols to use in a concrete project setting. E.g. Wooldridge [1] proposes several general criteria such as social welfare, guaranteed success or individual rationality that can be used for comparing candidate mechanisms. When implementing the corresponding protocols, developers should be enabled to concentrate on the domain-aspects of protocols abstracting away from their realization via message passing. From the micro level questions further requirements on protocol support are deduced.

Agent objectives (question 4) that have been settled during design should be conserved within the implementation, providing an intentional stance [15] with respect to the conversational behavior of agents, which facilitates explainability and predictability of communication. Moreover, agent developers should be enabled to use the same concepts offered by the agent architecture also for the implementation of agent conversations (question 5). A seamless integration allows exploiting the full potential of the architecture and requires the protocol support to be specifically tailored towards a suitable target architecture. Finally, the integration of domain logic with the generic protocols (question 6) should allow a clear separation of both aspects, facilitating the independent further development of both aspects and e.g. understandability and maintainability of application code. The integration should be done on an abstract level promoting the domain-view and hiding message level details.

Starting point for the approach presented in this paper is the belief-desire-intention model of agency (BDI-model) [5]. Interaction goals are introduced for expressing the objectives that the individual communication partners exhibit, serving as the connectives between a generic interaction protocol and the BDI architecture. Goals are advantageous, because they represent the motivations of an agent in an abstract manner, intentionally leaving open the means that could be used for their pursuit, thereby abstracting away from low-level message handling. In addition, goals also facilitate the handling of exceptional situations (e.g. cancelling an interaction by automatically using a separate protocol, when an interaction goal has been dropped). Details regarding the deduction of interaction goals from protocol descriptions and the integration of domain specific behavior by the application developer are presented next.

3.1   Domain Interaction Analysis

In this section, a process is proposed allowing to deduce descriptions of goal-oriented interaction protocols by analyzing normal AUML protocol representations [3]. In Fig. 1 a schematic view of an AUML-based goal-oriented interaction protocol is depicted. It is assumed here that on each side of the protocol a designated protocol goal is defined that exists for the whole lifetime of the role during

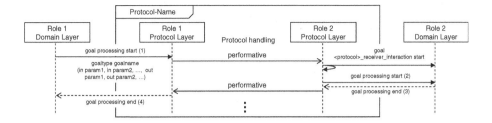

Fig. 1. Protocol analysis with AUML interaction diagrams

protocol execution. This provides an explicit notion of an ongoing conversation on both sides and allows for e.g. querying which conversations are currently pursued, which states they are in and additionally aborting an unwanted interaction by dropping the corresponding goal. In contrast to the original AUML representation each role is divided into two distinct parts. The original protocol layer (middle) is domain-independent and responsible solely for dialog control and execution of protocol specific actions. The protocol layer is augmented by the newly introduced domain layer (left resp. right) which encapsulates domain-relevant actions. The separation of protocols into these distinct parts helps to make explicit the interfaces between the domain and protocol parts. The first task now consists in finding out at which positions in each role of the protocol domain-specific activities are necessary, who initiates these activities and when they will be finished. In the diagram for each such action a goal description needs to be defined. This description consists of a pair of arrows indicating the beginning and ending of the domain activity and which part of a role initiates the activity within the other part. E.g. in the schematic view one can see that the domain layer of role 1 initiates the protocol execution via activity activation within the protocol layer of role 1 and finally fetches the results of its execution (arrows 1 and 4). Similarly, during protocol execution the protocol layer of role 2 needs a domain activity being executed and delegates it to the domain layer of role 2 (arrows 2 and 3). In a second step the goal descriptions need to be refined by specifying the more concrete goal signatures. This means it has to be analyzed what kind of domain activity is needed and which information needs to be transferred forth and back between the domain and protocol part of a role. The kind of activity determines the general goal type to be used, e.g. *query* for information retrieval or *achieve* for task execution. A definition of useful goal types can be found in [16] and is supported by influential methodologies and modeling approaches such as KAOS [17] and Tropos [18]. In the last step the signatures will be completed by adding detailed in- and out-parameter descriptions which have to be deduced from the informal activity descriptions.

3.2   Integration of Domain Behavior

The domain interaction analysis process results in the specification of the individual interaction goals of the participating agents. Interaction goals solve the problem of connecting protocol execution and agent architecture (question 5) as the agent applies its general reasoning strategies to handle these goals. From the viewpoint of the protocol execution, these goals are abstract, i.e., the behavior triggered by these goals is transparent. For the application developer, the interaction goals represent the access point for supplying the domain-dependent behavior (question 6), capturing the activities to be performed for each interaction goal. Goal parameters provide access to the relevant domain and communication data (e.g. the subject-matter of a negotiation), which can be used while executing arbitrary domain tasks. After finishing the domain tasks, the results are made available in the out-parameters of a goal. The goal specification therefore provides a clean interface, allowing the domain behavior accessing necessary information and making results of domain tasks available.

4   Realization Within Jadex

The goal-oriented protocols approach is realized within the Jadex BDI agent system [19]. Jadex aims at facilitating the development of multi-agent systems by introducing abstract notions such as beliefs, goals and plans. It provides a sound architecture and framework for programming goal-oriented agents using established technologies like XML and Java. Goal-oriented protocols are a further step towards this aim, allowing to abstract away from low-level message passing.

4.1   Realization Approach

The domain interaction analysis process allows deriving generic interaction points from AUML protocol descriptions, which are described in terms of goals. During protocol execution, these goals have to be handled or posted from protocol-specific but domain-independent agent behavior. In BDI agent systems such as Jadex, JACK or Jason (see [4]) such behavior can be captured in generic plans which have to be written once, and can be reused in different applications employing the same protocols. A problem with this approach is that plans are not sufficiently expressive for representing self-contained functionalities.

Hence, Jadex implements the extended capability concept [20], which allows to capture BDI-specific agent functionality as a reusable module. Capabilities group together functionally related beliefs, goals, and plans and exhibit a clearly defined interface of accessible beliefs or goals. To support the development of agents based on goal-oriented protocols, a so called *Protocols capability* has been realized as part of the current Jadex release. Based on the derived interaction goals generic plans for standardized FIPA protocols[1] such as Request, (Iterated)ContractNet, as well as English- and Dutch-Auctions have been implemented. While those plans are encapsulated inside the capability, the capability exposes the necessary goals needed to control the protocol execution.

---

[1] See http://www.fipa.org

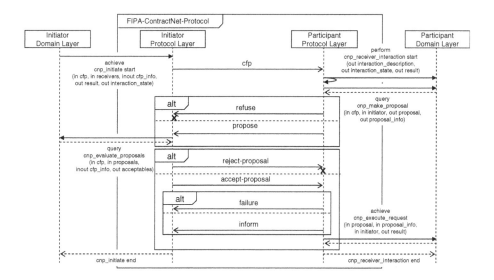

Fig. 2. Goal-oriented AUML contract-net specification (based on [21])

4.2   Example Protocol: Goal-Oriented Contract-Net

Figure 2 shows the result of the domain interaction analysis for the contract-net protocol [21]. On the initiator side the *achieve cnp_ initiate* goal states that a task should be delegated using a contract-net negotiation. It has mandatory in-parameters for the call-for-proposal description (in-parameter *cfp*) and the potential participants (in-parameter *receivers*) and an optional parameter for additional local information (inout-parameter *cfp_ info*). When the cfp message is received by the participant, a *cnp_ receiver_ interaction* goal is automatically created for managing the interaction at the receiver side. The termination of these goals (*cnp_ initiate* resp. *cnp_ receiver_ interaction* end) denotes the end of the interaction and can be observed by the domain layer.

During the automatic protocol execution three interaction points have been identified at which the protocol layers need to initiate domain activities. First the initiator side sends the cfp-description to all potential participants and waits for their replies. On the participant side the *query cnp_ make_ proposal* goal is used to retrieve a proposal (out-parameter *proposal*) for the received cfp-description (in-parameter *cfp*). Additional information to the proposal itself can be stored in the optional out-parameter *proposal_ info*. The proposal (or a refuse message in case no proposal was retrieved) will be automatically sent back to the initiator side. The initiator side uses the *query cnp_ evaluate_ proposals* goal to let the domain layer determine which of the received proposals (in-parameter *proposals*) should be accepted (out-parameter *acceptables*). For this decision it may use the original *cfp* and *cfp_ info* values. The gained information is used to automatically send accept resp. reject messages to the participant side. Every participant whose proposal has been accepted utilizes the *achieve cnp_ execute_ request* goal instructing the domain layer to execute the proposed action (in-parameter *proposal*). The result of the execution (out-parameter *result*) will be transferred back to the initiator side and will be stored in the original *cnp_ initiate* goal.

4.3 Goal-Oriented Contract-Net Implementation

Relevant parts of the contract-net implementation are shown in Fig. 3. The interface of the capability mainly consists of the goals derived from the interaction analysis discussed beforehand (lines 7-17). The protocol layer is realized by the plans encapsulated within the capability (lines 18-23). Exemplarily, the specification of the *cnp_ receiver_ plan* is shown. This plan will be created in response to the receipt of a call-for-proposal message (*cnp_ cfp*, line 21) and implements the participant role of the protocol. The actual code of the plan is contained in the Java CNPReceiverPlan class (cf. line 20) and not shown here. For message handling the plans make use of predefined message types (lines 24-32) derived from the FIPA protocol specifications. As an example, the call-for-proposal message (*cnp_ cfp*, lines 25-31) is further illustrated. Besides some parameter specifications, e.g. for performative and protocol type (lines 26-29), this message contains a match expression (line 30), for configuration purposes as described below.

Agents might contain several protocol capabilities for different purposes and need to decide in which capability an incoming message should be processed.

```
1    <capability name="Protocols" package="jadex.planlib">
2      <beliefs>
3        <belief name="cnp_filter" class="IFilter " exported="true">
4          <fact>IFilter . NEVER</fact>
5        </belief> <!-- Other beliefs omitted for brevity . -->
6      </beliefs>
7      <goals>
8        <achievegoal name="cnp_initiate" exported="true">
9          <parameter name="cfp" class="Object"/>
10         <parameter name="cfp_info" class="Object"/>
11         <parameterset name="receivers" class="AgentIdentifier"/>
12         <parameterset name="result" class="Object" direction="out"/>
13       </achievegoal>
14       <querygoal name="cnp_evaluate_proposals" exported="true">...</querygoal>
15       <querygoal name="cnp_make_proposal" exported="true">...</querygoal>
16       <achievegoal name="cnp_execute_task" exported="true">...</achievegoal>
17     </goals>
18     <plans>
19       <plan name="cnp_receiver_plan">
20         <body>new CNPReceiverPlan()</body>
21         <trigger><messageevent ref="cnp_cfp"/></trigger>
22       </plan> <!-- Other plans omitted for brevity. -->
23     <plans>
24     <events>
25       <messageevent name="cnp_cfp" type="fipa" exported="true">
26         <parameter name="protocol" class="String" direction="fixed">...</parameter>
27         <parameter name="performative" class="String" direction="fixed">
28           <value>SFipa.CFP</value>
29         </parameter> <!-- Other parameters omitted for brevity. -->
30         <match>$beliefbase.cnp_filter.filter  ($messagemap)</match>
31       </messageevent> <!-- Other events omitted for brevity. -->
32     </events>
33   </capability>
```

Fig. 3. Cutout of the Protocols.capability.xml

Therefore, the *cnp_filter* belief (lines 3-5) provides a filter used within the match expression. The belief (which turns off the participant role using IFilter.NEVER) can be overridden for specifying which calls for proposals should be handled.

5   Example Application

To illustrate how the goal-oriented approach can be used in practice the book-trading scenario from [12] is used, where personal buyer and seller agents are responsible for trading books according to instructions given by their principals. The market-based coordination strategy follows the contract-net protocol, equally respecting the goals of buyer and seller agents. It is assumed that buyers take the initiator role of the protocol while sellers play the responder role. The goal-oriented implementation of the booktrading example is part of the Jadex distribution and is divided into files specific to the buyer resp. seller agent, as well as common files (e.g. ontology and GUI classes). Both agents store Order objects in their beliefbase, which represent the current buy or sell orders entered by the agents principals through the user interface of each agent.

5.1   Buyer Agent Implementation

In Jadex, an agent type is described by a so called agent definition file (ADF). Important parts of the buyer agent ADF are shown in Fig. 4. Instances of the

```
1   <agent name="Buyer" ...>
2     <goals>
3       <achievegoal name="purchase_book" recur="true" recurdelay="10000">
4         <parameter name="order" class="Order"/>
5         <targetcondition>Order.DONE.equals($goal.order.getState())</targetcondition>
6         <failurecondition >$beliefbase. time > $goal.order. getDeadline(). getTime()</failurecondition >
7       </achievegoal>
8       <achievegoalref name="df_search"><concrete ref="dfcap.df_search"/></achievegoalref>
9       <achievegoalref name="cnp_initiate"><concrete ref="procap.cnp_initiate"/></achievegoalref>
10      <querygoal name="cnp_evaluate_proposals">
11        <assignto ref="procap.cnp_evaluate_proposals"/>
12        <parameterset name="winners" class="Object" direction="out">
13          <values evaluationmode="dynamic">
14            new Object[]{ select one Integer $price from $goal. proposals
15              where ((Order)$goal.cfp_info). getAcceptablePrice () >= $price.intValue()
16              order by $price  }
17          </values>
18        </parameterset> <!-- Other parameters omitted for brevity. -->
19      </querygoal>
20    </goals>
21    <plans>
22      <plan name="purchase_book_plan">
23        <parameter name="order" class="Order">
24          <goalmapping ref="purchase_book.order"/></parameter>
25        <body>new PurchaseBookPlan()</body>
26        <trigger><goal ref="purchase_book"/></trigger>
27      </plan>
28    </plans>
29  </agent> <!-- Other elements omitted for brevity. -->
```

Fig. 4. ADF excerpt of the buyer agent

```
1   public void body() {
2       IGoal df_search = createGoal("df_search");
3       df_search. getParameter("description "). setValue(getPropertybase(). getProperty("service_seller "));
4       dispatchSubgoalAndWait(df_search);
5       AgentDescription[] result = (AgentDescription[]) df_search. getParameterSet("result "). getValues();
6       if (result . length == 0) fail();
7       AgentIdentifier [] sellers = new AgentIdentifier [result . length];
8       for (int i = 0; i < result . length; i++)
9           sellers [i] = result [i]. getName();
10
11      Order order = (Order)getParameter("order").getValue();
12      IGoal cnp = createGoal("cnp_initiate ");
13      cnp.getParameter("content"). setValue(order. getTitle ());
14      cnp.getParameterSet("receivers "). addValues(sellers );
15      dispatchSubgoalAndWait(cnp);
16
17      order . setExecutionPrice (( Integer )( cnp.getParameterSet("result "). getValues()[0]));
18      order . setExecutionDate(new Date());
19  }
```

Fig. 5. The purchase book plan of the buyer

purchase_ book goal (lines 3-7) are created when new orders are added through
the user interface. To be continuously retried whenever it fails, the goal has a
recurdelay of 10 seconds (line 3). For holding the Order object entered through
the GUI, the goal has one parameter *order* (line 4). In the target condition, the
goal is considered to be reached, when the order is done, i.e., the desired book
was successfully bought (line 5). When the book could not be obtained before
the order deadline, the goal fails (line 6). To search for agents providing specific
services and to initiate a contract-net interaction, the *df_ search* goal (line 8) and
the *cnp_ initiate* goal (line 9) are included. During the execution of the contract-
net interaction, which is performed inside the generic protocols capability, an
instance of the *cnp_ evaluate_ proposals* goal (lines 10-19) is posted, when all
proposals have been collected and need to be rated against each other. In the
booktrading domain, the buyer agent compares the prices of the proposals to
the acceptable price as given in the order from the user (lines 14-16). When
no acceptable proposal is present, the query goal automatically fails due to an
empty *winners* parameter set, otherwise the interaction will terminate with the
buyer accepting the cheapest proposal (due to ordering defined in line 16). In
the plans section (lines 21-28), the *purchase_ book_ plan* is defined (line 22-27),
which is triggered by the *purchase_ book* goal (line 26). The *order* parameter
from the goal is mapped to a plan parameter (lines 23-24), while the body tag
(line 25) refers to the Java class implementing the plan.

The body of the *purchase_ book_ plan* is shown in Fig. 5. It contains two main
parts: First, it has to determine negotiation partners using a *df_ search* subgoal
(lines 2-9). In a second step a parallel negotiation with all suitable sellers is
performed represented by the *cnp_ initiate* subgoal (lines 11-15). When no error
occurs during the negotiation (in which case the plan would immediately fail and
exit), the result is finally stored in the Order object (lines 17-18) making the goal
succeed due to its target condition. When the goal is aborted before the plan
finishes (e.g. if the deadline passes during an ongoing interaction), the plan and

its subgoals will also be aborted, in which case the interaction is automatically terminated using the standardized FIPA-Cancel-Meta-Protocol (cf. [21]).

5.2   Seller Agent Implementation

Domain activities of the seller are triggered by the generic goals of the protocols capability, which are included as shown in Fig. 6. When a call-for-proposal message is received, the *cnp_ make_ proposal* goal (lines 3-19) is created automatically, allowing the agent to decide about making an offer. This query goal is defined declaratively by specifying directly the out-parameter values (lines 6-18), hence no plan is necessary to handle the goal. Instead, the current beliefs of the agent are checked, and if the agent currently whishes to sell the requested book (identified by the title in line 9), the acceptable price (line 16) is returned as a proposal. When the buyer accepts the proposal, a *cnp_ execute_ task* goal is created to complete the transaction. This goal is handled by an *execute_ order_ plan* (not shown), which may handle delivery and payment issues.

```
1   <agent name="Seller" ...>
2      <goals>
3         <querygoal name="cnp_make_proposal">
4            <assignto ref="procap.cnp_make_proposal"/>
5            <parameter name="cfp" class="Object">...</parameter>
6            <parameter name="proposal_info" class="Object" direction="out" optional="true">
7               <value evaluationmode="dynamic">
8                  select one Order $order from $beliefbase . orders
9                  where $order.getTitle (). equals ($cfp) && $order.getState(). equals (Order.OPEN)
10                 order by ($beliefbase . time − $order.getStartTime())
11                    / ($order. getDeadline(). getTime()−$order.getStartTime())
12              </value>
13           </parameter>
14           <parameter name="proposal" class="Object" direction="out">
15              <value evaluationmode="dynamic">
16                 ((Order)$goal. proposal_info ). getAcceptablePrice ()
17              </value>
18           </parameter>
19        </querygoal>
20        <achievegoalref name="cnp_execute_task">
21           <concrete ref="procap.cnp_execute_task"/></achievegoalref>
22     </goals> <!−− Plans and other elements omitted for brevity. −−>
23  </agent>
```

Fig. 6. ADF excerpt of the seller agent

The example shows the clean separation of protocol execution and domain activities, letting application developers focus on domain behavior. Moreover, architectural concepts such as goals and plans can be used as usual also for implementing interaction behavior. Finally, the code is more simple compared to a functionally equivalent implementation of the booktrading scenario in JADE as described in [12]. Although the JADE implementation uses generic classes as well for the contract-net implementation, the buyer and seller implementations are 30-50% larger than the corresponding Jadex implementations presented here.

6   Summary and Outlook

This paper tackles questions concerning the interaction of agents in a multi-agent system, and focuses on the mirco level of interactions, i.e., how to describe and implement interaction protocols from the viewpoint of single agents. Central questions are how to derive and accurately represent the individual objectives in the course of an interaction and how to relate interactions to the agent architecture and to domain-specific behavior. A review of related work reveals that existing approaches do not offer a unified domain-centric view to all these questions, and instead mostly focus on concrete message sequences.

Based on these findings, a new approach is proposed, which brings together an abstract BDI-centered view on domain activities with predefined interaction protocols. As result *goal-oriented interaction protocols* are derived leading to a reduced effort for realizing agent communications. Advantages of the approach are that interaction objectives are conserved in the implementation and a tight integration into the internal agent architecture is achieved. Moreover, the domain layer is separated from the protocol layer facilitating understandability, maintainability and reusability of code. A generic realization and an example application have been presented, demonstrating the feasibility of the approach. Future work can be undertaken in areas such as dynamic protocol selection or execution. E.g., a protocol engine would allow executing abstract user defined protocols additionally to the standardized protocols of the Protocols capability.

References

1. Wooldridge, M.: An Introduction to MultiAgent Systems. John Wiley & Sons, Chichester (2001)
2. Ferber, J.: Multi-Agents Systems. Addison-Wesley, Reading (1999)
3. Bauer, B., Müller, J., Odell, J.: Agent UML: A formalism for specifying multiagent software systems. Software Eng. and Knowledge Eng. 11(3), 207–230 (2001)
4. Bordini, R., Dastani, M., Dix, J., El Fallah-Seghrouchni, A.: Multi-Agent Programming: Languages, Platforms and Applications. Springer, Heidelberg (2005)
5. Bratman, M.: Intention, Plans, and Practical Reason. Harvard Press (1987)
6. Dinkloh, M., Nimis, J.: A tool for integrated design and implementation of conversations in multiagent systems. In: Bordini, R.H., Dastani, M., Dix, J., Seghrouchni, A.E.F. (eds.) Programming Multi-Agent Systems. LNCS (LNAI), vol. 3346, pp. 187–200. Springer, Heidelberg (2005)
7. Cabac, L., Moldt, D.: Formal semantics for AUML agent interaction protocol diagrams. In: Odell, J.J., Giorgini, P., Müller, J.P. (eds.) AOSE 2004. LNCS, vol. 3382, pp. 47–61. Springer, Heidelberg (2005)
8. Rooney, C., Collier, R.W., O'Hare, G.M.P.: VIPER: A VIsual Protocol EditoR. In: De Nicola, R., Ferrari, G.L., Meredith, G. (eds.) COORDINATION 2004. LNCS, vol. 2949, pp. 279–293. Springer, Heidelberg (2004)
9. Ehrler, L., Cranefield, S.: Executing agent UML diagrams. In: Autonomous Agents and Multi-Agent Systems (AAMAS 2004), pp. 906–913. IEEE, Los Alamitos (2005)
10. Scheibe, A.: Ausführungsumgebung für FIPA Interaktionsprotokolle am Beispiel von Jadex (in German). Diplomarbeit, University of Hamburg (2003)

11. Cheong, C., Winikoff, M.: Hermes: Designing goal-oriented agent interactions. In: Müller, J.P., Zambonelli, F. (eds.) AOSE 2005. LNCS, vol. 3950, Springer, Heidelberg (2006)

12. Bellifemine, F., Caire, G., Greenwood, D.: Developing Multi-Agent systems with JADE. John Wiley & Sons, Chichester (2007)

13. Whitestein Technologies: Semantic Communication User Manual, 2.0.0 (2006)

14. Ricci, A., Viroli, M., Omicini, A.: CArtAgO: An infrastructure for engineering computational environments in MAS. In: Weyns, D., Parunak, H.V.D., Michel, F. (eds.) E4MAS. LNCS, vol. 4389, pp. 102–119. Springer, Heidelberg (2006)

15. McCarthy, J.: Ascribing mental qualities to machines. In: Philosophical Perspectives in Artificial Intelligence. Humanities Press, pp. 161–195 (1979)

16. Braubach, L., Pokahr, A., Moldt, D., Lamersdorf, W.: Goal Representation for BDI Agent Systems. In: Bordini, R.H., Dastani, M., Dix, J., Seghrouchni, A.E.F. (eds.) Programming Multi-Agent Systems. LNCS (LNAI), vol. 3346, pp. 44–65. Springer, Heidelberg (2005)

17. van Lamsweerde, A.: Goal-Oriented Requirements Engineering: A Guided Tour. In: Requirements Engineering (RE 2001), pp. 249–263. IEEE Press, Los Alamitos (2001)

18. Giorgini, P., Kolp, M., Mylopoulos, J., Pistore, M.: The Tropos Methodology. In: Methodologies and Software Engineering for Agent Systems, Kluwer, Dordrecht (2004)

19. Pokahr, A., Braubach, L., Lamersdorf, W.: Jadex: A BDI Reasoning Engine [4]

20. Braubach, L., Pokahr, A., Lamersdorf, W.: Extending the Capability Concept for Flexible BDI Agent Modularization. In: Bordini, R.H., Dastani, M., Dix, J., Seghrouchni, A.E.F. (eds.) Programming Multi-Agent Systems. LNCS (LNAI), vol. 3862, pp. 139–155. Springer, Heidelberg (2006)

21. Foundation for Intelligent Physical Agents (FIPA): FIPA Contract Net Interaction Protocol Specification, Document no. FIPA00029 (December 2002)

VWM: An Improvement to Multiagent Coordination in Highly Dynamic Environments

Seyed Hamid Hamraz[1], Behrouz Minaei-Bidgoli[1], and William F. Punch[2]

[1] Department of Computer Engineering,
Iran University of Science and Technology, Tehran, Iran
hamid_hamraz@comp.iust.ac.ir, b_minaei@iust.ac.ir
[2] Department of Computer Science & Engineering, East Lansing,
Michigan State University, MI, USA
punch@cse.msu.edu

Abstract. This paper is aimed to describe a general improvement over the previous work on the cooperative multiagent coordination. The focus is on highly dynamic environments where the message transfer delay is not negligible. Therefore, the agents shall not count on communicating their intentions along the time they are making the decisions, because this will directly add the communication latencies to the decision making phase. The only way for the agents to be in touch is to communicate and share their beliefs, asynchronously with the decision making procedure. Consequently, they can share similar knowledge and make coordinated decisions based on it. However, in a very dynamic environment, the shared knowledge may not remain similar due to the communication limitations and latencies. This may lead to some inconsistencies in the team coordination performance. Addressing this issue, we propose to hold another abstraction of the environment, called Virtual World Model (VWM), for each agent in addition to its primary internal world state. The primary world state is updated as soon as a new piece of information is received while the information affects the VWM through a synchronization mechanism. The proposed idea has been implemented and tested for Iran University of Science and Technology (IUST) RoboCupRescue simulation team, the 3rd winner of the 2006 worldcup competitions.

1 Introduction

A multiagent system (MAS) consists of a group of agents that interact with each other [1, 2]. The research on MAS aims to provide methods and structures for better management of the agents' behavior. The present work is focused on cooperative MAS in which the agents coexist in a highly dynamic environment, such as the test beds provided by RoboCup [3]. The key point in such systems is *coordination* since the agents share a common goal and have to perform optimal joint actions in order to maximize a global payoff function.

P. Petta et al. (Eds.): MATES 2007, LNAI 4687, pp. 98–108, 2007.

1.1 Previous Work on Coordination

Addressing the above problem, previous research focuses on the use of game theoretic techniques [4], communication [5, 6], social conventions [7] and learning [8, 9]. Nevertheless, all these approaches call for exhausting the whole joint action space whose size grows exponentially with the number of agents. A more recent work is a coordination graph (CG) [10], in which the global payoff is decomposed to local ones, and consequently, each agent should only coordinate with its directly connected agents in the CG rather than the whole team. The agents can then apply the Variable Elimination algorithm (VE) [10] or other approximate alternatives such as Max-Plus [11, 12] or Simulated Annealing [13] in order to coordinate with each other.

The mentioned approaches offer coordination mechanisms from the perspective of the *decision making procedure* rather than the *form of implementation*; most of the methods can be implemented *centralized* or *distributed*, with or without utilization of *explicit communication* - depending on the MAS infrastructure and the features of the environment. For example, in [12] the Max-Plus algorithm has been presented both in the formats of centralized and distributed implementations while the procedure of the decision making has remained similar for both forms of the implementations. The only difference is that in the centralized implementation, one agent decides and informs others whereas in the distributed implementation, all of the agents individually make the same decision. Another example is what is reported in [14]; while the VE algorithm inherently calls for communication among the agents, it has been applied in a distributed manner without any kind of communication due to almost full perceptibility of the environment.

1.2 Explicit and Implicit Communication for Coordination

Communication is ordinarily an essential part for developing coordination in a MAS. From the perspective of the present research, the communication can be realized in two manners:

1. Explicit Communication: *Transferring the intentions (decisions) between the agents along the time they are making the decisions.*
2. Implicit Communication: *Transferring the beliefs (knowledge of the environment) asynchronously with the decision making procedure.*

It is generally argued that communication can add unacceptable delays in information gathering and should be kept minimal [15]. Fortunately, one important benefit that coordination with the implicit communication has over the explicit one is that the delay of message passing is not directly added to the time required for decision making.

Centralized implementations call for explicit communication which is an unwanted feature while the environment is so dynamic that the delay of message passing substantially degrades the team performance. Therefore, we are interested in distributed methods that do not exploit explicit communication; they may utilize implicit communication or even no communication. However, for completely removing communications, the environment should be considerably observable like what is reported in

[14], or it should be so simple that the local perception and the *locker-room agree-ments*[1] [16] suffice for coordination. To sum up, the domain of discussion here is situations where the *infrastructure of the MAS* and also the *context-specific restrictions in the MAS environment* obligate the designer to implement the coordination mechanism in a distributed format without the utilization of explicit communication.

There are various papers reporting an implementation of a coordination mechanism without explicit communication, e.g. [14, 17]. These approaches exploit the locker-room agreements and the implicit communication format for coordination. Put another way, the agents perceive the environment and communicate their observations and beliefs (if applicable) to construct rich conceptualizations the same as the outer environment, and consequently, the same as each other. Both the agents' internal illustrations and their locker-room agreements are the source of knowledge for their decisions. Hence, the agents can make coordinated and complementary decisions since they hold rather similar illustrations of the environment.

1.3 Problem Statement

Nonetheless, there is a subtle point which has not been clearly addressed in the previous work. Although the agents try to keep their internal world states up-to-date, they may encounter some inconsistencies in their states with respect to each other. The reason is the differences in the knowledge they acquire, i.e. each agent has its own point of view to the environment. For instance, an agent may perceive a new phenomenon in the world and broadcast it to other agents. During the time required for transferring the message, the agent holds a different illustration of the environment with respect to its teammates and this may generate an inconsistency in the team coordination. One may think that the inconsistency is just a temporal noise which is brushed off after the message transmission is accomplished. It's correct, but in a very dynamic environment, such temporal inconsistencies are generated (and overlapped) again and again, and therefore, the agents always experience some noise while they are trying to coordinate their actions.

What is the solution? A simple one is to avoid the inconsistencies! For example, in the above mentioned scenario, the agent who has transmitted the message can simply ignore the new perceived data until it ensures (with a rate of probability) that the message is received by its teammates. In this way, the agents can avoid the inconsistencies as much as possible while coordinating with each other. However, on the other hand, the newly perceived data is missed for a period of time, and so the agent is always a little behind of its changing environment even in its local domain of perception. In general, the agents for diminishing the inconsistencies should apply a synchronization mechanism. Instead, the mechanism may prevent the agents' internal world states from being real-time[2] in order to synchronize the agents' views. Thus, there is a tradeoff between *avoiding the inconsistencies* and *holding real-time world models*.

---

[1] Predetermined multiagent protocols accessible to the entire team, e.g. the instructions that a coach gives to the players prior to the game.

[2] Real-time internal world state means that the state holds whatever information the agent has received from its environment up to the time - while the synchronization mechanism may not let the received information immediately affect the state.

1.4 Present Paper

This paper aims to provide a structure that appropriately exploits the encountered tradeoff. The main idea is to maintain two world views for each agent. The primary one is being intrinsically updated as the agent receives the information via local perceptions and communications. The other view, called Virtual World Model (VWM), is updated through a synchronization mechanism which tries to diminish the inconsistencies with respect to the other agents' VWMs. Therefore, as pointed before, VWM is rather the consistent view, and so it is a good source for making high-level coordination decisions while the primary world view holds the real-time knowledge of the environment and is suitable for making individual low-level decisions.

The paper is structured as follows: In Sect. 2, the VWM from a general perspective is discussed. High- and low-level decision making is defined, and the agent architecture bearing VWM is presented. Section 3 discusses the VWM in the domain of RoboCupRescue Simulation System (RCRSS) as a case study, where an implementation of VWM for the IUST team, the third winner of the world cup 2006 competitions is presented. We will demonstrate the experimental results in Sect. 4, and finally, Sect. 5 summarizes and concludes the work.

2 VWM in General

The problem was described in the previous section. In this section we describe the general approach for resolving the problem.

2.1 High-Level and Low-Level Decision Making

Decision making in a MAS includes the following general, yet simplified, steps (as depicted in Fig.1):

1. Extracting a global task from the MAS aim.
2. Decomposing the global task into simpler subtasks.
3. Assigning the subtasks to the agents.
4. Accomplishment of the subtasks by the agents and consequently conquering the global task.

Agents, after realizing step 3, should achieve consistent results on what the *team's current global task* and the *contribution of each agent to the task* are[3]. Therefore, realization of the first three steps calls for a coordination plan in the team. On the other hand, the last step is completely agent-dependent, i.e. the agents are not required to concern about other team members while realizing this step. We will refer to the first three steps as the high-level (coordination) and the last as the low-level (agent-dependant) decision makings.

---

[3] Remember that we are talking about distributed implementation of the coordination algorithms, i.e. each agent shall realize all the four steps locally.

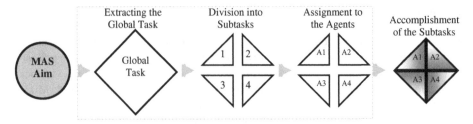

Fig. 1. Decision making phases in a MAS. The three steps surrounded by the dotted rectangle represent the coordination (high-level) part of decision making.

2.2 Agent Architecture

Figure 2 shows an overall architecture of an agent bearing the VWM. The local sensory and the communication information directly affect the primary world model of the agent, while the *synchronizer* symbolizes a mechanism which tries to update the VWM in a way that all the team members (at least the members who are connected in the corresponding coordination graph) hold similar knowledge in their VWMs. In other words, the synchronizer tries to filter the inconsistencies in the agents' VWMs as much as possible.

The decision making part of the agent is divided into two major units. The high-level decision making unit, which utilizes the VWM, is responsible for the high-level part of the decision, and the low-level unit exploits the <u>high-level coordination decision</u> and the <u>real-time knowledge in the primary world model</u> for producing the final low-level action decisions. As an example, consider a soccer team and two players: P_1 and P_2. P_1 utilizes its VWM and determines that it should pass the ball to P_2 in area A of the field. On the other hand, P_2 utilizes its VWM and understands that it is the receiver of a pass and will receive the ball in A. By now, both agents have made the

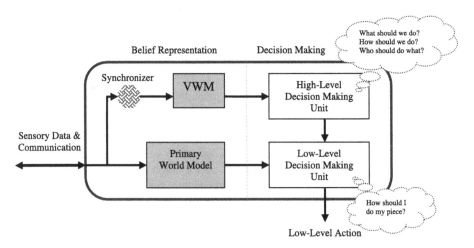

Fig. 2. Overall architecture of an agent bearing the VWM. Note that the agent has two main parts: *Belief representation* and *Decision Making*. The parts work completely asynchronously, i.e. the communication latencies never interfere with the time required for decision making.

high-level decision, and since both of them have exploited their VWMs, the decisions are consistent with each other. In the next step, as the agent-specific low-level actions, P_1 decides how it should kick the ball in order to send it to A, and P_2 will also decide how to intercept the ball while it is coming closer - both exploiting their real-time acquired knowledge in their primary world models. In this way, both agents can make consistent coordination decisions and submit real-time low-level actions to the environment.

3   Case Study: VWM in RCRSS

The critical part of the above architecture is the synchronizer mechanism, which guaranties a consistent coordination if it is realized well. However, the design and implementation of this part is an ad-hoc procedure, i.e. depending on the MAS infrastructure and the features and restrictions of the environment, the mechanism should be devised. In this section, we step through implementation of such architecture in the RCRSS as a case study.

3.1   RCRSS in Brief

RCRSS is a real-time distributed simulation system that is constructed from several modules connected through a network [18, 19]. The system totally simulates the phenomena after an earthquake. Rescue team acts as several independent agents in the simulated environment. There are three modules of rescue agents in RCRSS: *ambulance*, *fire* and *police*. Each module consists of two types of agents: *platoon* and *center* (Fig.3). There usually exists at most one center and *0-15* platoons in each module. Agents perceive the environment within a radius of $10m$ once a cycle[4]. They can also communicate with other rescue agents; that is the agents can utter natural voice or telecommunicate. Natural voice can be heard by humanoids (i.e. rescue agents and civilians) within a radius of $30m$. Telecommunication network is shown in Fig.3. Agents can broadcast message to their directly connected nodes in the graph.

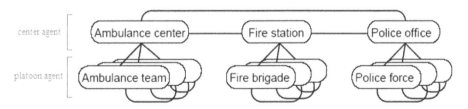

Fig. 3. Telecommunication Network

In order to make the communication sessions more realistic, some limitations have been applied. First, agents can not transmit a message more than 256 bytes in length. Second, platoon agents are not supposed to utter more than 4 messages per cycle.

---

[4] Time quantum of the simulation, during which only one action can be performed by each agent.

Utterance limit for center agents is twice as much as the number of platoons of the same type of the center agent. The third limitation is for hearing capability. Each time a message is received by an agent, it just reads who the sender is, and then it can use or discard the content of the message, depending only on who the sender is. The number of used messages per cycle must not exceed the hearing limit, which holds the same value as utterance limit for both platoons and centers.

3.2   Communication and World Modeling in the IUST Team

Since the RCRSS is a partially-observable environment, agents communicate their sensory inputs every cycle. We implemented the following strategy regarding the communication limitations.

When a platoon agent receives sensory information (i.e. at the start of cycle), it broadcasts the new useful information. The broadcast message is heard by all the connected nodes in the telecommunication graph, i.e. all the platoons and the center of the same type. Suppose that there are *10* platoon agents in a module - each of which transmitting the newly sensed information at the beginning of cycles. Consequently, each of them receives others' *9* messages per cycle while it can not consider more than *4* of them. Therefore, it misses a big fraction of the discovered information by the module members. Avoiding this problem, the platoon agents will not listen to any of the *9* messages; they discard the messages coming from other platoons. Instead, their center will listen to all of the *9* messages as it has the capability of hearing them. It gathers all of the new information, adds into it its own sensory information and the *new data coming from other center agents*, and rebroadcasts it. If the gathered information is too much to be fitted in one message, the center can split it into two or more messages. In this way, the redundant data can be omitted during information gathering phase by the center, and the *9* short messages are converted to one or more longer messages. Therefore, the platoons can receive almost all the discovered information from their center.

Using the new data coming from other centers, when the center is going to rebroadcast the gathered information, creates the link between modules, i.e. platoons will also get aware of discoveries by the other modules' platoons. For example, when a police broadcasts its recently perceived information, the police office will catch it. The office will then rebroadcast the information and its message will be caught by the fire station (ambulance center). The station (ambulance center) will also broadcast the information, and therefore fire brigades (ambulances) will finally receive the new piece of data.

Up to this point, the rescue agents communicate their beliefs of the environment and they can hold rich world models. Note that the communication of beliefs is accomplished in a centralized manner. However, the decision making procedure is realized completely distributed. Implementing any specific strategy which requires coordination among the team members can now be done, i.e. the agents utilize their world models for making both high- and low-level part of their decisions. However, as we exemplified before, there are always some inconsistencies in the agents' world models with respect to each other due to the message propagation latencies, and this may lead to some coordination inconsistencies. In order to filter the inconsistencies and to implement the proposed architecture, we did as follows.

3.3 IUST VWM Structure and the Synchronization Mechanism

The VWM structure is composed of all the variables in the environment that are required for making coordination decisions. In other words, it consists of the data which should be synchronized for the team members.

In the previous part, it is mentioned that each center agent gathers the received information and rebroadcasts it. Keep in mind that the center agent's broadcasts are heard by all of the homogeneous platoons (Fig. 3), e.g. the police office messages are heard by all polices. Therefore, if we forget about the network problems and assume that a transmitted message will certainly reach the targets[5], it can be indicated that all homogeneous platoons receive exactly the same messages from their center.

Hence, the key point for designing the synchronizer mechanism for our special case is that *all the homogeneous platoons receive similar knowledge from their center*. The mechanism is to only let the data receiving from the center agent affect the VWM, rather than the data obtained from other channels, e.g. local perception. As an example, when a police receives its local sensory information, it only updates its primary world model. Also, this information is looped back to all of polices via the police office in a cycle. At this point, the police can update its VWM, because it knows that other polices have also received the same data and they update their VWMs. In this manner, all the platoon agents from the same type can hold consistent knowledge in their VWMs[6].

4 Experimental Results

We utilized the VWM for various coordination tasks in our team such as coordination in searching the city for buried civilians, in how to collectively extinguish a fire block, in how to get distributed among buried civilians for rescuing them and in etc (remember that all of the tasks were implemented in a distributed manner). As a result, we experienced a gentle coordination without any noise in most cases. Moreover, we were exempt of changing the communication mechanism or adding a new protocol while trying to implement a new strategy which demands coordination; all we required to do was to implement the new decision making routines regarding that the knowledge required for the high-level (low-level) decision making routines should be supplied by the VWM (primary world model). In this section, the extract result of coordination in a specific task for both cases of absence and presence of VWM is presented.

---

[5] The issue of message loss is considered in the experimental results.

[6] For instance, all fire brigades have the same VWMs that are different from those of ambulances and polices. Therefore, we can exploit VWM only for intra-module coordination jobs, e.g. among police agents rather than between, for example, polices and fire brigades. Although we might be able to apply a synchronizer mechanism which led to similar VWMs for the whole rescue team, it was sufficient for our purpose to coordinate homogeneous agents using VWM, and implement inter-module coordination jobs using the agents' primary world models.

4.1 Searching Buried Civilians

Police platoons are assigned to clear debris from the roads. After accomplishing the task and opening the main routes, they are assigned to search the city in order to find buried civilians to help the ambulance module. We decided to implement the following strategy for this issue.

1. The number of living polices is calculated.
2. The city is divided into a few pie pieces equal to the number of the living polices.
3. The police agents should be distributed among pieces in a way that their total movement in order to reach their pieces becomes minimal.
4. Each police agent should perform the local search in its piece.

Because of highly dynamic environment, this process should be done dynamically (i.e. at the beginning of each cycle). For instance, a police may die, and therefore its piece may not be searched if the pieces are not assigned dynamically. The first three steps are the coordination and the last one is the final agent-dependent decision making phase. Evaluating the effect of VWM on the quality of coordination, we implemented the above algorithm utilizing once the VWM and once the primary world model for the high-level decision (The first three steps above).

All polices at cycle c perform the steps above, i.e. each police carries out the above listed steps locally. Each of them generates a *police-to-piece* allocation model, i.e. who should search which piece. Therefore, a pool of the models, generated by different police agents, is held for c. Among the pool, the one which is more frequent (has more identical[7] models) is said to be the base decision for c. Each police, who has generated a model rather than the base one in a cycle, is said to be deviated at that cycle.

Figure 4 shows the average results over *10* different simulations. The horizontal axis in the diagram represents the message loss percentile[8] while the vertical axis shows the percentage of agents who were deviated. Agents make the above coordination decision almost *300* times per simulation. Hence, the total average is extracted from near *3000* cycles of decision making by the police platoons.

It is clear that how VWM can decrease the rate of deviation in the team; the rate for VWM is always below the one for primary world model. Situations where there exists some message loss show that even with an incomplete synchronizer mechanism[9] the VWM idea is able to improve the quality of coordination. Another noticeable point is that although the deviation for the VWM disappears completely when the message loss shrinks to zero, the value for the primary world model never disappears and is leveled off in a greater-than-zero point. This value of deviation percentage represents the pure impact of the message delay, which is completely vanished by the utilization of VWM.

---

[7] Two models are said to be identical if they represent exactly similar allocations of polices to pieces, i.e. the number of pieces are the same and the same polices are allocated to the same pieces for both of them.

[8] We programmed the agents to randomly ignore messages. Due to TCP implementation of RCRSS networking, the situation of no message loss could also be tested.

[9] A complete synchronizer mechanism lead into exactly similar VWMs, however, an incomplete one is just able to decrease the inconsistencies. The incompleteness in our case is initiated from the loss of messages.

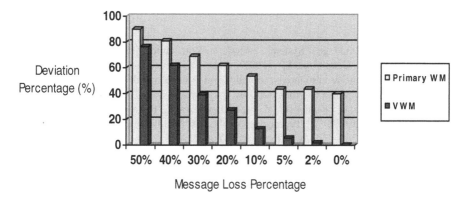

Fig. 4. Percentage of agents who were deviated from the base decision (what made by majority of the agents) is shown both for the primary world model and the VWM

5 Summary and Concluding Remarks

In this paper, we concentrated on highly dynamic environments where the designer of the MAS has decided to implement the coordination mechanism in a distributed format without using any explicit communication. The agents in such systems try to exploit a shared knowledge, which is present in their independent world models, in order to coordinate their decisions and produce an optimal joint action. It is discussed that the agents may suffer from some inconsistencies in their world models with respect to each other. The reason is the difference in the agents' viewpoints to the environment. Resolving the inconsistencies, we propose another abstraction of the environment, the VWM, for each agent, which is tried to be kept consistent to others' through a synchronization mechanism. It is also declared that the synchronization policy may defect the VWM from being real-time, and that is why we haven't omitted the primary world model in our proposed architecture. The decision making procedure in the agents is divided into two major parts: the coordination part which should produce consistent result for all the team members, and the agent-dependant part. Therefore, for the coordination part, agents exploit the synchronized knowledge in their VWMs, and for the other part, the agents exploit their real-time primary world models.

Finally, we applied our proposed architecture in the RCRSS, which was utilized for different tasks demanding coordination. As a result, we experienced gentle coordination without noise in most cases. As a specific experience, we described how the police agents collectively search the city for buried civilians. The algorithm was implemented once with and once without utilization of the VWM and the result was compared, for different rates of message loss. The VWM was able to diminish the inconsistencies and improve the quality of coordination even when there was a considerable amount of message loss.

References

1. Weiss, G. (ed.): Multiagent Systems: a Modern Approach to Distributed Artificial Intelligence. MIT Press, Cambridge, MA (1999)
2. Vlassis, N.: A concise introduction to multiagent systems and distributed AI. Informatics Institute, University of Amsterdam (2003)
3. Kitano, H., Asada, M., Kuniyoshi, Y., Noda, I., Osawa, E.: Robocup: The robot world cup initiative. In: AGENTS '97: Proceedings of the first international conference on Autonomous agents, pp. 340–347. ACM Press, New York (1997)
4. Osborne, M.J., Rubinstein, A.: A Course in Game Theory. MIT Press, Cambridge (1994)
5. Carriero, N., Gelernter, D.: Linda in context. Communications of the ACM 32(4), 444–458 (1989)
6. Gelernter, D.: Generative communication in Linda. ACM Transactions on Programming Languages and Systems 7(1), 80–112 (1985)
7. Boutilier, C.: Planning, learning and coordination in multiagent decision processes. In: TARK '96: Proceedings of the 6th conference on Theoretical aspects of rationality and knowledge, pp. 195–210. Morgan Kaufmann Publishers Inc, San Francisco, CA (1996)
8. Tan, M.: Multi-agent reinforcement learning: Independent vs. cooperative learning. In: Huhns, M.N., Singh, M.P. (eds.) Readings in Agents, pp. 487–494. Morgan Kaufmann, San Francisco, CA (1997)
9. Claus, C., Boutilier, C.: The dynamics of reinforcement learning in cooperative multiagent systems. In: AAAI/IAAI, pp. 746–752 (1998)
10. Guestrin, C., Koller, D., Parr, R.: Multiagent planning with factored MDPs. In: Advances in Neural Information Processing Systems, vol. 14, The MIT Press, Cambridge (2002)
11. Vlassis, N., Elhorst, R., Kok, J.R.: Anytime algorithms for multiagent decision making using coordination graphs. In: Proc. of the International Conference on Systems, Man and Cybernetics, The Hague, The Netherlands (2004)
12. Kok, J.R., Vlassis, N.: Using the max-plus algorithm for multiagent decision making in coordination graphs. In: Bredenfeld, A., Jacoff, A., Noda, I., Takahashi, Y. (eds.) RoboCup 2005. LNCS (LNAI), vol. 4020, pp. 1–12. Springer, Heidelberg (2006)
13. Dawei, J., Shiyuan, W.: Using the simulated annealing algorithm for multiagent decision making. In: Proceedings of RoboCup International Symposium, Bremen, Germany. LNCS, vol. 4434, Springer, Heidelberg (to appear, 2007)
14. Kok, J.R., Spaan, M.T.J., Vlassis, N.: Non-communicative multi-robot coordination in dynamic environments. Robotics and Autonomous Systems 50, 99–114 (2005)
15. Tews, A., Wyeth, G.: Thinking as one: Coordination of multiple mobile robots by shared representations. In: Intl. Conf. on Robotics and Systems (IROS) (2000)
16. Stone, P., Veloso, M.: Task decomposition, dynamic role assignment, and lowbandwidth communication for real-time strategic teamwork. Artificial Intelligence 110, 241–273 (1999)
17. Isik, M., Stulp, F., Mayer, G., Utz, H.: Coordination without negotiation in teams of heterogeneous robots. In: Proceedings of RoboCup International Symposium, Bremen, Germany (2006)
18. Morimoto, T.: How to develop a RoboCupRescue agent (for RoboCupRescue Simulation System version 0) (last visited 20070702) (2002),
   http://ne.cs.uec.ac.jp/~morimoto/rescue/manual/index.html
19. RoboCupRescue Simulation League, TC and OC: RoboCup 2006 Rescue Simulation League Rules (2006)

Dynamic Configurable Auctions for Coordinating Industrial Waste Discharges

Javier Murillo, Víctor Muñoz, Beatriz López, and Dídac Busquets

Institut d'Informàtica i Aplicacions
Campus Montilivi, edifice P4, 17071 Girona
{jmurillo,vmunozs,blopez,busquets}@eia.udg.es
http://iiia.udg.es/

Abstract. The use of auctions for distributing resources in competing environments has produced a large variety of auctions types and algorithms to treat them. However, auctions have some problems when faced with some real-world applications containing renewable and perishable resources. In this paper we present a mechanism to deal with such issues by dynamically configuring some of the auction parameters taking into account the past experience. The mechanism has been used to coordinate industrial discharges and a Waste Water Treatment Plant, so that the treatment thresholds of the plant are never exceeded. We have performed some simulations to evaluate the system, and the results show that with this mechanism the coordination between the industries improves the treatment of the water.

1 Introduction

Auctions are becoming popular to coordinate agents that share resources [1]. There are two major actors in an auction: bidders and auctioneers. The bidder demands the resources, while the auctioneer provides them and decides which bidder should be assigned each resource, in what is called the winner determination or clearing market algorithm.

There is a myriad of different mechanisms to implement auctions, depending on many parameters [2]. However, recent works, such as [3], point out that current auction mechanisms may have some problems in the emerging e-service markets. The reasons for that are the renewable and perishable nature of the resources being auctioned. On one hand, renewability requires that the auctioneer offers the resources every time they become free. Thus, auctions should be repeated (recurrent auctions). On the other hand, a perishable resource cannot be stored or left unused if we are trying to optimize the resource utility.

In the scenario in which the auctioneer is repeating the auction process with the same consumers, it seems appropriate to think on using the auctioneer's experience to improve its decision (clearing the market). Such improvements involve avoiding the same winner each time (dominant bidder) [3] in order to incentivize participation. In addition, such experience can also be used to prevent failures, that is, to build robust solutions. This issue is specially important in

P. Petta et al. (Eds.): MATES 2007, LNAI 4687, pp. 109–120, 2007.

industrial environments, as the one we are working on: waste water treatment management.

A waste water treatment plant (WWTP) accepts the contaminant waste discharges of different industries. The sum of all contaminants arriving at the WWTP should be under its design parameters, otherwise the water cannot be fully treated and the river can be contaminated. Currently, this goal is achieved by assigning a fixed amount of authorized discharges to each industry. As an alternative and more flexible coordination mechanism, we propose the use of an auction process in which the capacity of the WWTP is sold. However, the uncertainty of the application domain, due to uncontrolled discharges, or even the rainfall, can cause some incidences, leading to the failure of the solution established in the auction process, and causing terrible ecological consequences to the river basin. For this reason, the use of past experience that improves the decision process is crucial.

In this paper we present a multiagent framework in which industrial agents coordinate their discharge activities thanks to a recurrent auction mechanism that is dynamically configured according to the experience of the system. The paper is organized as follows. First we describe the multiagent system deployed, based on the waste water treatment system. Then, the auction and the methods to configure it are described. Next, some implementation details are provided. We continue by giving some results and we end with some conclusions.

2 Waste Water Discharge System and Agent Technology

The treatment of the waste water discharged from industries is vital to assure the quality level of the river. For this purpose, the water is treated in a waste water treatment plant (WWTP) [4]. Each plant has several hydraulic and contaminants capacity constraints that are defined according to its expected use (industries and cities in the surroundings that generate the waste). For example, a plant for a city of 128,000 equivalent inhabitants would have the following capacities: maximum flow allowed of 40,000 m^3/d, with at most 100 g/m^3 of Nitrogen, 650 gO/m^3 of Biological Demand of Oxygen (DBO) and 550 g/m^3 of Solids in Suspension (SST).

Discharges come from industries, as well as from cities. In our first approach to the problem, we concentrate on industries, assuming that the city discharges can be aggregated to the closest industry.

Laws regulate the amount of waste water each industry can discharge, as well as the maximum levels of the contaminant components. Moreover, each industry has to pay a given amount per unit of treated water. In addition, the industry can be billed if it discharges some non authorized waste water.

In this distributed scenario, there is a single resource (the flow entering the WWTP) and several consumers that wish to use the resources (the industries). In order to support resource coordination, we have proposed to replicate the scenario in a multiagent system, in which each industry is represented by an *industry agent* and the WWTP by the *WWTP agent* (see Fig. 1). The WWTP

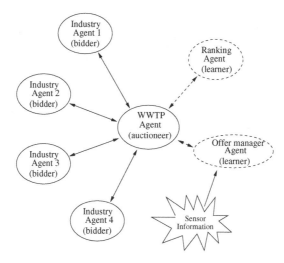

Fig. 1. Multiagent system for WWTP

agent uses an auction process to assign discharge authorizations to the industries. Each time a conflict between industry discharges is detected, the authorization to discharge in the conflicting period is auctioned.

The multiagent approach allows to keep information of each consumer (industry) in privacy, an important issue since discharges are related to the manufacturing activity of industries. For collaboration purposes, each industry agent provides the WTTP agent in advance with a scheduling of the discharges it plans to perform for a given day. With this information, the WWTP agent can detect any overflow situation and coordinate the different industry discharges. If an industry is not allowed to discharge, it could derive the waste water to a buffer that allows the temporary retention of it up to a certain limit. If the buffer is full, the industry can either change its manufacturing activity to avoid the discharge or to discharge the waste water even if it is not authorized to do so. This is an internal decision of the industry agent that, among other issues, takes into account company policies and economic incentives (billing, cost of stopping production, etc.). The multiagent system, however, has been designed with the aim to avoid arriving to such extreme situations.

3 Dynamic Auction Configuration Through Autonomous Agents

The flow is a perishable resource: it cannot be stored and leaving it unused decreases its utilization. So at some extend, the flow behaves as a e-service, inhering the problems of such kind of goods. However, the benefits of auctioning the maximum flow capacity should be balanced with the risk of other factors as the rain and agent behavior that are out of the scope of the auctioneer.

In order to deal with such factors, the auctioneer can dynamically change the amount of flow to be auctioned. For doing so, each auction is configured by means of several parameters that are set up with the help of other additional agents that take care of the previous experience of the system, namely, the *priority agent* and the *offer-manager agent*.

Finally, note that we are dealing with a recurrent auction since the process is repeated each time a conflict arises among the different industry agents schedules (see Fig. 2). In this section we describe the mechanism of the recurrent auction and the agents that are used to set up its configuration

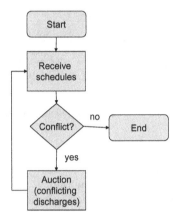

Fig. 2. Recurrent auction flow

3.1   Recurrent Auction of Perishable Resources

For a given day, each industry provides the WWTP agent with its discharges schedule. The WWTP agent analyzes them, trying to find conflicting situations regarding its design constraints. A conflict arises when, for example, the addition of the flows scheduled by the industries exceeds the hydraulic capacity of the WWTP. It could also happen that although the flow is not above the maximum WWTP capacity, one or more of the components (Nitrogen, Biological Demand of Oxygen, etc.) exceed the permissible levels.

Even though there could be more than one conflict for a given day, they are being treated sequentially, resulting in a recurrent auction process. The parameters that set up the auction are the following:

- Agent priority list
- WWTP capacities
- Time interval
- Winner determination algorithm

First, the agent priority parameter is included to deal with the bidder drop problem of recurrent auctions [3]. This problem is related to an uneven wealth distribution of winners, so that poor bidders may starve. Dominants agents, which have been the winners on the latest auctions, have a low priority, while loser agents have a high priority. The agent priority list is computed by the ranking agent based on the previous auction outcomes, as shown below.

Second, the WWTP capacities refers to the resources thresholds to be auctioned. These thresholds are being set by the offer-manager agent based on the previous experiences of the rainfall and the trust on the agents involved in the auction, as detailed at the end of this section.

Third, the time interval is set by the WWTP agent and corresponds to the period in which industry agents have conflicting discharges.

Finally, the winner determination parameter establishes the algorithm used to clean the market. There are several algorithms in the literature, whose performance depends on the problem dimensionality, among other issues. For example, we are using a linear programming algorithm [5] since it outperforms other algorithms when dealing with low scale problems; however, with large scale problems, genetic algorithms may be more appropriate.

Once the auction is configured, it can be started. The WWTP agent sends a call for bids to all the industry agents involved in the conflict. The WWTP agent provides information on the interval to be auctioned. Then, each agent answers with its bid. Each bid is composed by the features of the discharge to be performed during the interval and the price they would pay for the discharge. The price is related to the industry's retention capacity. If it has enough buffer capacity to keep the discharge, the bid price is low; otherwise it is high since the industry has no way to retain that discharge.

The bids received from the industry agents are modified by the WWTP agent according to its priorization. For doing so, we are currently multiplying the price by the agent priority. So bids with high priority (that corresponds to agents which have lost the latest auctions) increase their chances of being the winners. In this sense, we are trying to achieve a fair behavior of the overall process, trying to avoid extreme situations in which an agent that continuously loses is forced to perform the discharges without authorization. Finally, the WWTP agent cleans the auction by providing the list of winners.

If an industry agent loses an auction, it reschedules the discharge and sends its new schedule to the WWTP agent. When the WWTP agent has all the new discharge schedules, it checks again for conflicts. This process is iterated, until a complete schedule without any conflict is obtained (see Fig. 2).

3.2 Bidder Ranking

The ranking agent is in charge of providing a ranking of all the bidders involved in an auction process. It takes into account the outcomes of the bidders in past auctions. The ranking is expressed as a priority value p in $[0, 1]$. The ranking agent keeps a list of successes and failures for each bidder. A success is considered when the bidder wins the auction, while a failure is considered when the industry agent loses. Let $succ_i$ be the number of successes of agent i, and $fail_i$ the number of failures. Then, the priority of agent i is computed as follows [6]:

$$p_i = \frac{fail_i + 1}{succ_i + fail_i + 2} \tag{1}$$

Thus, all agents have an initial priority of 0.5. If an agent loses an auction, its priority is increased; otherwise, it is decreased.

3.3 Preventing Failures

The offer-manager agent is in charge of computing the thresholds of the WWTP's capacities according to the context of the auction so that possible failures can be avoided. This context include the trust on the bidders involved in the auction, and other external factors such as the weather forecast.

On one hand, the offer-manager agent keeps a trust list of all industry agents. This trust value is computed according to the information provided by the industry sensors. These sensors are in the industry pipes in order to bill industries, and can also be used to check whether the amount of discharges produced by the industry corresponds to the contracted ones.

For each agent, the number of uncomplied-contracts ($uncomp$) is being kept, as well as the number of complied-contracts ($comp$). An uncomplied-contract is the one in which the industry agent has lost the auction, but it has performed the discharge anyway. Conversely, if the agent fulfills the auction contract it is considered a complied-contract. Then, using the following equation, the trust t_i of the industry agent i is computed as follows [6]:

$$t_i = \frac{comp_i + 1}{uncomp_i + comp_i + 2} \tag{2}$$

All agents have the same neutral trust at the beginning. As the experience of the system evolves, the trust on the agents is modified, becoming a trustworthy (trust close to 1) or untrustworthy ($t \simeq 0$) agent.

When an untrustworthy agent participates in an auction, it means that there is a risk that the agent performs a discharge even if it does not get the contract. Since this situation is very dangerous for the ecology of the river basin, the offer-manager agent reserves part of the current WWTP capacities for dealing with possible inappropriate discharges. For each WWTP capacity (flow and contaminants) the offer-manager agent computes a trust reduction ΔC_i^{trust}. Let be U the set of untrustworthy agents involved in the auction, that is, agents with a trust level under 0.5. Then, ΔC_i^{trust} is computed as follows:

$$\Delta C_i^{trust} = g(f(c_i^1, t^1), \ldots, f(c_i^{|U|}, t^{|U|})) \tag{3}$$

where t^j is the trust degree of the j-th untrustworthy agent in the conflict, c_i^j is the amount requested by this agent for the i-th capacity of the WWTP, and f and g are functions that compute the individual and collective reduction caused by all the agents in U.

On the other hand, a second factor related to prevention is the rain. In order to take into account this factor we use the information of the weather forecast.

When the weather forecast informs about possible rainfall, the WWTP capacities are also modified. Rain could affect in several ways the WWTP behavior. As a first approach, we decrease the WWTP capacities according to the following equation:

$$\Delta C_i^{rain} = p_r(rain) \cdot rainfall \qquad (4)$$

where $p_r(rain)$ is the probability of rain in the weather forecast, and *rainfall* is the expected amount of rain.

Once the trust and rain reductions have been computed, the auction is set up with the following capacity thresholds:

$$C_i' = C_i - \Delta C_i^{trust} - \Delta C_i^{rain} \qquad (5)$$

where C_i is the design threshold of capacity i of the WWTP.

It is important to note that decreasing the WWTP capacities could be understood as a resource waste. However, wasting the resource could be better than causing an ecological disaster in the river basin. The goal of the above equations is to establish a tradeoff between both factors.

4   Implementation

We have implemented a prototype of the system to evaluate the coordination mechanism. We have used the Repast environment [7], a free open source software framework for creating agent based simulations using the Java language. The simulation reproduces the process and the communication between the WWTP and the industries performing waste discharges. We have created an agent that represents the WWTP, another one for each of the industries and the ranking agent. The offer-manager agent is not yet implemented.

The bid with which the industry agent participates in an auction is computed taking into account the urgency for performing the discharge, based on the buffer occupation of the industry:

$$bid = \frac{\text{buffer occupation}}{\text{total buffer capacity}} \qquad (6)$$

In case an industry agent has to reschedule its discharges, its behavior is the following: it first tries to store the rejected discharge into the buffer. The discharge of the buffer is then scheduled as the first activity of the agent after the conflict finishes. The rest of discharges are shifted so that they do not overlap. If the buffer cannot contain the current discharge, the industry performs it anyway.

As a first evaluation of the system, we have supposed that the industries always obey the WWTP decisions, as long as they have enough buffer capacity. We will introduce different industry behaviors in future experiments to have more realistic scenarios.

Figure 3 shows the application user interface. The graphical representation shows the buffer occupation levels of the industries and the occupation degree of the WWTP.

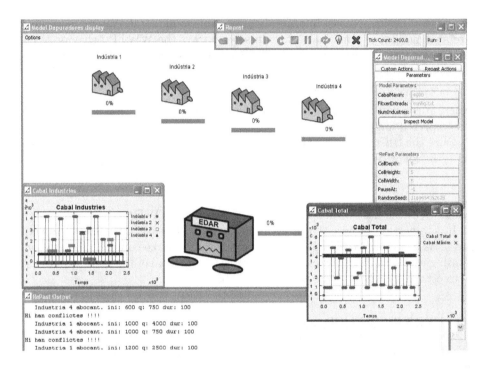

Fig. 3. User interface

5 Results

In order to perform the simulation, we have used a set of real data in a period of 24 hours with 4 industries. So far we have only considered the hydraulic capacity. In the near future we will consider different contaminant components.

Figure 4 shows an example of the behavior of the system without any coordination, while Fig. 5 shows the behavior of the system with the same example when using the recurrent auction mechanism with priorities. In the first figure we can see that the WWTP capacity is being exceeded seven times, while in the second the maximum capacity is never exceeded. When using coordination, there have been some losers in the auctions, but even though some industries had to reschedule their discharges, they have never caused unauthorized discharges. This shows that the priority mechanism favours the industries with high urgency to perform their discharges, so that their buffers do not overflow. However, the overall discharge plan when using coordination is almost 6 hours longer due to rescheduling. This could cause some problems with the scheduling of the following day.

In Fig. 5 we can observe that sometimes the WWTP flow is underused. If industries were allowed to perform multiple discharges (from the buffer and from the production process) at the same time, the reschedule delays could be shortened. We need to deal with this possibility in future work.

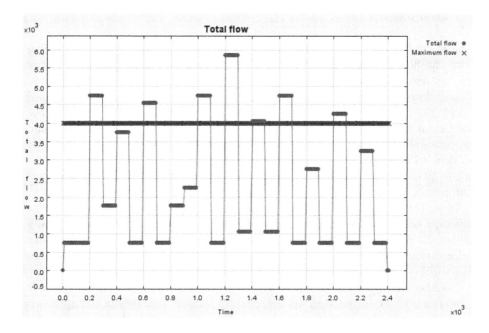

Fig. 4. Behavior without coordination

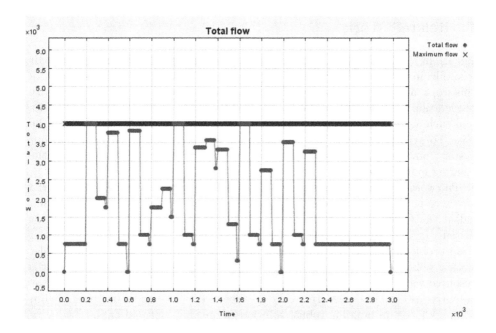

Fig. 5. Behavior with coordination

6   Discussion

The results shown that auctions could be an adequate mechanism for dealing with the flow resource in our waste water domain. Auctions allow to keep in privacy agents information, allowing the combination of the different schedules. Other classical approaches (as for example linear or constraint programming) could take the different discharges and built a global schedule, by imposing the individual schedules to the industries. Even that a negotiation process could be established in this classical scenario, from our understanding it is easier to deal with a conflict at a time (in which at most one discharge by industry is involved) that with a set of discharges (schedules imposed by a central authority).

In addition, we think that the recurrent auctions presented here, with the dynamic configuration of its parameters, can also be extended to share other perishable resources as, for example, communication bandwidth. The use of our priorization model could be used in this kind of environments to get the maximum utility for an auction while providing a fair solution over time.

We also know that the proposed models of priority and trust are quite simple (equations 3 and 4), but they are sufficient to show the validity of our approach on finding such fair solutions over time. Our future work, however, includes the study of better computations, as for example to include the length of the interactions in the trust computation following [6].

7   Related Work

Recurrent auctions have been addressed in recent works in e-service markets. For example, in [8] auctions are used to assign advertising time in a public display. In this work, an heuristic strategy for bidders is implemented based on the history observation and the detected audience. The displaying period is divided in cycles and each agent keeps information about the number of cycles it has won in the past. So agents are using its experience for learning its bidding policy. In our system, however, we focus on the use of the experience in order to improve the clearing market process.

The work presented in [3] also uses recurrent auctions in order to deal with the e-service networking markets. The authors present a novel auction mechanism, called the Optimal Recurring Auction, which tries to overcome the problems arisen when dealing with perishable resources, as the e-service ones: the bidder drop problem and the resource waste problem. We are also tackling the bidder drop problem but with a different strategy: the use of priorities. Regarding the resource waste, we are not so much interested on the maximum utility of the resource, as [3], but on assuring that the resource will never be overused. So our strategy focus on building robust solutions more than optimal ones.

Regarding auctions, it is also important to distinguish between recurring, continuous and iterative auctions. Recurring auctions, as the one described in this paper, are related to auctions that are repeated over time, getting a solution in each execution. Continuous auctions [2] are auctions that accept bids anytime, and clear the market as soon as offers arrive. Finally, iterative auctions are the ones that are repeated, but in each round, the solution is considered an approximation. The auction ends whenever the agents repeat the bids or each agent wins some bid [9].

Concerning waste water treatment, there is recent interest on developing distributed approaches. For example, in [10] a negotiation approach to deal with the coordination of different WWTPs of the same river basin is proposed in order to improve the contaminants discharges. Even that our work could be extended to n WWTP (using, for example, a distributed auction mechanism such as the one proposed in [11]), we are currently focusing on the coordination of the industries governed by a single WWTP.

Finally, we would like to point out that our offer-manager mechanism has been influenced by the research work on resource management of broadband networks. In this field, some logical paths are reserved for backup purposes providing more flexibility to the dynamic management of the network when an incidence occurs [12]. The offer manager agent of our architecture tries to capture this room capacity of the WTTP for backup purposes.

8   Conclusions

In this paper we have presented a recurrent auction mechanism that has been applied to a waste water treatment system. The auction is used to coordinate the contaminant discharge plans of the industries in a global plan that does not exceed any WWTP capacity. Auction configuration is set up according to the past system experience. First, a priority mechanism tries to avoid starvation of poor bidders by feeding the auction process with a prioritized list of agents. And second, an offer-management mechanism is used to set up the resource capacities in order to prevent possible incidences during the execution of the contract auctions.

Results show that our approach achieves the goal of keeping the incoming flow below the WWTP capacity, ensuring that the water is completely treated before going to the river. Although the results are promising, we need to study in more detail the delay consequences of our current solution. However, we believe that auction technology could be more flexible with the industries discharges while taking more profit of the perishable resource involved.

Acknowledgments. Many thanks to the LEQUIA research group for providing the opportunity to work with them in this problem.

This research project has been partially funded by the Spanish MEC project TIN2004-06354-C02-02 and DURSI AGAUR SGR 00296 (AEDS).

References

1. Chevaleyre, Y., Dunne, P., Endriss, U., Lang, J., Lemaître, M., Maudet, N., Padget, J., Phelps, S., Rodríguez-Aguilar, J., Sousa, P.: Issues in multiagent resource allocation. Informatica 30(1), 3–31 (2006)
2. Kalagnanam, J., Parkes, D.: Auctions, bidding and exchange design. In: Simchi-Levi, D., Wu, S., Shen, Z. (eds.) Handbook of Quantitative Supply Chain Analysis: Modeling in the E-Business Era, pp. 143–212. Springer, Heidelberg (2004)
3. Lee, J.S., Szymanski, B.: Auctions as a dynamic pricing mechanism for e-services. In: Hsu, C. (ed.) Service Enterprise Integration, pp. 131–156. Springer, New York (2006)
4. Tchobanoglous, G., Burton, F., Stensel, H.: Wastewater Engineering. Treatment and Reuse, Metcalf and Eddy, Inc., 4th edn. McGraw-Hill, New York (2003)
5. GLPK: GLPK (GNU Linear Programming Kit),
   http://www.gnu.org/software/glpk/
6. Patel, J., Teacy, W., Jennings, N., Luck, M.: A probabilistic trust model for handling inaccurate reputation sources. In: Herrmann, P., Issarny, V., Shiu, S.C.K. (eds.) iTrust 2005. LNCS, vol. 3477, pp. 193–209. Springer, Heidelberg (2005)
7. REPAST: Recursive agents simulation toolkit, http://repast.sourceforge.net/
8. Payne, T.R., David, E., Jennings, N.R., Sharifi, M.: Auction mechanisms for efficient advertisement selection on public displays. In: Brewka, G., Coradeschi, S., Perini, A., Traverso, P. (eds.) ECAI, pp. 285–289. IOS Press, Amsterdam (2006)
9. Parkes, D.: Iterative Combinatorial Auctions: Achieving Economic and Computational Efficiency. Dissertation proposal, University of Pennsylvania (2000)
10. Rendón-Sallard, T., Sánchez-Marré, M., Aulinas, M., Comas, J.: Designing a multi-agent system to simulate scenarios for decision-making in river basin systems. In: Polit, M., Talbert, T., López, B., Meléndez, J. (eds.) Artificial Intelligence Research and Development. Frontiers in Artificial Intelligence and Applications, vol. 146, pp. 291–298. IOS Press, Amsterdam (2006)
11. Gradwell, P., Padget, J.: Markets vs. auctions: approaches to distributed combinatorial resource scheduling. In: Gleizes, M.P., Kaminka, G., Nowé, A., Ossowski, S., Tuyls, K., Verbeeck, K. (eds.) EUMAS, Koninklijke Vlaamse Academie van Belie voor Wetenschappen en Kunsten, pp. 487–488 (2005)
12. Vilá, P.: Dynamic Management and Restoration of Virtual Paths in Broadband Networks based on Distributed Software Agents. PhD thesis, University of Girona (2004)

Distributed Clustering
of Autonomous Shipping Containers
by Concept, Location, and Time

Arne Schuldt and Sven Werner

Centre for Computing Technologies (TZI)
University of Bremen, Am Fallturm 1, D-28359 Bremen
{as, sw}@tzi.de

Abstract. Recent developments in logistics show an increasing trend towards autonomous control. Intelligent software agents, that represent logistic objects like shipping containers, plan and schedule their way through a logistic network. This paper addresses the aspect of cooperation. A special focus lies on the second step of the model for cooperation, namely team formation. The question is by which criteria shipping containers, or logistic objects and agents in general, can form clusters. Starting from the particular demands of the logistics domain this paper argues in favour of conceptual, spatial, and temporal properties. A framework that takes concept, location, and time into account is introduced and demonstrated by an example application.

1 Introduction

Logistics plays an important role in a globalised economy. Trade between different parts of the world demands reliable transport networks. The challenge when dealing with logistic processes is to cope with the complexity and the dynamics that are inherent in these processes. Thus, recent developments show an increasing trend towards autonomous logistics. From the artificial intelligence point of view, such processes can be modelled by software agents which act on behalf of the represented logistic entities in a multiagent system [1].

Today, shipping containers form one of the most important logistic objects as they handle most of the intercontinental transport of packaged goods [2]. In the history of logistics, the concept of containerisation as a medium for intermodal transport is a relatively new one. It has been established since 1956 when Malcom Purcell McLean (1913 – 2001) started to employ containers on a large scale [3]. Containers revolutionised the area of transport logistics as they allow the transfer of goods between different means of transport without the necessity for repacking. In particular, this massively decreases the time required for loading goods onto ships. An important property of shipping containers is that they exhibit standardised sizes which makes them highly interchangeable. Hence, they provide a high degree of abstraction from the concrete goods carried.

P. Petta et al. (Eds.): MATES 2007, LNAI 4687, pp. 121–132, 2007.

Represented by software agents, containers are capable of autonomously planning the transport from their source to a sink. In some situations it might be useful or even necessary to cooperate with other containers in order to meet this objective. A common approach addressing this purpose is the model for cooperation [4]. The question remains what are the criteria by which shipping containers can be grouped together. This paper argues in favour of conceptual, spatial, and temporal properties. The same properties have, for instance, also been applied for information retrieval from the semantic web (e. g. [5,6]).

The remainder of this paper is structured as follows: Section 2 discusses the addressed scenario and Sect. 3 presents related work. The identified clustering criteria are introduced in Sect. 4. A compatible clustering protocol is presented in Sect. 5 and its implementation is dealt with in Sect. 6. As a case study, it is subsequently applied to an example problem in Sect. 7. Eventually, a conclusion follows in Sect. 8.

2   Scenario

This paper addresses the area of forward logistics which deals with procuring products from all over the world. These goods are packed into shipping containers in order to be loaded onto container vessels. The particular focus of this paper lies in an onward carriage scenario, that begins as soon as the containers arrive at their scheduled port of discharge (Fig. 1). The task is then to find an appropriate warehouse in which the contained goods can be received. This is challenging due to the underlying complexity and dynamics. The complexity is caused by the high throughput of containers as well as the parameters influencing the decision, e. g., date of arrival, port of discharge, properties of the goods, and capacities, just to name a few. Containers are sometimes delayed or even lost. This prevents static planning and leads to highly dynamic processes. Approaching this challenge with centralised methods (such as [7]) is, therefore, only efficient to a minor degree.

As discussed in Sect. 1 the idea is therefore to apply an autonomous approach in which the planning and scheduling is carried out locally by the containers themselves. In the process of solving this task the containers' content plays an important role. With regard to the subsequent distribution it is desirable for a company to concentrate similar goods as early as possible. As an example, multiple containers with T-shirts that are scheduled to be sold together should be jointly received in the same warehouse. Proceeding this way allows similar products to be delivered together by truck to the distribution centres. Otherwise, the goods would have to be shipped from multiple warehouses which increases the probability of empty space on the trucks. While this is an argument for the coordination of multiple containers of the same company, there exist also reasons for preventing containers from being clustered. Consider, for instance, fresh fruits. Due to their perishability, they can only be received in a refrigerated warehouse. A second example is that of jewellery which can only be stored in secured warehouses. Furthermore, damaged goods cannot be received in any conventional warehouse; they have to be delivered to a selector who repairs them. These examples illustrate that some goods cannot be received arbitrarily together with

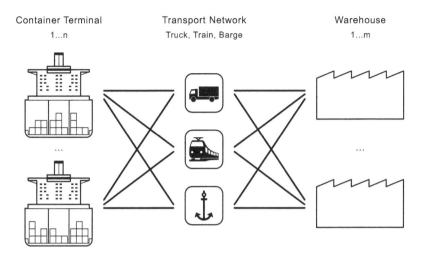

Fig. 1. Containers arriving at a container terminal have to find an appropriate warehouse. Thereby, they also have to choose an available transport network.

others in the same warehouse. The above considerations on the content of containers shall be summarised as their *concept*.

It is clear that the content of containers alone is not sufficient to decide whether they should be clustered. Furthermore, the *location* of containers is relevant. As an example, transporting containers by train is much cheaper than loading them onto trucks. Nevertheless, this is only the case if a certain number of containers is transported together on the same train. Thus, a shipping container has to find partners that share a common location and destination. This directly leads to the third criterion, namely *time*. The containers should additionally be scheduled for a similar date of delivery. Otherwise, some of them are forced to wait for the others; possibly longer than their own scheduled date of delivery.

The above applications indicate the necessity for the clustering of similar shipping containers belonging to the same company. The clustering criteria that can be derived from these examples are concept, location, and time.

3   Related Work

As discussed above, the task is to establish meaningful groups of shipping containers. Clustering algorithms partition a given set of objects into distinct groups. The objective is to achieve a maximal distance between different clusters and a minimal distance between the members of each cluster. Previous algorithms such as k-means [8] generally have a centralised perspective on the data to be clustered. Hence, they cannot be applied to the distributed problem at hand.

Distributed clustering approaches can be found in the area of wireless sensor networks [9]. Like the logistics domain, the application of sensor networks is highly distributed. In general, sensors are spread within a certain area in order to observe specific phenomena. Their primary tasks are acquiring data from the environment as well as transmitting the collected data to a base station. Since the individual sensors act independently of a central power supply, saving energy resources is a crucial task. Therefore, clustering algorithms for sensor networks aim at optimising energy consumption and communication costs. A common approach is to cluster sensors by spatial proximity. The routing of data messages is then organised in a hierarchical way [10]. Each cluster collects the sensor data of its region, aggregates it, and transmits it to the base station. A prominent approach is LEACH, which stands for low-energy adaptive clustering hierarchy [11]. In this method some sensor nodes choose to be cluster-heads. The remaining nodes join the cluster that requires minimum communication energy (generally the spatially closest cluster-head). In order to equally distribute the power consumption for long-range communication the cluster-heads are regularly changed, which also leads to a new cluster partitioning.

In order to judge an application to logistic object agents, it is necessary to discuss differences between sensor networks and the logistics domain. While it seems suitable for sensor networks to form clusters just by spatial proximity and residual energy, this is not the case for shipping containers. By contrast, as described in Sect. 2, further criteria apart from location have to be taken into account. Even w. r. t. location, it is not always reasonable to consider only quantitative spatial distances. In contrast, qualitative relationships between shipping containers (e. g., same destination) are of particular interest. Moreover, the continuous re-clustering in order to distribute power consumption conflicts with the objective of long-term cooperation. Finally, in a sensor network, generally all nodes exist right from the start. In the logistics domain, such a predetermined date does not exist as shipping containers might also join the network later on.

4   Clustering Criteria

The approach presented in this paper is based on the so-called model for cooperation [4]. This model defines a formalisation for cooperative problem solving (CPS) approaches. The CPS process is divided into four steps: recognition of potential for cooperation, team formation, plan formation, and team action. The particular focus of this paper is on forming a distinct team that is capable of realising a certain goal, i. e., the second step. The detection of a potential for cooperation is considered to be agreed upon in the first step in which an agent concludes that some of its goals could be reached by a group of agents. Furthermore, the third and fourth step are carried out after applying the presented method and are also out of the scope of this paper.

In order to address the task of team formation, it is necessary to compare the properties of the respective agents. As described in Sect. 2 the presented approach takes concept, location, and time constraints of agent properties into account. These properties are considered relevant to agents that have to deal with transport problems and that may take advantage of forming clusters. After applying the proposed team formation step in terms of the model for cooperation, the formed cluster of agents is supposed to be adequate for realising the desired goal. However, it is also possible that this phase may not succeed, since failure is also a possible outcome of the model for cooperation.

4.1   Conceptual and Spatial Constraints

The knowledge concerning the content of shipping containers is represented by an ontological approach based on description logics [12]. Description logic is a decidable fragment of first-order logic. The modelling consists of concepts representing sets of objects and roles as relationships between these objects. Figure 2 shows an example ontology that consists of three major parts: article, property, and location. The first part arranges the transported goods by their type into a taxonomical hierarchy. The taxonomy allows the recognition of more general classes of goods; for instance, it can be concluded that T-shirts are textiles. A second part of the ontology comprises properties that goods may have. By introducing further roles it is possible to model that, say, fruits are perishable or jewellery is valuable. In contrast to the type of goods, which generally never changes, the properties may change (although rather seldom). As an example, goods might be damaged during transport. Furthermore, the location of goods can be integrated as an ontological concept, which is the third part. Thus, further restrictions can be realised, e. g., a class comprising all containers with valuable jewellery that are currently at a container terminal. Changes in this part of the description are most likely as goods are transported between different locations.

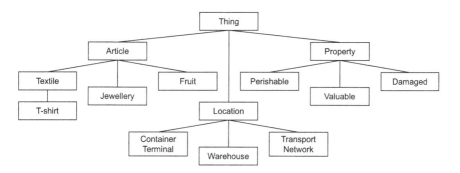

Fig. 2. An example ontology for goods with three major parts: article, property, and location. The lines connecting concepts indicate taxonomical relations.

As discussed above, the ontological descriptions of logistic objects change over time. The time-span in which an ontological concept holds can be characterised with the help of the following definition of temporal intervals:

Definition 1 (Temporal Interval). *A temporal interval τ is defined by a start point t_s and an end point t_e, where $t_s < t_e$:*

$$\tau = (t_s, t_e); t_s, t_e \in \mathbb{N}, t_s < t_e$$

Based on this definition, the ontological concept of a container agent during a given time-span can be defined as a subclass of the universal concept $\top$:

Definition 2 (Agent Concept). *Let α be an agent. The ontological concept of α during τ is represented by*

$$\mathsf{c}(\alpha, \tau) \sqsubseteq \top$$

4.2 Agent Clusters

In order to achieve a common goal, container agents are capable of clustering. The lifetime of the whole cluster can thereby exceed the membership of a single agent. Furthermore, each agent can leave a cluster and rejoin later. Therefore, the membership of an agent cannot be characterised by a single temporal interval. By contrast, a set of intervals has to be applied (which might also be empty):

Definition 3 (Cluster Membership). *Let α be an agent, let γ be a cluster. The membership of α in γ is defined by a set of temporal intervals:*

$$\mathsf{m}(\alpha, \gamma) = \{\tau_1, \ldots, \tau_n\}, n \in \mathbb{N}$$

Before joining a cluster, a container has to determine its similarity to the cluster. This procedure is a special case of the so-called matchmaking problem [13]. It denotes the decision whether advertisements offered by business entities or agents match requests issued by other agents. An approach proposed by [14] addresses this task by considering the formal semantics of ontology-based knowledge representation techniques. They propose five different degrees of match between two concepts c_1 and c_2: exact $c_1 \equiv c_2$, plug-in $c_1 \sqsupseteq c_2$, subsume $c_1 \sqsubseteq c_2$, intersection $\neg(c_1 \sqcap c_2 \sqsubseteq \bot)$, and disjoint $c_1 \sqcap c_2 \sqsubseteq \bot$.

Like agents, clusters are also characterised by concepts that hold within given temporal intervals. During its membership, the concept of each agent is supposed to be subsumed by the cluster concept:

Definition 4 (Cluster Concept). *Let γ be a cluster. The ontological concept of γ during τ is represented by*

$$\forall_{\alpha \in \gamma} \forall_{\tau_i \in \mathsf{int}(\tau, \mathsf{m}(\alpha, \gamma))} \mathsf{c}(\alpha, \tau_i) \sqsubseteq \mathsf{c}(\gamma, \tau) \sqsubseteq \top$$

Apart from subsumption, Definition 4 also uses the auxiliary function int, that computes for a given set of temporal intervals their intersection with a reference interval. This ensures that the concept of the cluster members is only compared for those times that are covered by τ:

$$\mathsf{int}(\tau, \{\tau_1, \ldots, \tau_n\}) = \{(\tau \cap \tau_i) \mid i \in \{1, \ldots, n\} \wedge (\tau \cap \tau_i) \neq \emptyset\} \tag{1}$$

Besides matching containers and clusters, the approach can also be applied in order to find appropriate warehouses. As an example, it can be deduced from the ontology that a cluster of containers carrying damaged T-shirts can be received in a warehouse that is capable of receiving damaged textiles.

4.3   Temporal Constraints

As discussed in the previous section, the concept (including location) of container agents plays an important role during cluster formation. So far, the application of time has been limited to checking whether agents meet a cluster concept during a given temporal interval. Besides, some applications also demand certain temporal relationships between the agents within a cluster. Figure 3 illustrates three shipping container examples. First, if containers plan to be transported by the same truck, one after another, their temporal intervals have to be disconnected (i.e., without overlap). Second, if one container conducts the planning for the whole group, its membership has to subsume the memberships of all other agents. Finally, if containers plan to share a train, their expected dates of arrival at the station should correspond, i.e., the respective intervals must share a common end.

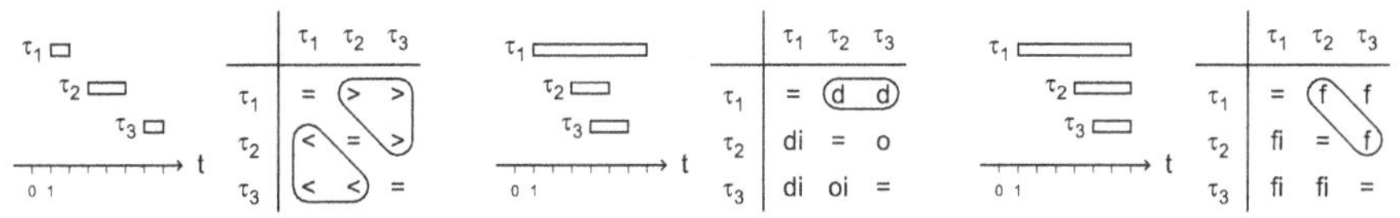

Fig. 3. Three examples for relations between sets of temporal intervals within an agent cluster and the respective temporal matrices

A classical approach for temporal reasoning is formed by Allen's qualitative relational system [15] (qualitative in the sense that it abstracts quantitative data to a semantically defined representation) which is depicted in Fig. 4:

Definition 5 (Temporal Relation). *Let τ_i, τ_j be temporal intervals. The position $\tau_{i\tau_j}$ of τ_j w.r.t. τ_i is then characterised as*

$$\tau_{i\tau_j} \in \{<, >, m, mi, o, oi, s, si, d, di, f, fi, =\}$$

However, these 13 relations characterise pairs of temporal intervals. Hence, this paper proposes a generalised approach of predicates about arbitrary sets of temporal intervals in order to meet the above requirements.

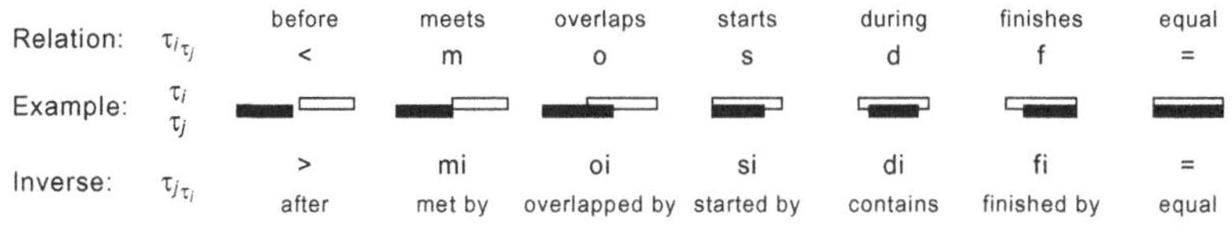

Fig. 4. The 13 relations that have been proposed by Allen [15] in order to characterise the qualitative relationship between two temporal intervals

In order to reason about temporal intervals within a cluster, it is first necessary to obtain all these intervals. This is achieved by the following auxiliary function:

$$\text{allIntervals}(\gamma) = \bigcup_{\alpha \in \gamma} m(\alpha, \gamma) \tag{2}$$

Since the above set is not necessarily sorted (accordingly to start and end points), it is transferred into an ordered list by a further auxiliary function:

$$\text{orderedIntervals}(\gamma) = \langle \tau_1, \ldots, \tau_n \rangle, \tau_i \in \text{allIntervals}(\gamma),$$

$$\forall_{\tau_i = (t_{s_i}, t_{e_i})} \begin{cases} t_{e_i} \leq t_{e_{i+1}} & \text{iff} \quad t_{s_i} = t_{s_{i+1}} \\ t_{s_i} < t_{s_{i+1}} & \text{else} \end{cases} \tag{3}$$

Based on these auxiliary functions, it is then possible to define the matrix M_γ that comprises the relations for all pairs of temporal intervals of a cluster:

Definition 6 (Temporal Matrix). *Let γ be an agent cluster. The matrix*

$$M_\gamma = \langle \tau_1, \ldots, \tau_n \rangle \times \langle \tau_1, \ldots, \tau_n \rangle, \tau_i \in \text{orderedIntervals}(\gamma)$$

characterises the relations $\tau_i \tau_j$ between all temporal intervals in γ with $\tau_i \tau_j$ being the entry in row τ_i and column τ_j.

Figure 3 gives these matrices for the depicted configurations. Restrictions like those discussed in the introductory paragraph of this section can be defined as predicates on the temporal matrices. For instance, in the first example the only relations that are allowed to occur in the whole matrix are $\{<, >\}$. Thereby, the matrix' main diagonal is excluded as it relates each interval to itself, which always results in $=$. For the second example, it has to be ensured that there exists one row comprising at most the relations $\{s, d, f, =\}$. In order to determine the third example it is sufficient to examine pairs of subsequent intervals (which is a diagonal of the matrix). The occurring relations are restricted to $\{f, =\}$. The general definition for these three types of predicates is as follows:

Definition 7 (Temporal Matrix Restriction). *Let γ be an agent cluster. Restrictions on its temporal matrix M_γ can be described by a set ρ of temporal relations and one of the following predicates:*

$$\text{wholeMatrix}(M_\gamma, \rho) = \forall_i \forall_j \ (\tau_i \tau_j \in M_\gamma \wedge i \neq j) \rightarrow \tau_i \tau_j \in \rho$$
$$\text{matrixRow}(M_\gamma, \rho) = \exists_i \forall_j \ (\tau_i \tau_j \in M_\gamma \wedge i \neq j) \rightarrow \tau_i \tau_j \in \rho$$
$$\text{matrixDiagonal}(M_\gamma, \rho) = \forall_i \ \tau_i \tau_{i+1} \in M_\gamma \rightarrow \tau_i \tau_{i+1} \in \rho$$

5   Clustering Protocol

The clustering criteria presented in Sect. 4 are based on semantic knowledge and qualitative relations. Although they are not restricted to specific clustering

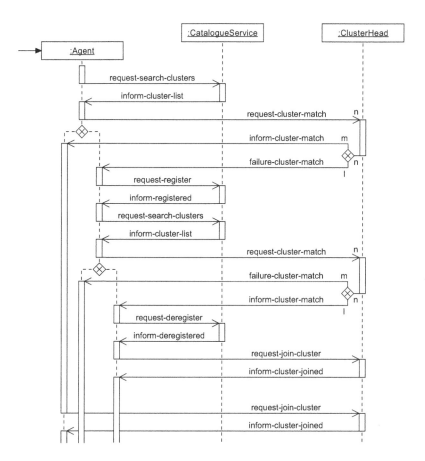

Fig. 5. The protocol flow of the distributed clustering approach for autonomous agents described by an AUML sequence diagram (exceptional messages are omitted for the sake of readability)

algorithms, they cannot be applied with arbitrary methods. As an example, the algorithms discussed in Sect. 3 are not applicable since they demand quantitative distances. This section presents a clustering protocol (Fig. 5) for autonomous agents that is capable of considering the criteria introduced.

As soon as an agent is created, it queries a catalogue service for existing clusters. Subsequently, it communicates its properties to all cluster-heads. Clusters matching the properties of the agent send positive answers. If the requesting agent receives a positive answer, it joins the respective cluster. Otherwise, the agent chooses to register as a cluster-head itself.

The above method suffers from a potential problem: concurrency. Querying the catalogue and registering oneself as a cluster-head is not an atomic operation. Hence, other agents with the same properties can register in between. In order to address this issue, the agent has to send its properties to all cluster-heads that have been registered in between as soon as its registration is finished. If the agent finds another cluster-head exhibiting the same properties and an earlier registration time-stamp, it deregisters and joins the earliest cluster found.

The asymptotic communication complexity of the protocol is $O(mn)$. This can be explained by the fact that all n agents contact at most all m clusters, whereby $m \leq n$. For most applications, m is considered to be even much smaller than n, which means $m \ll n$. The main benefit of this protocol, however, is the high degree of autonomy that is left to the individual agent, since the catalogue service does not make any decisions for the agents.

6   Implementation

The protocol is implemented within the Java-based agent-framework JADE [16]. The simulation is synchronised; it is based on time-slots of one day each. The implementation contains three types of agents. The first one is the shipping container creator agent. It uses real-world data from existing containers and defines agents representing the containers accordingly. The creation is conducted at the respective time-slots. The second agent type represents the shipping container itself. Having determined its respective values for concept, location, and time, this agent type proceeds following the protocol presented in Sect. 5. All communicative actions are conducted according to the FIPA request protocol. They apply the standardised achieve rational effect classes offered by the JADE framework. Due to long response delays of JADE's standard directory facilitator (DF) implementation, a third agent type is defined. This agent administers a list of existing clusters and is called a catalogue service agent: the agent holds a list comprising the agent ids of all cluster-heads. Additionally, it features three basic operations: adding clusters, removing clusters, and questioning the cluster list.

7   Case Study

In order to test the clustering criteria introduced and the performance of the proposed algorithm, a case study is conducted. The goal is to demonstrate that the approach can overcome the limitations of other approaches regarding distribution and semantic knowledge. Furthermore, its applicability to real-world problems has to be examined. As an example application, similar containers located anywhere are expected to form clusters in order to be jointly received in a common warehouse. The purpose is to reduce the subsequent distribution costs as discussed in Sect. 2. The lifetimes of the agents are thereby expected to overlap pairwise without a gap in between.

The case study is carried out with real-world data from about 2,400 containers that were actually in operation during three months in 2006. The containers join the network distributed over this time-span. A manual data inspection reveals that there exist 215 clusters; so this is the expected outcome of the experiment. Due to the asymptotic complexity, it is expected that the number of conversations and the computation time will develop almost quadratically.

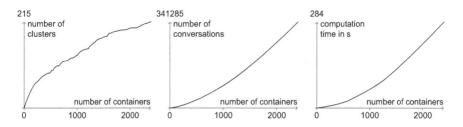

Fig. 6. The number of clusters (left) and conversations (centre) and the time needed for computing the simulation (right) in relation to the number of containers

The average results of 50 test runs are given in Fig. 6. The number of clusters in relation to the total number of agents is depicted on the left hand side. The exact shape of the curve strongly depends on the underlying data. As a result it can, however, be discovered that the final number of clusters is 215 for all test runs, i. e., the algorithm is capable of solving the addressed problem. The total number of conversations (Fig. 6 centre) is 341,285. This is below the expected asymptotic complexity. This result can be explained by the fact that not all clusters exist right from the start. Nevertheless, the plotted part of the curve indicates the expected quadratic shape. This observation also corresponds with the computation time that is depicted on the right hand side of Fig. 6. On a computer with Windows XP and an Intel Centrino Duo processor with 2.16 Gigahertz, the total time for clustering is 284 seconds.

8   Conclusion

This paper introduces a framework that allows agents representing autonomous shipping containers to form clusters by concept, location, and time. The conceptual, spatial, and temporal properties are thereby represented as semantic knowledge and qualitative relations. The case study conducted demonstrates the applicability to problems in the shipping container domain. The method presented does not make special assumptions about the objects represented. Hence, it is not limited to containers and can also be applied in order to realise clustering of other logistic objects (e. g., autonomous packages). As concept, location, and time are general properties, it is also possible to apply the approach in multiagent systems that model domains not related to logistics.

The clustering algorithm presented exhibits two main features. First, it is capable of handling the above semantic features. Second, it is highly distributed and leaves all decision-making to the autonomous agents. A question for future research is how to further reduce communication efforts. Shipping containers are often located within greater logistic entities, such as container vessels or terminals. Therefore, it seems promising to install them as proxies that cache and bundle communication with the catalogue service and the clusters.

References

1. Weiss, G. (ed.): Multiagent Systems. A Modern Approach to Distributed Artificial Intelligence. MIT Press, Cambridge, MA (1999)
2. Günther, H.O., Kim, K.H. (eds.): Container Terminals and Automated Transport Systems. Springer, Heidelberg (2005)
3. Levinson, M.: The Box: How the Shipping Container Made the World Smaller and the World Economy Bigger. Princeton University Press, Princeton, NJ (2006)
4. Wooldridge, M., Jennings, N.R.: The Cooperative Problem Solving Process. Journal of Logic & Computation 9(4), 563–592 (1999)
5. Hübner, S., Spittel, R., Visser, U., Vögele, T.J.: Ontology-Based Search for Interactive Digital Maps. IEEE Intelligent Systems 19(3), 80–86 (2004)
6. Visser, U.: Intelligent Information Integration for the Semantic Web. LNCS, vol. 3159. Springer, Heidelberg (2004)
7. Dantzig, G.B.: Application of the Simplex Method to a Transportation Problem. In: Koopmans, T.C. (ed.) Activity Analysis of Production and Allocation, pp. 359–373. John Wiley & Sons, New York (1951)
8. MacQueen, J.: Some Methods for Classification and Analysis of Multivariate Observations. In: Fifth Berkeley Symposium on Mathematical Statistics and Probability, pp. 281–296 (1967)
9. Akyildiz, I.F., Su, W., Sankarasubramaniam, Y., Cayirci, E.: Wireless Sensor Networks: A Survey. Computer Networks 38, 393–422 (2002)
10. Al-Karaki, J.N., Kamal, A.E.: Routing Techniques in Wireless Sensor Networks: A Survey. IEEE Wireless Communications 11(6), 6–28 (2004)
11. Heinzelman, W.R., Chandrakasan, A., Balakrishnan, H.: Energy-Efficient Communication Protocol for Wireless Microsensor Networks. In: 33rd Hawaii International Conference on System Sciences. vol. 8, pp. 8020–8029 (2000)
12. Baader, F., Calvanese, D., McGuinness, D., Nardi, D., Patel-Schneider, P.F. (eds.): The Description Logic Handbook. Cambridge University Press, Cambridge (2003)
13. Shvaiko, P., Euzenat, J.: A Survey of Schema-Based Matching Approaches. Journal on Data Semantics 4, 146–171 (2005)
14. Li, L., Horrocks, I.: A Software Framework for Matchmaking Based on Semantic Web Technology. International Jounal of Electronic Commerce 8(4), 39–60 (2004)
15. Allen, J.F.: Maintaining Knowledge about Temporal Intervals. Communications of the ACM 26(11), 832–843 (1983)
16. Bellifemine, F., Caire, G., Greenwood, D.: Developing Multi-Agent Systems with JADE. John Wiley & Sons, Chichester (2007)

Coordinating Competitive Agents in Dynamic Airport Resource Scheduling

Xiaoyu Mao[1,2], Adriaan ter Mors[1,3], Nico Roos[2], and Cees Witteveen[3]

[1] Almende B.V, 3016 DJ Rotterdam, The Netherlands
[2] MICC/IKAT, Universiteit Maastricht, The Netherlands
[3] EWI, Technische Universiteit Delft, The Netherlands
{xiaoyu,adriaan}@almende.com

Abstract. In real-life multi-agent planning problems, long-term plans will often be invalidated by changes in the environment during or after the planning process. When this happens, short-term operational planning and scheduling methods have to be applied in order to deal with these changed situations. In addition to the dynamic environment, in such planning systems we also have to be aware of sometimes conflicting interests of different parties, which render a centralized approach undesirable. In this paper we investigate two agent-based scheduling architectures where stakeholders are modelled as autonomous agents. We discuss this approach in the context of an interesting airport planning problem: the planning and scheduling of deicing and anti-icing activities. To coordinate the competition between agents over scarce resources, we have developed two mechanisms: one mechanism based on *decommitment penalties*, and one based on a more traditional (Vickrey) auction. Experiments show that the auction-based mechanism best respects the preferences of the individual agents, whereas the decommitment mechanism ensures a fairer distribution of delay over the agents.

1 Introduction

Aircraft *deicing* and *anti-icing* is required in winter time when frost, snow, and ice form on the wings and fuselage of an aircraft. Such a layer of frost or ice on aircraft surfaces influences the aircraft's aerodynamic properties which may cause a loss of lift that could result in a crash. Deicing refers to the removal of frost, snow, or ice from aircraft surfaces, while anti-icing is the application of a layer of viscous fluid onto aircraft surfaces that should prevent snow or ice from accumulating. Since the deicing and anti-icing operations are always performed together, in the remainder of this paper we will not distinguish them and will use the term *deicing* to refer to both deicing and anti-icing.

The planning and scheduling of deicing activities at airports is an important and challenging part of airport departure planning. Like other real-life planning problems, long term planning can be invalidated by the dynamic changes in the environment during or after the planning process. In these cases, short-term operational planning and scheduling methods have to be applied. In addition to

P. Petta et al. (Eds.): MATES 2007, LNAI 4687, pp. 133–144, 2007.
© Springer-Verlag Berlin Heidelberg 2007

the dynamic environment, in such planning systems we also have multiple self-interested parties that often have conflicting interests, which makes a centralized approach less appropriate.

The dynamic nature of the aircraft deicing problem stems from the fact that in many temperate climate zones as found in Western Europe, the process of deicing is not part of the original flight plan, and thus it has to be scheduled as part of *operational* (i.e., short-term) planning. Moreover, during wintry conditions involving snow and ice, airport capacities will be greatly reduced — again, in temperate climate zones, this is not taken into account in the flight schedules — putting a great strain on the re-planning capabilities of all parties involved. These parties are self-interested and often have conflicting interests. For instance, airlines and pilots will be concerned with the effects of deicing on their flight schedules, air traffic control will be responsible for safe flight movements, the airport itself will strive for a maximum utilization of its facilities (runways, gates, etc.), and the ground servicing companies performing the deicing will want to operate as efficiently as possible. To resolve the dependencies between self-interested parties, we need some form of coordination.

In this paper, we investigate two coordination mechanisms: *i*) coordination based on decommitment penalties and *ii*) a Vickrey auction mechanism. The decommitment-penalties mechanism aims at minimizing the total delay on the airport, and distributing this delay evenly over the agents in the system. The auction mechanism aims to find an allocation of slots that matches the preferences or priorities of the agents (for instance, a fully-loaded Airbus 380 aircraft with many passengers on board may value its punctual departure higher than a half-empty Fokker 50).

This paper is organized as follows. In Sect. 2, we will describe the background of the airport deicing scheduling problem, and we link it to the problem of multi-agent scheduling. In Sect. 3 we will give a formal model of the deicing scheduling problem and we will introduce a simple solution scheme. The agent coordination mechanisms will be discussed in Sect. 4; in Sect. 5 we will show the experimental comparison of the auction and decommitment coordination mechanisms. Section 6 concludes with a look to the future.

2   Background and Related Work

Like many real world problems, the problem of managing deicing resources exhibits characteristics of both planning and scheduling. It is a scheduling problem in the sense that aircraft tasks have to be allocated to resources over time, and it is a planning problem in the sense that an aircraft has a number of choices with regard to which deicing resource to make use of — and this choice of deicing resource has implications for other airport planning problems like arrival planning, departure planning, and taxiway planning. Nevertheless, the management of deicing resources can best be characterized as a scheduling problem as it involves only a small, fixed number of choices, and because the focus is more on time and resource constraints, rather than on ordering of actions (cf. [1]).

If agents were to schedule completely independently of each other, the union of their plans would show many conflicts. In the airport deicing domain, these conflicts will concern the simultaneous use of scarce resources. We therefore define the problem of multi-agent scheduling as follows:

Definition 1 (Multi-Agent Scheduling). *Given a set of agents each with a set of tasks to schedule, and a set of resources to schedule them on, each agent should find an individual schedule for its tasks in such a way that none of the resource capacity constraints are violated.*

Obviously, satisfying all resource constraints will not happen by magic; the agents will need some coordination mechanism that will safeguard these constraints. Therefore, we can summarize the multi-agent scheduling problem as follows:

Multi-Agent Scheduling = Distributed Scheduling + Coordination

Within multi-agent scheduling research, two main tracks can be identified: cooperative agent scheduling and competitive agent scheduling (or selfish scheduling). The scheduling of deicing resources has characteristics of both cooperative and competitive scheduling, as the aircraft/airline agents are competing for access to scarce resources, whereas deicing-resource agents are collaborating in order to maximize resource utilization. In this paper, we will focus our attention on mechanism design for selfish agents.

Since the work of Nisan and Ronen [2] on mechanism design, in 1999, selfish scheduling has recently been studied by many researchers. Some researchers consider the machines to be the selfish agents machines [3,4,5], while others associate an agent with a single task or job [6,7]. However, all these works differ from our paper since they dealt with scheduling problems in a static environment.

Related work on dynamic selfish scheduling is by Vermeulen et al. [8], who developed a Pareto-optimal appointment exchanging algorithm in a patient-scheduling problem. The objective is to improve upon the initial schedule, constructed using first come, first served, by letting patient-agents exchange their slots. It is quite similar to the work of Paulussen et al. [9] where the agent coordination mechanism is a dynamic schedule-repair affair that can be classified as an after-scheduling coordination mechanism. Although Vermeulen's slot swapping mechanism may be a valuable optimization tool in a dynamic schedule repair context, there is still a need for a coordination mechanism that finds a satisfying initial schedule.

In this paper we present and compare two coordination mechanisms for obtaining an initial schedule: the first is based on an auction for selling deicing slots, the second is based on decommitment penalties. In previous research, auction-based scheduling methods have been well studied since they respect the natural autonomy and private information in decentralized systems [10,11,12]. In contrast to these previous approaches, we investigate the auction-based scheduling scheme in a dynamic scheduling environment. Decommitment research has been primarily used to enable agents to explore new opportunities from the domain or from other agents [13,14]; an example is a package-delivery agent that decommits the contract for one package so that it is able to accept a more profitable package to deliver [13]. Another use of decommitment penalties is to allow agents to speculate on future events [15]. We propose that the concept of decommitment penalties can also be used to coordinate agents, by associating a penalty with the occurrence of an agent decommitting from a slot because it could not make the agreed time. In this sense, the decommitment mechanism curbs the greedy tendency of agents to grab the deicing station resource as early as possible, before other agents have a chance to take it. Now, every agent gets that chance, but it has to suffer the consequences if it miscalculated its ability to make its slot.

3   Modelling the Aircraft Deicing Scheduling Problem

In this section we will present a formal model of the aircraft deicing scheduling problem and discuss how uncertainty in the environment influences the scheduling process.

Definition 2 (Aircraft Deicing Scheduling Problem). *The aircraft deicing scheduling problem is a tuple $\langle A, D, c, \tau, p, P, l \rangle$ where*

- *A is a set of n aircraft agents,*
- *D is a set of m deicing station resources,*
- *$c : D \to \mathbb{N}$ is a capacity function specifying the number of aircraft that can simultaneously be serviced at the deicing station (i.e., the number of bays),*
- *$\tau : A \to \mathbb{R}$ is a function associating a Target Off-block Time with every agent, which is in fact the time aircraft is able to leave the gate for deicing,*
- *$p : A \to \mathbb{R}$ is function that specifies the deicing process duration for a certain aircraft,*
- *$P : \mathbb{R} \times A \to \mathbb{R}$ is a function that gives the the probability that an incident will happen to a certain agent,*
- *$l : \mathbb{R} \times A \to \mathbb{R}$ is a function that assigns a cost to the delay of an aircraft.*

The incident probability $P(t, a_i)$ indicates the probability that an incident will occur in the interval $[t, \tau(a_i)]$, i.e., the time during which the aircraft agent will receive ground services at the gate. The occurrence of such an incident may delay the Target Off-block Time, and rescheduling will therefore be needed for an aircraft having a deicing slot right after τ. The aircraft delay cost function $l : \mathbb{R} \times A \to \mathbb{R}$ maps delay in minutes to cost, reflecting the fact that different agents may have different value systems.

A solution to an instance $\langle A, D, c, \tau, p, P, l \rangle$ is a multi-agent schedule given by the vector $S = \langle (d_1, I_1), \ldots, (d_n, I_n) \rangle$ where (d_i, I_i) is a tuple in which $d_i \in D$ is the deicing station assigned to agent a_i during interval I_i such that

$$I_i = [s_i, \; s_i + p(a_i)] \land s_i \geq \tau(a_i) \tag{1}$$

where s_i is the deicing start time of a_i. A feasible schedule satisfies the following resource constraints: at every point in time t, the deicing resource utilization for every resource does not exceed its capacity:

$$\forall t \forall d \in D | \{a_j \in A \mid (d, I_j) \in S \wedge t \in I_j\}| \leq c(d) \qquad (2)$$

Given a Target Off-block Time for each aircraft agent a_i, an individual agent tries to minimize its delay $dl_i = s_i + p(a_i) - \tau(a_i)$. For the set of all agent schedules, we can define two optimization criteria: the first is to minimize the total delay cost of all aircraft: $\min \sum_{a_i \in A} l(dl_i, a_i)$ as a measure of social welfare; another criterion is to minimize the sum of standard deviations in individual aircraft delay, which reflects the fairness of resource allocation at the airport.

Although the list of things that can go wrong in airport deicing operations is too extensive to fit into an elegant model of agent reasoning with uncertainty, observations from real and simulated deicing operations lead us to conclude that many incidents are concentrated in the ground servicing of the aircraft. For example, if the apron in front of an aircraft accumulates too much snow, it becomes difficult for ground servicing vehicles like baggage carts to reach the aircraft, and push-back vehicles cannot find the grip required to tow an aircraft away from the gate. Hence, there is a great deal of uncertainty surrounding the Target Off-block Times of aircraft.

If an aircraft agent is considering at time t whether to reserve (or bid for) the deicing slot starting at time t_s ($t_s \geq t$), then two factors are relevant:

1. $\delta_1 = \tau(a) - t$: If δ_1 is large, then there are many ground servicing tasks that still need to be performed, in which case the probability that something will cause a delay is considerable.
2. $\delta_2 = t_s - \tau(a)$: If the reserved slot is very far away from the Target Off-block Time, then a small delay during ground handling will not necessarily mean that the deicing slot will be missed.

In this paper, we assume that the probability-of-decommitment only depends on δ_1 and no incidents will occur after ground services are finished. Hence, we assume that the probability-of-decommitment function has the following form:

$$P(t, a) = \begin{cases} 0 & \tau(a) < t \\ \min(c, \alpha \cdot (\tau(a) - t)) & \text{otherwise} \end{cases} \qquad (3)$$

where c and α are constant values between 0 and 1. The constant c provides an upper bound on the probability of having an incident, even if t is an arbitrarily early time of requesting the de-icing slot. The constant α regulates the rate of incident-occurence. If α is very large, then even when a de-icing slot is requested close to the off-block time, there is a high probability of suffering an incident.

4   Coordination Mechanisms

In this section we will describe two coordination mechanisms: coordination using a Vickrey auction to sell deicing slots to the highest bidder and coordination through decommitment penalties.

A simplifying assumption we will make for both coordination settings is that there is only a single deicing station having a single deicing bay. Having multiple deicing stations makes the problem more interesting from a combinatorial optimization point of view, but it is not especially relevant to our investigation into the relative merits of auctioning and decommitment.

4.1 Vickrey Auction Mechanism

Bidding for a (deicing) slot is a straightforward way of distributing the scarce deicing slots over the self-interested aircraft agents[1]. Our idea is that the aircraft agents with the highest need get the best slots. In the airport scheduling case, the different preferences of the aircraft agents can be the result of, for example, the number of passengers aboard an aircraft, or the level-of-service that an airline wishes to maintain. If we assume that an agent may not sell a slot to another agent in case it has to decommit, then the value of the slot is a *private value*. In private value auctions all auction types give the same result according to the revenue equivalence theorem. Therefore, we choose the Vickrey auction (a closed-bid, second price auction), because of its property that (rational) agents are encouraged to bid their true value. Hence, deicing of aircraft should occur in the order of agents who are willing to pay the most. We will now describe how we set up the auction.

The deicing station will initiate a new auction when the start of next free deicing slot (starting at t_{nextslot}) is approaching, e.g. half an hour before t_{nextslot}. In each auction, the deicing station auctions off the next available deicing slot (alternative auction schemes like accepting bids for multiple deicing slots are less appropriate given the dynamic nature of the setting). To determine its value for a certain slot, an aircraft agent a should first check whether the start time of this slot t_{nextslot} is greater than its Target Off-block Time $\tau(a)$; if it is not, then the agent can't make use of this slot. In case $\tau(a) < t_{\text{nextslot}}$, an agent needs to estimate the delay it will incur by not obtaining the current slot. If there are m other aircraft in the system that also need deicing, then the value of the $(m+1)$-th slot is 0, because all competing agents can be served before this time. Then, the private value for agent a of the slot starting at t_{nextslot} is:

$$pv(a) = l(t_{m+1} - t_{\text{nextslot}}, a) \tag{4}$$

However, not all aircraft agents in the system will be able to compete for the next slot, in case their Target Off-block Times are greater than t_{nextslot}. Therefore, the number m may be smaller than the total number of agents (left) A^* in the system. At the same time, we cannot simply equate m to the number k of *direct competitors* —agents having a $\tau < t_{\text{nextslot}}$— because after the first

---

[1] Note that in the General Motors paint station problem [11], the roles of the agents are reversed: there, the resource agents have needs due to e.g. switching costs from one colour of paint to another. In our deicing problem, the jobs (aircraft agents) have needs, based on their flight schedules and other considerations such as service levels that must be maintained towards their customers.

k aircraft have been serviced, more agents will be ready for deicing. Finding the set A_c of competing agents can be done simply by extending, agent by agent, the set of direct competitors for a slot (see Algorithm 1). Note that in case of insufficient deicing capacity, the set A_c will quickly equal the set of all agents that have not yet received deicing.

Algorithm 1. Calculate the set A_c of agents competing for slot $t_{nextslot}$

$t_{next} := t_{nextslot}; A_c := \phi$
boolean $isDone := false$
while $!isDone$ **do**
    $A' := \{a \in (A^*) | \tau(a) \leq t_{next}\}$
    $A^* := A^* \setminus A'$
    $A_c := A_c \cup A'$
    $t_{next} := t_{next} + |A'| \cdot p(n)$
    if $A' = \phi$ **then**
        $isDone := true$
    end if
end while
return A_c

Having described how to determine the number of competitors for a slot, we now return to the definition of an agent's private value for a slot.

Formula 4 ignores the possibility that incidents can occur during other ground services that will cause an agent to miss its reserved slot. Taking into account the incident probability $P(t, a)$, we get the following private value:

$$pv(a) = l(t_{m+1} - t_{\text{nextslot}}, a) \cdot (1 - P(t, a)) \tag{5}$$

Equation 5 thus expresses that an agent's private value of a slot decreases as the probability increases that it will not make that slot. In the next subsection, we will introduce an alternative coordination mechanism that focuses not so much on agent preferences, but more on the effects of decommitting on the schedule of an agent.

4.2 Decommitment Penalty Mechanism

When an aircraft agent reserves a particular time slot at a resource such as a deicing station, it will commit to turn up at that deicing station at the specified time. If the aircraft fails to show up, it has to pay a decommitment penalty to the deicing station. Hence, with the introduction of decommitment penalties, agents have an incentive to reserve as late as possible; after all, if it reserves a slot five minutes from now, it will be fairly certain it can make this slot. On the other hand, if an agent waits too long to reserve the next available free slot, another aircraft might reserve it. Therefore, the agent will also have an incentive to reserve a slot as early as possible.

Our approach to coordination using decommitment penalties can be described as follows. An agent can reserve any free slot at a deicing station, as the deicing station will accept all requests. However, with a certain probability incidents occur that make it impossible for the aircraft to be present at the deicing station at the agreed time. When such an event occurs, it must decommit and pay a decommitment penalty, which we assume to be an airport-wide constant δ. We assume that the availability of the deicing resource is known to all aircraft agents. Therefore, an aircraft agent a can see when the first available slot starts, and it has to solve the following decision problem:

Do I reserve the currently first available slot, or do I reserve a slot at a later time?

To judge whether the decision to reserve now has any merit, the agent needs to estimate the probability it will have to decommit from the slot. For this, we can make use of Equation 3. Judging the option of reserving a slot at a later time is more difficult, as it needs to predict the availability of deicing slots in the future. This availability depends on at least the following factors:

1. the passage of time; if a slot is available 10 minutes from now, then, if no-one else takes it, there will be a slot 5 minutes in the future 5 minute from now,
2. other agents can reserve slots while an agent is waiting to decide.

Trying to incorporate all these factors into a realistic model is a formidable task, especially as the slot-reserving behaviour of agents may be subject to their perception (and prediction) of other agents' behaviour. Therefore, we will make the following simplifying assumptions to make the task of foretelling the future a more tractable one:

- If an agent has to decommit from a slot, then it will have to find a new slot. Apart from the time lost in decommitment, we assume that the number of aircraft needing deicing per hour stays constant throughout the day. Hence, an agent will not suddenly find itself in a departure peak, after having to decommit.
- When an aircraft opts to postpone its decision to reserve a slot until the next round, and it turns out that another agent has reserved the previously earliest slot, then the start time of the new earliest slot is simply the start time of the old slot plus the deicing time, which we assumed to be equal for all aircraft.

Armed with these simplifications, we can develop a strategy for an aircraft agent.

Strategy (Deicing Slot Reserving Strategy). *Reserve the earliest available slot if the expected cost of reserving this slot is less than the expected cost of reserving a slot the next round[2]; otherwise, postpone the reservation decision until the next round.*

---

[2] We assume a short and constant period of time in between two rounds of the agent's decision process.

We will now introduce a number of functions to be able to define the expected cost of reserving the earliest available slot, which takes into account the results of having to decommit. First of all, an agent has to pay the decommitment penalty δ; second, if t_d stands for the time decommitment occurs $(t_d < \tau)$, then the aircraft has wasted $(t_d - t)$ minutes (where t is the time at which the slot was reserved). We assume that this quantity $(t_d - t)$ will in fact delay deicing by $(t_d - t)$ minutes. As the delay cost $l(dl, a)$ defined in Def. 2 is a linear function, we can calculate the expected cost of decommitment for agent a as:

$$E_{dcp}(t, a) = \delta + \frac{l(\tau(a) - t, a)}{2} \qquad (6)$$

Using the above definitions, an aircraft agent a can calculate the expected cost of reserving a slot at time t with earliest available slot time t_s:

$$E_{\text{res}}(t, t_s, a) = P(t, a) \cdot E_{dcp}(t, a) + (1 - P(t, a)) \cdot l(t_s + p(a) - \tau(a), a) \qquad (7)$$

Note that a more realistic model for the cost of reserving a slot would be forward recursive: in case an aircraft has to decommit, it will have to try to get a slot again in subsequent rounds, again with the possibility of having to decommit, adding to its cost. Equation 7 effectively cuts off this forward recursion after one step, by taking into account only the immediate cost for decommitment.

To determine the expected cost $E_{\text{wait}}(t, t_s, a)$ of reserving a slot in the next round, we need the current time t, the time of the next reservation decision t^+, the start time of the first available deicing slot t_s, and the start time of the second available slot (in our case t_s plus the standard deicing time), then the expected cost of waiting until the next round is given by the following function:

$$E_{\text{wait}}(t, t_s, a) = P_T(t) \cdot E_{\text{res}}(t^+, t_s + p(a), a) + (1 - P_T(t)) \cdot E_{\text{res}}(t^+, t_s, a) \qquad (8)$$

in which $P_T(t)$ stands for the probability of another agent having reserved the next available slot between time t and t^+. This probability function is based on the number of aircraft in the system, and the scarcity of the deicing resources. We assume aircraft take-off times are independent of each other and are uniformly distributed over time, and so we model the probability $P_T(t)$ with a Poisson distribution $f(k; \lambda) = \frac{e^{-\lambda}\lambda^k}{k!}$ where:

$$P_T(t) = 1 - f(0, \frac{t^+ - t}{|D| \cdot T}) = 1 - e^{-\frac{|A| \cdot (t^+ - t)}{|D| \cdot T}} \qquad (9)$$

and T is the time in minutes over which these aircraft are distributed (e.g., we could have a simulation run of $T = 300$ minutes in which $|A| = 100$ aircraft have to be deiced using $|D| = 4$ deicing stations).

Equation 8 basically expresses that by not reserving a slot this round, there is a chance that another agent reserves the previously earliest available slot, and you consequently have to schedule a later slot, which will result in more delay; on the other hand, if no agent has reserved the slot starting from t_s, then this possibility is still open to you at time t^+. By this time, the probability of decommitment will have lowered (i.e., $P(t^+, a) < P(t, a)$), and thus reserving this slot at time t^+ will have a lower expected cost.

The agent strategy we propose in this section is simple: in case $E_{\text{res}} < E_{\text{wait}}$, the agent will reserve at time t the slot starting at t_s, otherwise it will wait until the next round. In the next section, we will investigate whether reasoning about decommitment in this way results in improved performance.

5   Experimental Results

In this section, we will compare the two coordination mechanisms of Sect. 4 with each other, and also with a naive, baseline scheduling strategy, which we have termed the Naive Scheduling Strategy (NSS). This strategy schedules deicing slots on a first come, first served basis. When an aircraft arrives at the airport, NSS assigns to this aircraft the first available slot after its target off-block time.

We judge the algorithms on two criteria: the first one is the total delay cost of all aircraft, given by the sum of the delay costs of all agents. Recall that the delay cost of one agent a is given by $l(dl, a)$, where dl is the agent's delay in minutes — this means that we do not take auction fees and decommitment penalties into account when calculating the global cost. Hence, this criterion measures the efficiency of the coordination mechanisms. As a second criterion, we also record the standard deviation of delay in minutes, summed over all agents. The standard deviation can be interpreted as a measure of fairness: if it is low, then all agents suffer a comparable amount of delay.

We conducted these experiments using only a single deicing station with a single deicing bay, and a deicing time of 5 minutes. Target Off-block Times (τ) are randomly distributed over 5 simulation hours. Deicing slots may be allocated after the initial five hours; in fact, the simulation continues until all aircraft have received a deicing slot. For these parameters, the number of aircraft n that can maximally be serviced without any delay equals $n = \frac{5 \times 60}{5} = 60$, assuming a maximally convenient distribution of τ. This means that with a random distribution of τ, we can expect some delays regardless of the scheduling strategy in case we have more than 60 aircraft. Some further parameter values include: the delay cost per time unit in the function l for agent a is randomly distributed over $[0.5, 1.0]$; a fixed value for the decommitment penalty $\delta = 50$; and the maximum decommitment probability $c = 1.0$; In the auction setting, slots are auctioned half an hour in advance; and the time in between two rounds in decommitment penalties is set to 5 minutes. The number of aircraft in the experiment ranges from 10 to 90. The results of the experiments are displayed in Figure 1.

The first thing that catches the eye in Figure 1 is that the NSS strategy is outperformed by the two other mechanisms on all counts, except for runs having a very small number of aircraft, in which the auction setting does not perform very well. The reason for this is that in the auction setting we sell slots starting from specific times, such as 10:00, 10:05, etc. In case there is a mismatch with aircraft Target Off-block Times, for example if $\tau(a_i) = 10:03$ for some aircraft a_i, then small delays will be incurred by the aircraft. As competition for the deicing resources increases, these small delays become less significant.

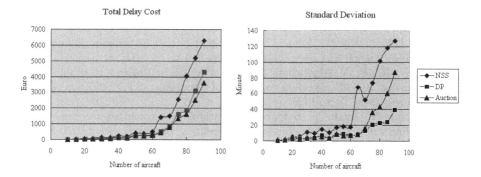

Fig. 1. Total delay cost and standard deviation in NSS, Decommitment Penalty (DP) and Auction

Another observation is that as soon as the airport starts getting congested —from around 70 aircraft— the standard deviation for the auction mechanism shoots up, leaving the decommitment mechanism 'behind'. Note that Figure 1 shows that for the less efficient NSS strategy, airport congestion starts from around 60 aircraft.

As a final remark, we can conclude that the auction mechanism is the most efficient choice for congested airports in terms of total delay cost. However, when there are relatively few aircraft that need to be deiced, the auction mechanism (at least in its current implementation) is not as efficient. The increased efficiency of the auction mechanism does come with a price, however, namely that delay is distributed more unevenly over the aircraft.

6   Conclusion and Future Work

In this paper we have proposed an agent-based model for the scheduling of aircraft deicing services. We introduced two agent coordination mechanisms — a Vickrey auction and a mechanism based on decommitment penalties. The former best caters to the preferences and relative priorities of the agents, the latter one ensures the fairest distribution of delay over the agents. Both mechanisms outperform a naive coordination mechanism based on first come, first served.

Options for future work are too numerous to list exhaustively. We would like to investigate other scheduling strategies in conjunction with the mechanisms presented in this paper. Also, our results currently rely on some simplifying assumptions, and it would be interesting to see whether the conclusions of this paper hold up if we relax some of these assumptions. Another extension is to look at the relation with other airport planning and scheduling problems. In itself, the deicing problem as formulated in the formal model of Sect. 3 is not that exceptional. What makes the problem interesting to look into is its relation to other planning problems, possibly involving other planning agents.

References

1. Smith, D.E., Frank, J., Jónsson, A.K.: Bridging the gap between planning and scheduling. Knowl. Eng. Rev. 15(1), 47–83 (2000)
2. Nisan, N., Ronen, A.: Algorithmic mechanism design. In: Proceedings of the Thirty-First Annual ACM Symposium on Theory of Computing (STOC'99), pp. 129–140. ACM Press, New York (1999)
3. Andelman, N., Azar, Y., Sorani, M.: Truthful approximation mechanisms for scheduling selfish related machines. In: Diekert, V., Durand, B. (eds.) STACS 2005. LNCS, vol. 3404, pp. 69–82. Springer, Heidelberg (2005)
4. Auletta, V., Prisco, R.D., Penna, P., Persiano, G.: Deterministic truthful approximation mechanisms for scheduling related machines. In: Diekert, V., Habib, M. (eds.) STACS 2004. LNCS, vol. 2996, pp. 608–619. Springer, Heidelberg (2004)
5. Kovács, A.: Fast monotone 3-approximation algorithm for scheduling related machines. In: Brodal, G.S., Leonardi, S. (eds.) ESA 2005. LNCS, vol. 3669, pp. 616–627. Springer, Heidelberg (2005)
6. Angel, E., Bampis, E., Pascual, F.: Truthful algorithms for scheduling selfish tasks on parallel machines. Theor. Comput. Sci 369(1-3), 157–168 (2006)
7. Immorlica, N., Li, L., Mirrokni, V.S., Schulz, A.: Coordination mechanisms for selfish scheduling. In: Deng, X., Ye, Y. (eds.) WINE 2005. LNCS, vol. 3828, pp. 55–69. Springer, Heidelberg (2005)
8. Vermeulen, I., Bohte, S., Somefun, D., Poutré, J.L.: Improving patient schedules by multi-agent pareto appointment exchanging. In: Proceedings of 2006 IEEE International Conference on E-Commerce Technology (CEC/EEE 2006), San Francisco, California, June 26-29, p. 9 (2006)
9. Paulussen, T.O., Jennings, N.R., Decker, K.S., Heinzl, A.: Distributed patient scheduling in hospitals. In: IJCIA-03, pp. 1224–1232. Morgan Kaufmann, San Francisco (2003)
10. Attanasio, A., Ghiani, G., Grandinetti, L., Guerriero, F.: Auction algorithms for decentralized parallel machine scheduling. Parallel Comput. 32(9), 701–709 (2006)
11. Lewin, R.: Embracing Complexity: Exploring the Application of Complex Adaptive Systems to Business. Ernst & Young (1996)
12. Parkes, D.C., Ungar, L.H.: An auction-based method for decentralized train scheduling. In: Proceedings of the Fifth International Conference on Autonomous Agents, Montreal, Canada, pp. 43–50. ACM Press, New York (2001)
13. 't Hoen, P.J., Poutre, J.A.L.: A decommitment strategy in a competitive multi-agent transportation setting. In: AAMAS '03, pp. 1010–1011. ACM Press, New York (2003)
14. Sandholm, T., Lesser, V.: Leveled commitment contracts and strategic breach. Games and Economic Behaviour 25, 212–270 (2001)
15. Collins, J., Tsvetovas, M., Sundareswara, R., van Tonder, J., Gini, M., Mobasher, B.: Evaluating risk: flexibility and feasibility in multi-agent contracting. In: Proceedings of the Third International Conference on Autonomous Agents (Agents'99), Seattle, WA, USA, pp. 350–351. ACM Press, Seattle, WA (1999)

Large-Scale Agent-Based Pedestrian Simulation

Franziska Klügl[1] and Guido Rindsfüser[2]

[1] Dep. of Artificial Intelligence, University of Würzburg
Am Hubland, 97074 Würzburg, Germany
kluegl@informatik.uni-wuerzburg.de
[2] Emch & Berger Bern AG
Gartenstr. 1
CH-3008 Bern
guido.rindsfueser@emchberger.ch

Abstract. Pedestrian simulation is a challenging and fruitful application area for agent-based modeling and simulation in the traffic and transportation domain. In this paper we will present the concepts and results of a particular project study: an agent-based simulation of pedestrian traffic of the complete railway station of Bern during the most busy morning hours. Overall more than 40 000 agents are passing through during 1,5 virtual hours. Going beyond traditional approaches for microscopic pedestrian simulation, our simulated pedestrians are not only capable of moving without collisions between two pre-defined locations, but are able to flexibly plan and re-plan their way through the railway station. A short glance and some discussion about the potential of agent-based pedestrian simulation closes this contribution.

1 Introduction

Pedestrian simulation is a challenging and fruitful application area for agent-based modeling and simulation in the traffic and transportation domain: on one side design and implementation involve interesting issues especially related to scalability and individual realism. On the other side, agent-based modeling provides the foundation for simulations on a interesting and relevant level of detail and complexity for a variety of applications of pedestrian simulations: Availability of information, location of direction signs, consequences of orientation behavior, etc.

In this paper, we want to describe a successful application example of agent-based pedestrian simulation: The growing amount of travelers using the SBB railway station Bern and the wish to offer better services, shorter connections and higher frequencies led to the idea of a pedestrian simulation for testing different layout options or new train schedules. A simulation model was developed at the chair of Artificial Intelligence at the University of Würzburg together with traffic engineers from one of the leading Swiss traffic engineering companies, Emch & Berger AG, Bern. The simulation had to cover the busiest morning hours. During this time, an overall amount of about 80 trains with more than 40 000 traveler is

P. Petta et al. (Eds.): MATES 2007, LNAI 4687, pp. 145–156, 2007.

passing through the station heading to different destinations. Several thousand pedestrians are populating the railway station concurrently.

A multi-agent-simulation promised to be a good solution for two reasons: It allows for integrating higher-level decision making for realistic simulations beyond collision-free smooth movement. On the micro-level autonomous decision making entities are existing enabling validation or at least testing for plausible behavior on the level of individual agents. Secondly – in contrast to other paradigms for simulating pedestrians like cellular automata or force-based approaches – it can be designed in a way that both memory consumption and computational time is feasible for large number of pedestrians. However, design, implementation and simulation are still quite demanding.

The remainder of this contribution is structured as follows: We start by a short review of microscopic pedestrian simulation in general. After that we discuss issues of agent-based simulation and why we think that an agent-based approach is particularly apt for large-scale pedestrian simulations. Section 4.1 introduces the problem that was tackled by the SBBPedis project, followed by a short description of the agents and environmental model. Section 5 gives a short glance on the results of the project. The last sections summarizes the paper and gives some concluding thoughts.

2   Pedestrian Simulation

Traditionally, pedestrian simulation has been done using techniques such as flow-speed-density equations, which aggregate pedestrian movement into flows, average speed or density. This approach, derived from vehicular traffic simulation, may be simple and lead to feasible solutions, but it is not capable of taking into account the basic behaviors and interactions between the pedestrians [1]. Due to improvements in computing power, microscopic models became feasible for generating pedestrian flows and crowd behavior based on low-level behavior of pedestrians, including their interactions during movement as well as higher level cognitive abilities for flexible routing in detailed environments.

From beginning of the 90ies, there has been a remarkable progress in modeling pedestrian behavior on a microscopic level. Basically three types of microscopic models have been proposed:

1. Force-based models, like the *social force model*[2] are based on the assumption that the direction and speed of a pedestrian can be computed based on the combination of different forces that attract the pedestrian towards their goals but repel them from moving and static obstacles. These force-based models are quite brittle as the weights for the different forces have to be thoroughly balanced for producing reasonable behavior. An additional problem is that these models are quite slow when the density of pedestrians is high as many entities have to be considered for computing the final movement. There are additional problems when forces are exactly opposite, then pedestrians are trapped. For this reason, also for moving around obstacles sub-goals have to be introduced.

2. Cellular automata [3], [4], [5] are based on discrete spatial representations. The state of a cell captures static and dynamic potential fields that represent the local effect of obstacles or of other moving pedestrians. Additionally, as in the force-based approach, an additional potential field towards the goal of the pedestrian on a cell is integrated into the status of the cell. As the size of a cell is according to the space taken by a pedestrian (e.g. 40x40 cm), a huge amount of cells is necessary even for small size environments. This results in quite extensive memory requirements for such simulations. Using lazy evaluation and hybrid simulation, it is possible to improve this problem [6]. However, it seems to be problematic to tackle individual and heterogeneous goals in the simulated pedestrians movement. Thus, Cellular automata based approaches are mostly used for simulating evacuation dynamics where all pedestrians are heading towards the emergency exits or for simulating hiking on defined paths.

3. Sometimes also the above approaches are called "agent-based", due to their micro-scopic nature (see e.g. in [1]). True agent-based simulations use the idea of a simulated pedestrian based on the paradigm of an autonomously acting and interacting entity. Although it is in principle possible to integrate complex details of higher level information processing, most approaches for agent-based pedestrian simulation just deal with collision-free goal-oriented movement, not much more intelligent than the other micro-scopic approaches. Examples for agent-based pedestrian simulations are [7], [8], [1], [9], [10]. For a detailed overview in relation to public transport facilities see [11].

In [12], three microscopic models - representatives of the three categories - were compared in three situations (evacuation, public transport and shopping center) on implementation level for their capability of representing higher level decision making, efficiency and for technical aspects like simulation time and memory consumption. This study supported our hypothesis that agent-based approaches were best apt for large scale pedestrian simulations also including flexible planning and heterogenous destinations of pedestrians.

3   Agent-Based Pedestrian Simulation

Agent-based simulation of pedestrian behavior is an attractive way of reproducing pedestrian dynamics for several reasons. The most important advantage is that it is possible to integrate higher-level cognitive behavior for path planning, flexible information processing and orientation. Modeling the low-level movement in an agent-based manner is also attractive as it can be done in an efficient way in terms of memory and computational time. Another important advantage is that an agent-based simulation allows separating pedestrian behavior from particular spatial layout. This is due to the concept of a pedestrian as a self-contained, autonomous entity that is situated in its environment. Thus, environmental changes - basically modifications of the layout or train schedules - can be done without manipulations in the pedestrian model. The agent is adapting itself due to its perceptions. Therefore, such layout changes are rather cheap in modeling cost. Last, but not least, an agent-based model facilitates communication as the agent concept is intuitively clear to traffic engineers dealing with self-determined travelers.

Given the goal of our effort - simulating the pedestrian dynamics during the morning rush hours in the complete SBB railway station in Bern, we must take care for technical details affecting the feasibility of large scale pedestrian simulations. Against this background, the following issues for designing an appropriate agent model have to be considered:

- The basic question concerns how much information should be processed by each of the agents itself, and on what level granularity. An example is the path planning in world populated by dynamic and static obstacles. Should every agent construct a mental map with a detailed sequence of locations that it has to pass? This would result in smooth and realistic movement. The alternative would be that the agent plans its path on a very coarse level with only a few sub-goal positions and flexibly adapts its movement without long-distance sight. Obstacle avoidance can then result in unrealistic almost-bouncing. However, it is quite clear that realism is traded against computational time and memory consumption.
- Should the agents be capable of re-planing their path due to congestions, information signs etc. Such a behavior would be realistic, yet expensive. However, these replanning capabilities form one of the essential advantages of an agent-based approach in comparison to existing microscopic modeling paradigms (see Sect. 6.1).
- Environmental pre-processing versus computations done by the agent. This is similar to one of the basic differences between cellular automata approaches and social force models: In a cellular automata model the environment pre-computes the influences of all obstacles, the agent may only access this information instead of relying on its own perceptions. On the other side, in a force-based model, the particle - or here agent - would be responsible for all information processing itself. There is no environment capable of carrying such information. Thus, again computational time is traded against memory consumption.
- Another, more technical issue refers to the basic spatial representation: discrete or continuous space, three-dimensional space or multi-layer layout that is basically two-dimensional but has areas/points like stairways or elevators that connect the different areas without influencing pedestrian dynamics in a artificial way. At least for the latter, the solution is quite obvious: three-dimensional layout makes no sense if the simulated pedestrians just move in two dimensions and do not incorporate cognitive models of orientation e.g. related to visibility of signs on different heights, etc. The first issue - discrete or continuous map influences the options that a simulated agent has to move around obstacles.

4   SBBPedis

4.1   Questions Addressed by the Study

While thinking about infrastructure, facilities and operation for the year 2030, questions concerning the pedestrian flows within the SBB railway station in Bern arose. An assumed increase of plus 20-25% passengers using the station in the future, a higher frequency of train departures and arrivals and the limited possibilities in space for infrastructural development cause the need to undertake in-depth analysis.

The task was to set up a model of pedestrian behavior and to use it to simulate the pedestrian flow within the morning peak hour in the entire SBB railway station Bern. A special interest was to get detailed information (hints) about bottlenecks to be expected, pedestrian travel times and the needed time to change trains.

The situation for the year 2006 was build as reference scenario and also as the first application: There are two variants of this situation. Currently, a second traverse ("Passerelle") is closed for reasons of dilapidation. Should this overpass be renovated (*2006Pa*) or completely be demolished (*2006Re*), was one of the questions which's decision should be supported by simulation.

A second scenario is the situation *2030Ra*, which is based on assumptions of the increasing amount of passengers, an additional track, another timetable and some other operational items.

The simulated railway station area was chosen to include all train tracks, the main pedestrian movement areas, and the main static obstacles (e.g. elevators). 3 (5 in the *2006Pa* Scenario) areas were defined as pedestrian sources and targets (entrances and exits to the simulation system) in addition to the trains. All trains arriving and departing within the time from 6:30 to 8:30am are simulated based on the original timetables without any assumptions on delays. All passengers are simulated during the given time period based on observation data from the public transport provider SBB. Additionally, observation data from the public transport providers SBB and BLS were prepared to serve as basis for the amount of train changes for each individual train and passenger. In total, in every scenario more than 40'000 pedestrians are simulated within the given virtual time period.

For reproducing the pedestrian dynamics in the SBB railway station Bern during the morning rush hour, we used an agent-based model that combines simple, but flexible individual path planning with collision avoidance in continuous space and (virtual) multi-level layout. Details about the model are given in the following subsections.

4.2   Environmental Model

It is quite clear that the most important agents in our scenario are the simulated pedestrians. However, before giving details on their behavior and decision making, the environmental model will be discussed as it frames the pedestrian model:

In general, there is continuous space consisting of areas like the platforms, all stairways and ramps, the overpass as well as the underpass. Two important simplifications were made for the model:

- The curved geometry of the railway station was straightened, simplifying geometric representation and computations involving layout. However, this is quite a hard abstraction, as it influences orientation times especially for simulated pedestrians that are not familiar with the station. There are positions where hardly any exit, nor even a exit sign is visible.
- The multi-level property was resolved by arranging the different areas side by side with transfer areas between them. When an agent moves on such an area, it is transported automatically to the corresponding area without distorting movement. Thus, a 3D station representation is avoided.

Figure 1 shows the simulated layout of the scenario *2006Re*, i.e. the situation with the layout of 2006, yet the overpass under question has been completely removed.

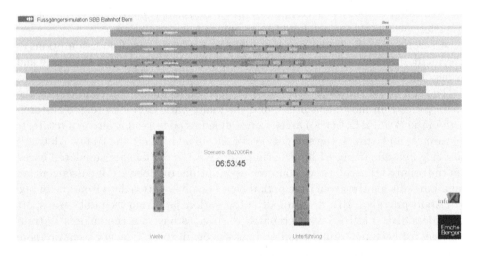

Fig. 1. Scenario *2006Re*: Layout of 2006, without renovated overpass. Larger dark areas represent the entries/exits of the railway station, smaller dark areas are the transfer areas connecting areas that should be on the same level. Tracks are light gray; platforms are framed by thin black lines.

In addition to the simulated pedestrians, three kinds of environmental entities are treated as sufficiently active so that they are modeled as agents: Sensors for data gathering, rail tracks and the doors of trains or of the overall station. Sensors are trivially counting pedestrians passing through their measurement areas. Tracks are also quite simple: They manage trains that arrive and depart on them. When a train arrives, the track generates the doors of the train that then generate new pedestrians leaving the trains through them. Thus, a train object is only a passive data structure; its existence during its stay-time on a track is represented by a number of temporary existing door-agents distributed along the edge of the platform. At the scheduled departure time the track closes and deletes the doors independently on how many simulated travelers are still waiting to enter. The track also sums up relevant statistical data for the departing train including the number of passengers that were not able to enter the train. Thus, there is no delay in departure.

As mentioned before, the third category of environmental agents are the doors of trains or the general exits of the railway station. Whereas the former are dynamic as they execute the schedule of train arrival and departure, the latter are permanent. Basically, these agents produce all pedestrian agents: At the initialization phase of the simulation, the arrival of every simulated pedestrian that will head towards a train, is scheduled by one of the doors of the railway station. It is computed based on a probability distribution determining how long before train departure pedestrians arrive at the train. Later at the appropriate time step, the simulated travelers are generated. On the other side, travelers passing the doors heading outside the railway station or entering a train are deleted from the simulation after storing relevant individual values like, walking time, etc.

4.3   Simulated Pedestrians

Figure 2 gives a short glance on the general architecture of a simulated pedestrian.

As mentioned before, simulated pedestrian agents are generated either by one of the main entries of the railway station or by one of the dynamic train door agents. At the beginning, they randomly determine an individual optimal velocity and select their final goal, e.g. a certain exit and determine their high-level path plan on the level of areas: they select which stairways to take, pass through overpass or underpass and head towards the selected exit. As the different areas of the railway station construct some hierarchic structure, an agent uses it for path planning and also for re-planning, from its entry point to the platform from where its goal train will depart, etc. The procedure is similar to the model of scene spaces [13] in spatial cognition.

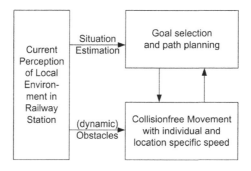

Fig. 2. Short overview over the architecture of a simulated pedestrian

When entering the station (or in the case of connecting train travelers leaving their train) heading towards the goal train, the simulated pedestrian analogously determines its path plan on the area level. However, the situation is a little bit more complex, as the final destination is just selectable, when the agent has reached the platform and the goal train is already there. If the pedestrian agent has to wait on the platform, a waiting position is randomly adopted. As we mainly simulate commuters, we assume that the agents know where the train will stop and restrict possible waiting positions accordingly. When the train arrives, all waiting agents select one of the near doors as their immediate destination. However, before being allowed to enter, all exiting agents are generated; thereafter simulated pedestrians may enter one of the doors. We assume that only one agent may enter or leave the door per second, however, when too many agents block the area before the door, this frequency may decrease. A small share of simulated pedestrians is not familiar with the layout of the railway station and has to invest some time into orientation. The share is higher for long-distance trains (30%) than for short-distance ones (1%). In this model, they move some time with reduced velocity when entering a platform.

Independently from whether they want to enter a train or leave the station, during their way through the railway station, the simulated pedestrians continuously evaluate whether their current planned path still is reasonable. They perceive not only local density around them - adopting side step behavior (with 80% probability to the right) or slowing down (depending on perceived density) - but also the direction of pedestrians near them. Thus, they can gather information that triggers them to re-plan their way through the railway station, e.g. taking another stairway than planned, when there is too much oncoming traffic or going to another door of the train when the queue in front of the previously selected is too long.

This restricted form of planing refers only to the level of areas, yet actual movement happens on a lower level of spatial resolution: Collision-free movement on platforms, stairways, etc. is realized quite simply using a set of rules which determine the directions and distances that are tested for determining a new direction and speed for avoiding collision with static and moving obstacles. Every simulated pedestrian moves with an individual desired speed that is determined at generation time. However, speed is influenced by the walking ground, so it is reduced when the agents enters a stairway heading upstairs, etc. It also tries to maintain an individual distance from other pedestrians or obstacles, edges, etc.

4.4   Implementation and Validation

The agent-based pedestrian simulation was implemented using SeSAm 2.1. (Shell for Simulated Agent Systems) that is a high-level modeling and simulation environment for agent-based simulation. Due to its visual programming environment it allows for rapid prototyping testing a variety of model variants; Simulation is quite efficient despite of explicit model interpretation due to the usage of code optimization techniques from compiler construction. SeSAm uses a time-stepped simulator, a time step corresponded here to 1 second real time, one position on the map corresponds to 10 cm. A simulated pedestrian is set to $40 \times 40 cm$.

SeSAm emulates parallelism by sequential agent updates with random shuffles. The basic system is open source and available via *www.simsesam.de*.

For model validation, data from a PDA-based observation at several stairways and all exits within the railway station in Bern were used. SBB provided numbers of travelers entering and leaving trains from counts. These number were used for generating simulated travelers. However, it turned out that the number of simulated traveler were much higher than the overall numbers of counted traveler at different positions within the station.

In addition to individual stay times that could be gathered due to the individual-based simulation, we also integrated sensors comparable to real world: Some kind of virtual photo sensors that counts all passing pedestrian agents or some form of mat noticing the number of agents moving over it.

Due to the discrepancies in overall traveler numbers, we could not find a satisfying resemblance, but saw that the peaks of travelers passing the "sensors" had some noticeable deviation. Assuming that trains were in time during measurement, we charged this problem to the low-level movement model. Thus, we calibrated its parameters using the automatic calibration tool described in [14] which improved the situation. However, a small delay of the peaks of passing pedestrians after train arrival remained. However, the simulated pedestrians movement was acknowledged as plausible by the experts of SBB.

5   Short Glance on Simulation Results

An agent-based simulation in principle offers a variety of possibilities to gather data that can be used for analysis – this is simply due to the explicit treatment of every actor in the simulation. Each attribute of each agent in every single time step may be stored during simulation.

One of the most interesting questions was to see how the new infrastructure and operation influence travel times and train changing times. The simulation showed some concentration results from modified operation. A significant increase (concentration) on short train changing times results from changing tracks for train arrival and departure (as one could expect).

In Fig. 3 the distribution of stay times for simulated dropout travelers is displayed for the scenario 2006Re and 2030Ra showing the result of changed train schedules.

Here, some unexpected effects can be seen. The expected and wanted shift to shorter travel times from scenario 2006Re to situation 2030 can be seen for the "short" times, whereas some 7% of the pedestrians will need really longer times. It turned out that the tense schedule in 2030Ra in combination with the increase of agent numbers did not allow the station to be almost emptied between train arrivals. In the simulation, this builds up a more and more populated station worsening the possibility to get through due to increased overall density. This is illustrated in Fig. 4. As to expect, densities where generally high at the entry areal of stairways. In the 2030 scenario, the complete underpass was jammed at around 9 a.m., leading to higher overall stay times.

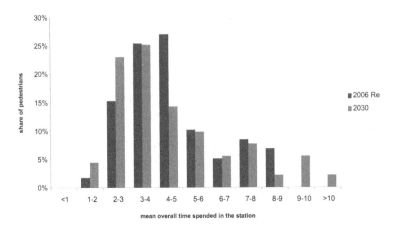

Fig. 3. Mean time that a simulated traveler needed to go from its train to one of the main exits

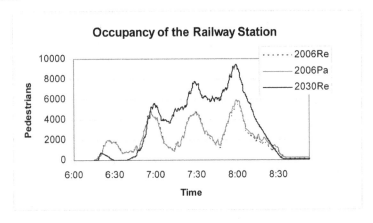

Fig. 4. Dynamics of overall number of pedestrian agents in the simulated railway station

Additional to all data analysis, the simulation system allows the researcher to save the complete simulation run as a video. Animation is in general not only useful for visualization and presentation, but also for face validation. Observing the pedestrian flows supports defining bottlenecks or leads to further questions or ideas of situations (scenarios) to be investigated.

6   Conclusion

6.1   Agent-Based Pedestrian Simulation Revisited

Simulating pedestrians did not start with the advent of agent-based simulation, but has been done before also microscopically in a quite successful manner. As in traffic simulation in general, one has to argue why and what questions can be answered better by agent-based simulation for justifying that well-understood ways of analysis are not used.

Although applied quite successfully in different application domains involving human decision making, one must not ignore that agent-based simulation raises problems beyond its technical feasibility. The formal basis of agent-based simulations is much weaker than e.g. in modeling using partial differential equations, cellular automata, or other microscopic modeling paradigms. This has consequences on the trustworthiness of simulation results as a complex agent-based model is hardly fully documentable for enabling others to reproduce the results or as most formal specification remain very abstract. Another disadvantage of an agent-based simulation in addition to the need for data on a very detailed level that is hardly available, is the effort in computational time and space. When a single simulation run needs several days (2-3 days in our study), experimentation becomes painful, reasonable calibration becomes impractical, etc.

However, to our opinion traffic simulation in general, and pedestrian simulation in particular has the potential to become the great success story for the application of agent-based simulation. Travelers are moving through space and time, simulated agents have all decision-making capabilities available at every point of time during simulation. Thus, agent-based simulation seems to be the best, if not the only modeling paradigm for reproducing the reaction of travelers to locally displayed or dynamic information, in our case to unforeseeable agent densities. Together with the simulation of true heterogeneity in equipment, preferences, this forms a good basis for analysis of future traffic situations involving Advanced Traveler Information Systems and sophisticated control measures in the network infrastructure. This project is a step further to show that agent-based simulations can be successfully used in real-world applications

6.2   Future Work

This project showed that it is conceptually and technically feasible to design and execute such large agent-based pedestrian simulations that can provide valuable data for analysts and offer a useful tool for planning pedestrian facilities. The project finally was terminated in February, 2007. Currently, a successor project is prepared by a further optimization of simulation speed based on some model refactoring. This successor project will integrate new movement areas as well as an extension by urban areas near the station to include the access ways to the station and the connection to a new planned underground station. This may result in a better representation of travel demand and distribution beyond the originally simulated railway station.

References

1. Teknomo, K.: Microscopic Pedestrian Flow Characteristics: Development of an Image Processing Data Collection and Simulation Model. PhD thesis, Department of Human Social Information Sciences, Graduate School of Information Sciences, Tohoku University, Japan (2002)

2. Helbing, D., Molnar, P.: Social force model for pedestrian dynamics. Physical Review E 51(5), 4282–4286 (1995)
3. Schadschneider, A.: Cellular automaton approach to pedestrian dynamics - theory. In: Schreckenberg, M., Sharma, S.D. (eds.) Pedestrian and Evacuation Dynamics, pp. 75–85. Springer, New York (2002)
4. Adler, J.L., Blue, V.J.: Cellular automata model of emergent collective bidirectional pedestrian dynamics. In: McCaskill, J.S., Packard, N.H., Rasmussen, S. (eds.) Artifcial Life VII, pp. 437–445. MIT Press, Cambridge (2000)
5. Burstedde, A., Kirchner, A., Klauck, K., Schadschneider, A., Zittartz, J.: Cellular automaton approach to pedestrian dynamics - applications. In: Schreckenberg, M., Sharma, S.D. (eds.) Pedestrian and Evacuation Dynamics, pp. 87–97. Springer, New York (2002)
6. Gloor, C., Stucki, P., Nagel, K.: Hybrid techniques for pedestrian simulations. In: Sloot, P.M.A., Chopard, B., Hoekstra, A.G. (eds.) ACRI 2004. LNCS, vol. 3305, pp. 581–590. Springer, Heidelberg (2004)
7. Osaragi, T.: Modeling of pedestrian behavior and its applications to spatial evaluation. In: AAMAS '04, pp. 836–843. IEEE Computer Society, Washington, DC (2004)
8. Willis, A., Kukla, R., Hine, J., Kerridge, J.M.: Developing the behavioural rules for an agent-based model of pedestrian movement. In: Proceedings of the European Transport Conference, pp. 69–80 (2000)
9. Toyama, M.C., Bazzan, A.L.C., da Silva, R.: An agent-based simulation of pedestrian dynamics: from lane formation to auditorium evacuation. In: AAMAS '06, pp. 108–110. ACM Press, New York (2006)
10. Dijkstra, J., Jessurun, J., de Vries, B., Timmermans, H.: Agent architecture for simulating pedestrians in the built environment. In: Bazzan, A.L.C., Chaib-Draa, B., Klügl, F., Ossowski, S. (eds.) 4th International Workshop on Agents in Traffic and Transportation at AAMAS-06, Hakodate Japan, pp. 8–16 (2006)
11. Daamen, W.: Modelling Passenger Flows in Public Transport Facilities. PhD thesis, Technische Universiteit Delft (2004)
12. Scherger, K.: Evaluation verschiedener Ansätze zur Simulation von Fußgängerverhalten. Master's thesis, Institut für Informatik, Universität Würzburg (2006)
13. Rüetschi, U.J., Timpf, S.: Modelling wayfinding in public transport: Network space and scene space. In: Freksa, C., Knauff, M., Krieg-Brückner, B., Nebel, B., Barkowsky, T. (eds.) Spatial Cognition IV: Reasoning, Action, Interaction; International Conference Frauenchiemsee. LNCS (LNAI), vol. 3343, pp. 24–41. Springer, Heidelberg (2005)
14. Fehler, M., Klügl, F., Puppe, F.: Techniques for analysis and calibration of multiagent simulations. In: Gleizes, M.-P., Omicini, A., Zambonelli, F. (eds.) ESAW 2004. LNCS (LNAI), vol. 3451, pp. 305–321. Springer, Heidelberg (2005)

Diagnosis of Plan Structure Violations

Nico Roos[1] and Cees Witteveen[2]

[1] Dept. of Computer Science, Universiteit Maastricht
P.O. Box 616, NL-6200 MD Maastricht
roos@micc.unimaas.nl
[2] Faculty EWI, Delft University of Technology
P.O. Box 5031, NL-2600 GA Delft
C.Witteveen@tudelft.nl

Abstract. Failures in plan execution can be attributed to errors in the execution of plan steps or violations of the plan structure. The structure of a plan prescribes which actions have to be performed and which precedence constraints between them have to be respected. Especially in multi-agent environments violations of plan structure might easily occur as the consequence of synchronization errors. While in previous work we have concentrated on the first type of failures, in this paper we introduce the idea of diagnosing plan structure violations. Using a formal framework for plan diagnosis, we describe how Model-Based Diagnosis can applied to identify these violations of plan structure specifications and we analyze their computational complexity.

Keywords: Model-Based Diagnosis, Plan execution, Coordination errors.

1 Introduction

Plan diagnosis deals with the identification of errors occurring during the execution of a plan. In previous work, we have presented methods for identifying such errors as failed executions of plan steps in multi-agent plans [1,2], equipment failures and malfunctioning agents causing the execution of plan steps to fail [3,4], and methods for assigning responsibility to agents in case plan execution failed [4]. In all these papers, however, we tacitly assumed that during plan execution the *plan structure* is not violated, i.e., all plan steps as specified in the plan are executed (correctly or incorrectly) and the order in which they are executed does not violate any precedence constraint.

In reality, however, violations of the plan structure may easily occur and might result in plan failure. For instance, consider a plan for loading a truck that has to visit several places to deliver cargo. Often, such a plan contains a specific ordering of loading actions guaranteeing that items are loaded in such a way that they can be unloaded in an efficient way. If, however, the structure of such a loading plan is violated, upon the delivery location it may force to unload other items in order to get the right item that must be unloaded, causing unnecessary delay and even violation of time constraints. Another example would be a plan for loading a ship that ensures a correct weight distribution by carefully ordering the items that have to be loaded. In this case, an incorrectly loaded ship may even disturb the stability of the ship in rough seas causing a total transport plan failure.

P. Petta et al. (Eds.): MATES 2007, LNAI 4687, pp. 157–169, 2007.

Multi-agent systems are particularly susceptible to such violations of plan structure occurring as a consequence of *synchronization problems* between agents. In such a multi-agent system a joint plan has to be executed by several agents each performing a subset of actions. Correct execution of the plan requires synchronization of their activities. Often, planning agents need not use special synchronization actions to synchronize their activities during plan-execution. Instead, synchronization is achieved by relying on specific starting times of actions specified in the plan itself or by relying on observations that indicate the completion of tasks performed by other agents. If, however, the execution of some crucial action is delayed or if observation errors lead to incorrect beliefs about the state of the world, violations of precedence constraints may easily occur. Also other failures of plan structure, as omitting or duplicating plan steps, might easily occur in multi-agent environments. For example, suppose that the set of plan steps to be executed by an agent overlaps with the set of plan steps to be executed by another agent. The first agent that is able to perform such a plan step will do so, enabling the other agent to skip the plan step. In such cases, without special synchronization actions, an agent might erroneously conclude that an action has already been performed (or not performed) by the other agent, taking the wrong action and causing the plan to fail. In any case, plan diagnosis should be able to identify such violations if they occur during the execution of a plan.

Remark. Identifying violations of precedence constraints is closely related to diagnosis of coordination errors. Kalech and Kaminka [5] apply classical model-based diagnosis [6,7] to identify coordination errors between *reactive agents*. Each reactive agent executes some *behavior* that may need to be coordinated with other agents. The coordination must ensure that certain constraints on behaviors are satisfied. Violation of these constraints implies that some agents behave abnormally in the sense that they fail to coordinate their behaviors.

The main difference with the work of Kalech and Kaminka is that here we have a (traditional non-behavior-based) plan in which coordination errors lead to violations of the plan's structure. Diagnosing plan structure violations also differs from other approaches to *plan diagnosis* proposed in the literature: [8,9,10,11,12,2,4].

In this paper, we extend the framework for plan diagnosis as described in [1,2]. In this model the state of the world is modeled by set of variables (objects) the values of which are changed by plan steps executed. This representation makes it possible to apply classical Model-Based Diagnosis (MBD) [6]) to identify anomalies in the execution of the plan. To simplify the presentation of diagnosis of violations of precedence constraints, we do not used the extension of the above mentioned model[1] presented in [3,4].

The remainder of this paper is organized as follows: Section 2 introduces the basic framework for plan-based diagnosis. Section 3 extends plan diagnosis to enable diagnosis of plan structure failures and Sect. 4 concludes the paper.

---

[1] In this extension we showed how our plan diagnosis approach can be conceived as a Discrete Event System (DES) [13,14,15,16]) of which the state is changed by unknown events causing anomalies in the plan execution. The here presented extensions of the former model that enable diagnosis of violations with respect to the structure of the plan can easily be incorporated in the latter, more elaborate, model.

2   Plans and Plan Execution

Before we discuss the idea of diagnosing plan structure failures, we start with a brief introduction to plan-based diagnosis.

2.1   Plans as Systems

We consider plan-based diagnosis as a simple extension of the model-based diagnosis approach, where the model is not a description of an underlying physical system but a *plan* of one or more agents. By executing the plan we change a part of the world.

To keep representational issues as simple as possible, we assume that for the planning problem at hand, the world can be simply described by a set $Var = \{v_1, v_2, \ldots, v_n\}$ of variables and their respective *value domains* D_i. A *state of the world* σ then is a value assignment $\sigma : Var \rightarrow \bigcup_{i=1}^{n} D_i$ to the variables. We will denote such a state simply by an element of $D_1 \times D_2 \times \ldots \times D_n$, i.e. an n-tuple of values.

We also introduce a *partial state* as an element $\pi \in D_{i_1} \times D_{i_2} \times \ldots \times D_{i_k}$, where $1 \leq k \leq n$ and $1 \leq i_1 < \ldots < i_k \leq n$. We use $Var(\pi)$ to denote the set of variables $\{v_{i_1}, v_{i_2}, \ldots, v_{i_k}\} \subseteq Var$ specified in such a partial state π. The value $\sigma(v_j)$ of variable $v_j \in Var(\pi)$ will be denoted by $\pi(v_j)$. The value of a variable $v_j \in Var$ not occurring in a partial state π is said to be *undefined* (or *unpredictable*) in π, denoted by $\bot$. Including $\bot$ in every value domain D_i allows us to consider every partial state π as an element of $D_1 \times D_2 \times \ldots \times D_n$.

An important notion in plan diagnosis is the notion of *compatibility* between partial states. Two states π and π' are said to be compatible, denoted by $\pi \approx \pi'$, if there is no essential disagreement about the values assigned to variables in the two states and they could be extended to the same complete state. That is,

$$\pi \approx \pi' \text{ if } \forall v \in Var\left[(\pi(v) = \bot) \vee (\pi'(v) = \bot) \vee (\pi'(v) = \pi(v))\right].$$

Actions, Plan Operators and Plan Steps. In the preceding section we used the term 'actions' in a rather informal way. From now on we will distinguish *plan operators* and *plan steps*, which are both covered by the term 'actions'.

A *plan operator* refers to a description of an action in a plan. In our model, plan operators are *functions* mapping partial states to partial states. More exactly, a plan operator o is a function that replaces the values in its range $ran_{Var}(o) \subseteq Var$ by other values (dependent upon the values of the variables in its domain $dom_{Var}(o) \subseteq Var$). Hence, every plan operator o can be modeled as a (partial) function $f_o : D_{i_1} \times \ldots \times D_{i_k} \rightarrow D_{j_1} \times \ldots \times D_{j_l}$, where $1 \leq i_1 < \ldots < i_k \leq n$ and $1 \leq j_1 < \ldots < j_l \leq n$. Note that the set of variables in a plan operator's range $ran_{Var}(o)$ may differ from the variables in its domain $dom_{Var}(o)$. This property ensures that most planning formalisms, such as STRIPS, can be modeled using our plan operators. Also note that if a variable occurs in a plan operator's range but not in its domain, its value will be set by the application of the plan operator independently of its previous value.

A plan operator o may be used at several places in a plan. A specific occurrence s of o is called a *plan step* mapping a specific partial state into another partial state. A plan step s as an occurrence of o then describes a specific *function application* of the function f_o at a specific place in the plan. Therefore, given a set $\mathcal{O}$ of plan operators, we consider a set $S = inst(\mathcal{O})$ of *instances* of plan operators in $\mathcal{O}$, called the set of plan steps. A plan step will be denoted by a small roman letter s_i. We use $type(s)$ to denote plan operator o of which the plan step s is an instance: $s \in inst(o)$. Moreover, we use $dom_{Var}(s)$ for $dom_{Var}(type(s))$ and $ran_{Var}(s)$ for $ran_{Var}(type(s))$.

Example 1. Figure 1(a) depicts two states σ_0 and σ_1 (the white boxes) each characterized by the values of four variables v_1, v_2, v_3 and v_4. The partial states π_0 and π_1 (the gray boxes) characterize a subset of values in a (complete) state. The plan steps s_1 and s_2 are instances of the plan operators o_1 and o_2, respectively. Plan operators are used to model state changes. The domain of the plan operator o_1 is the subset $\{v_1, v_2\}$, denoted by the arrows pointing to s_1. The range of o_1 is the subset $\{v_1\}$, which is denoted by the arrow pointing from s_1. Finally, the dashed arrow denotes that the value of variable v_2 is not changed by the plan step s_1 causing the state change.

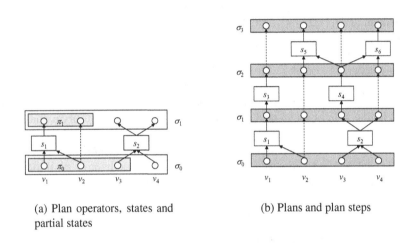

(a) Plan operators, states and partial states

(b) Plans and plan steps

Fig. 1. Plans, plan states and plan steps

Plans and Plan Execution. An executable plan is a tuple $P = \langle \mathcal{O}, S, \prec \rangle$ where $S \subseteq Inst(\mathcal{O})$ is a set of plan steps occurring in $\mathcal{O}$ and $(S, \prec)$ is a partial order. The partial order relation $\prec$ specifies an *execution relation* between these instances: for each $s \in S$ it holds that s is executed immediately after all plan steps s' such that $s' \prec s$ have been finished. We will denote the *transitive reduction*[2] of $\prec$ by $\ll$.

Without loss of generality, we assume that every plan step $s \in S$ takes one unit of time to execute and the execution of the first plan step starts at time $t = 0$. Using this assumption and the definition of the execution ordering $\prec$, the time t at which a plan step s will be executed is uniquely determined: Let $depth_P(s)$ be the depth of plan step s in plan $P = \langle \mathcal{O}, S, \prec \rangle$. Here, $depth_P(s) = 0$ if $\{s' \in S \,|s' \ll s\} = \varnothing$ and $depth_P(s) = 1 + max\{depth_P(s') \mid s' \ll s\}$, else. [3] Then the time t_s at which the plan step s is executed is $t_s = depth_P(s)$ and s will be completed at time $t_s + 1$. Let

---

[2] So $\ll$ is the smallest subrelation of $\prec$ such that the transitive closure $\ll^+$ of $\ll$ equals $\prec$.

[3] If the context is clear, we often will omit the subscript P.

P_t denote the set of plan steps s with $depth_P(s) = t$, let $P_{>t} = \bigcup_{t'>t} P_{t'}$, $P_{<t} = \bigcup_{t'<t} P_{t'}$ and finally, let $P_{[t,t']} = \bigcup_{k=t}^{t'} P_k$.

Example 2. Figure 1(b) illustrates a plan with precedence relations: $s_1 \ll s_3$, $s_2 \ll s_4$, $s_4 \ll s_5$ and $s_4 \ll s_6$. In this plan, the depth of s_1 and s_2 is 0, the depth of s_3 and s_4 is 1, and the depth of s_5 and s_6 is 2. Therefore, $P_0 = \{s_1, s_2\}$, $P_1 = \{s_3, s_4\}$ and $P_2 = \{s_5, s_6\}$.

Given a state σ at some time t and the set P_t of plan steps to be executed at time t we want to be sure that the next state σ' at time $t + 1$ is uniquely defined. If P_t contains two plan steps s and s' with overlapping ranges, i.e., if $ran_{Var}(s) \cap ran_{Var}(s') \neq \varnothing$, the final result of a variable v occurring in this intersection is not uniquely defined in σ'. We therefore assume the following condition to hold:

Determinism. If P is a plan and s, s' are plan steps in P such that $ran_{Var}(s) \cap ran_{Var}(s') \neq \varnothing$ then $depth_P(s) \neq depth_P(s')$.

It is not difficult to see that Determinism guarantees that a future plan state can be defined uniquely given a plan, the current time t and a partial state at time t.

2.2 Qualifications

As we already noted in the introduction, several types of failure can be distinguished: the execution of a plan step might fail, a plan step might be omitted, a plan step might be executed more than once (duplicated) or the precedence order between plan steps might be violated. If such a failure occurs, we say that a plan step is qualified as failed, missing or duplicated, or a precedence constraint is qualified as violated. Below we specify these qualifications in detail. In the next subsection we specify their consequence for plan execution. This will enable us to diagnose such failures.

Failing Plan Steps. The correct execution of a *plan step may fail* either because of an inherent malfunctioning, or because of a malfunctioning of an agent responsible for executing the action, or because of unknown external circumstances. In all these cases, we model the effects of a failed execution of a plan-operator by introducing a set of *health modes* H_s for each plan step $s \in S$. This set H_s contains at least the normal mode *nor*, the mode *ab* indicating the most general abnormal behavior, and possibly several other specific fault modes. The most general abnormal behavior of plan operator o is specified by the function f_o^{ab}, where $f_o^{ab}(d_{i_1}, d_{i_2}, \ldots, d_{i_k}) = (\bot, \bot, \ldots, \bot)$ for every partial state $(d_{i_1}, d_{i_2}, \ldots, d_{i_k}) \in dom(f_o)$.[4] To keep the discussion simple, we distinguish only the health modes *nor* and *ab*.

We will use the set of plan steps $F \subseteq S$ to denote the plan steps that are qualified as abnormal (failed). The behavior of each plan step $s \in F$ is specified by the function f_o^{ab} where $s \in inst(o)$. The plan steps $S - F$ are qualified as normal and the behavior of the of each plan step $s \in (S - F)$ is specified by the function f_o^{nor}.

Omitted and Duplicated Plan Steps. At first sight it may seem that omitted (missing) and duplicated plan steps could be treated as special cases of failing plan steps.

---

[4] This definition implies that the behavior of abnormal actions is essentially unpredictable.

For example, an omitted plan step $s \in inst(o)$ could be qualified as omitted by assuming a special health mode *omit* such that f_o^{omit} equals the identity function, while a plan step could be qualified as duplicated by assuming a health mode *dup* such that $f_o^{dup} = f^{nor} \circ f^{nor}$. The problem with this solution is that the execution of an omitted plan step still would take time and duplicating a plan steps would not increase execution time. Therefore, instead of assigning health modes, we propose another approach, where duplicated and omitted plan steps are indicated as the result of an explicit *plan transformation*. We specify this transformation using a special set D indicating the set of plan steps duplicated and M denoting the set of plan steps omitted (missing). The existing plan P then is transformed into a new plan $P_{M,D}$ reflecting the omitted and duplicated plan steps. This plan $P_{M,D} = \langle \mathcal{O}, S_{(M,D)}, \prec_{(M,D)} \rangle$ consists of the set of plan steps $S_{(M,D)} = S - M \cup \{s_{dup} \mid s \in D\}$, and the set of precedence constraints $\prec_{(M,D)} = \prec - \{(s, s'), (s', s) \mid s \in M\} \cup \{(s, s_{dup}), (s_{dup}, s') \mid s \in D, (s, s') \in \prec\}$. Here, the idea is that the duplicating plan step s_{dup} will be executed immediately after the original plan step s. Moreover, s_{dup} and s have the same behavior, since $type(s) = type(s_{dup})$.

Precedence Constraint Violations. A precedence violation occurs if a plan P specifies that some plan step s' is dependent upon a plan step s (i.e. $(s, s') \in \prec$) and the execution order of s and s' is *reversed*.[5] Instances of $\ll \subseteq \prec$ that are reversed are denoted by the set C. We have to take care that C is a closed set of violations. For example, if $s \prec s'$, $s' \prec s''$ then a violation of $s \prec s''$ not only implies that $(s, s'') \in C$, but also that $(s', s'') \in C$.[6] The plan $P^C = (\mathcal{O}, S, \prec \dagger C)$ is plan transformation from P where $\prec \dagger C$ is the updated set of precedence constraints generated by $\prec$ and the set of violations C: $\prec \dagger C = (\prec - C) \cup \{(s, s') \mid (s', s) \in C\}$.

Total Qualification. Having defined the plan steps that are qualifies as failed F, as missing M and as duplicated D, and the constraints that are qualified as violated by C, we define a total qualification of plan failures as: $Q = (F, M, D, C)$ and we denote a plan P with these qualifications by $P_Q = \langle \mathcal{O}, S, \prec, Q \rangle$. We keep in mind, however, that such a plan P_Q also implicitly defines a (complex) transformation of the original plan P.

2.3 Plan Execution

In general, a plan P executed in a given initial state π_0 will induce a sequence of states $\pi_0, \pi_1, \ldots, \pi_k$, where π_{t+1} is generated from π_t by applying the set of plan steps P_t to σ_t. To define this relation between partial states at different time points we denote a partial state π at a given time t by a tuple, also called a *timed state*, denoted by (π, t).

---

[5] Strictly speaking, a violation of $s \prec s'$ could also imply that s and s' are executed concurrently. Such a violation, however, leads to unpredictable outcomes because the *determinism* requirement is violated. This implies that we cannot distinguish between unplanned concurrent execution of plan steps and plan step execution failures. Therefore, this type of constraint violations will not be distinguished explicitly.

[6] In general, if $(s, s'') \in C$ then for all $s' \in S$ such that $s \prec s' \prec s''$ it holds that $(s', s'') \in C$.

This execution relation will be defined incrementally. We will start with a plan where the only failures that are allowed are plan step failures. Then the relation for plans with plan structure failures is defined by reducing them to the first case.

Execution of Failing Plan Steps. First, let us assume that M, D and C are empty sets, that is, we have a plan $P_{(F,\varnothing,\varnothing,\varnothing)}$. We will first specify how the derivability relation can be specified taking into account the set F of plan steps that might have failed [2].

We define the execution of a plan step as follows:

Definition 1. *We say that* $(\pi',t+1)$ *is (directly) generated by execution of the F-qualified plan* $P_{(F,\varnothing,\varnothing,\varnothing)}$ *from* (π,t), *abbreviated by* $(\pi,t) \rightarrow_{(F,\varnothing,\varnothing,\varnothing);P} (\pi',t+1)$, *iff for every* $v \in Var$ *the following conditions hold:*

1. *if* $v \notin ran_{Var}(P_t)$ *then* $\pi'(v) = \pi(v)$;
   Here, $ran_{Var}(P_t)$ *is a shorthand for the union of the sets* $ran_{Var}(s)$ *with* $s \in P_t$.
2. *if* $v \in ran_{Var}(s)$ *for some plan step* $s \in P_t - F$ *enabled in* π *(i.e.,* $dom_{Var}(s) \subseteq Var(\pi)$*), then* $\pi'(v) = f_o^{nor}(\pi)(v)$;
3. *else* $\pi'(v) = \bot$.

Omitted and Duplicated Plan Steps. We now extend the direct derivability relation $\rightarrow_{(F,\varnothing,\varnothing,\varnothing);P}$ for normal and failing plan steps with missing and duplicated plan steps. As was pointed out in the previous subsection, the idea is that missing and duplicated plan steps transform the original plan P into an new plan P'. Hence, the direct derivability relation of the original plan P with qualification $(F,M,D,\varnothing)$ can be simply defined as follows:

Definition 2. *The timed state* $(\pi',t+1)$ *is (directly) generated from* (π,t) *by execution of the plan* $P = \langle \mathcal{O},S,\prec \rangle$ *given the qualification* $(F,M,D,\varnothing)$, *abbreviated by* $(\pi,t) \rightarrow_{(F,M,D,\varnothing,);P} (\pi',t+1)$, *iff* $(\pi',t+1)$ *is (directly) generated from* (π,t) *by execution of the plan F-qualified plan* $P_{(F,\varnothing,\varnothing,\varnothing)}^{M,D} = \langle \mathcal{O},S_{(M,D)},\prec_{(M,D)} \rangle$.

That is, $(\pi,t) \rightarrow_{(F,M,D,\varnothing,);P} (\pi',t+1)$ *iff* $(\pi,t) \rightarrow_{(F,\varnothing,\varnothing,\varnothing);P^{M,D}} (\pi',t+1)$

Precedence Constraint Violations. Finally, we extend the direct derivability relation with a non empty set of violated precedence constraints. Constraint violations also modify the original plan P by eliminating constraints and by adding the reverse of the eliminated constraints. Hence, we define the execution relation analogous to the previous case:

Definition 3. *The timed state* $(\pi',t+1)$ *is (directly) generated from* (π,t) *by execution of the plan* $P = \langle \mathcal{O},S,\prec \rangle$ *given the qualification* $Q = (F,M,D,C)$, *abbreviated by* $(\pi,t) \rightarrow_{(F,M,D,C);P} (\pi',t+1)$, *iff* $(\pi',t+1)$ *is (directly) generated from* (π,t) *by execution of the plan* $P^{M,D,C} = \langle \mathcal{O},S_{(M,D)},(\prec \dagger C)_{(M,D)} \rangle$ *given the qualification* $(F,\varnothing,\varnothing,\varnothing)$.

That is, $(\pi,t) \rightarrow_{(F,M,D,C);P} (\pi',t+1)$ *iff* $(\pi,t) \rightarrow_{(F,\varnothing,\varnothing,\varnothing);P^{M,D,C}} (\pi',t+1)$.

General Derivability. We extend the direct derivability relation to a general derivability relation in a straightforward way:

Definition 4. *For arbitrary values of* $t \leq t'$ *we say that* (π', t') *is (directly or indirectly) generated by execution of* P^Q *from* (π, t), *denoted by* $(\pi, t) \rightarrow^*_{Q;P} (\pi', t')$, *iff the following conditions hold:*

1. *if* $t = t'$ *then* $\pi' = \pi$;
2. *if* $t' = t + 1$ *then* $(\pi, t) \rightarrow_{Q;P} (\pi', t')$;
3. *if* $t' > t + 1$ *then there must exist a unique state* $(\pi'', t' - 1)$ *such that* $(\pi, t) \rightarrow^*_{Q;P}$
   $(\pi'', t' - 1)$ *and* $(\pi'', t' - 1) \rightarrow_{Q;P} (\pi', t')$.

Note that $(\pi, t) \rightarrow^*_{(\varnothing, \varnothing, \varnothing, \varnothing); P} (\pi', t')$ denotes the normal execution of a normal plan $P_\varnothing$. Such a normal plan execution will also be denoted by $(\pi, t) \rightarrow^*_P (\pi', t')$.

3   Plan Diagnosis

In our framework, a diagnosis is a qualification that resolves conflicts between the observed and predicted values of variables. To establish plan diagnosis in our framework we need to make *observations*. Our framework provides a natural candidate for representing such observations: an observation $obs(t)$ at time t can easily be represented by a timed state (π, t). Note that this implies that we do not require observations to specify a complete state. Suppose that during the execution of a plan P we have an observation $obs(t) = (\pi, t)$ and an observation $obs(t') = (\pi', t')$ at some later time $t' > t \geq 0$. We would like to use these observations to infer a qualification $Q = (F, D, M, C)$ for the plan. First, assuming a normal execution of P, we can predict the partial state of the world at a time point t' given the observation $obs(t)$: if all plan steps behave normally, no plan steps are omitted or duplicated and no constraint is violated, we predict the timed state $(\pi'_\varnothing, t')$ such that $obs(t) \rightarrow^*_{(\varnothing, \varnothing, \varnothing, \varnothing); P} (\pi'_\varnothing, t')$.

Such a prediction has to be compared with the actual observation $obs(t') = (\pi', t')$ made at time t'. It is easy to see if the predicted state and the observed state match: in that case we should be able to find a state σ such that both the observed state π' and the predicted state $\pi'_\varnothing$ are contained in σ, that is, $\pi' \sqsubseteq \sigma$ and $\pi'_\varnothing \sqsubseteq \sigma$. Hence, $\pi'_\varnothing$ and π' are *compatible* states, i.e. $\pi' \approx \pi'_\varnothing$ holds.

If this is not the case, the execution of some plan steps must have gone wrong, some plan steps might have been omitted or duplicated, or some precedence constraint might have been violated. Therefore, we have to determine a qualification $Q = (F, M, D, C)$ such that the predicted state π'_Q derived using Q is compatible with π'. Hence, we have the following straight-forward extension of the diagnosis concept in MBD to plan diagnosis (cf. [6]):

Definition 5. *Let* $P = \langle \mathcal{O}, S, \prec \rangle$ *be a plan with observations* $obs(t) = (\pi, t)$ *and* $obs(t') = (\pi', t')$, *where* $t < t' \leq depth(P)$ *and let* $obs(t) \rightarrow^*_{Q;P} (\pi'_Q, t')$ *be a derivation using the qualification* Q.
   Then Q *is said to be a* qualification diagnosis *of* $\langle P, obs(t), obs(t') \rangle$ *iff* $\pi' \approx \pi'_Q$.

It is easy to show that such a diagnosis can always be proven to exist if for every variable v there exists at least some plan step s and some time $t \leq t'' \leq t'$ such that $s \in P_{t''}$ and $v \in ran_{Var}(s)$.

Example 3. Consider the plan depicted in Fig. 2.a. Let $obs(0) = (\pi_0, 0)$, $obs(3) = (\pi_3', 3)$ and let π_3' be equal to π_3 except that there is a deviation in the value of v_1, v_2 and v_4 at time $t = 3$ (as indicated by the black dots).

Suppose that changing the execution order of plan steps s_4 and s_7 enables us to correctly predict the value of variable v_4, and omitting plan step s_6 enables us to predict the value of variable v_2. Then $Q = (\{s_5\}, \{s_6\}, \varnothing, \{(s_7, s_4)\})$ is a qualification diagnosis as depicted in Fig. 2.b.

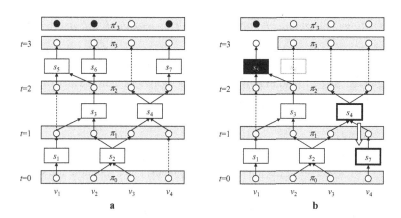

Fig. 2. Plan execution before and after a qualification diagnosis together with an observation deviating from the expected observation, as indicated by the black dot

3.1 Identifying Diagnoses

Let the size $\|Q\|$ of a qualitative diagnosis $Q = (F, D, M, C)$ be equal to the sum of the cardinalities of the sets involved, i.e. $\|Q\| = |F| + |D| + |M| + |C|$. Intuitively, we should aim at finding diagnoses of minimum size. In general, finding such minimum diagnoses is an NP-hard problem, and it turns out that the same holds for plan diagnosis, too, even if we restrict our attention to the diagnosis of failing plan steps. In this section, therefore, we will restrict our attention to the complexity of finding *pure F, D, M or C* diagnoses.

Identifying F-diagnoses. Identifying an arbitrary F-diagnosis is trivial: qualify every plan step as abnormal. This will constitute a diagnosis. Finding a subset-minimal F-diagnosis is also easy, but finding a minimum (cardinality-minimal) F-diagnosis is NP-hard [17].[7]

Minimizing the *size* of a diagnosis, however, is only one option in finding a suitable diagnosis. It is usually preferred if the normal health state of a plan step is more likely than an abnormal one. Another criterion that is useful is the *information content* of a diagnosis. We say that a qualification diagnosis Q is more informative than another one

---

[7] It is not difficult to show that for every qualification diagnosis of size m there exists an F-diagnosis (where every component except the F-component is empty) with size less than or equal to m, explaining the same set of observations.

Q' iff $Var(\pi'_{Q'}) \subset Var(\pi'_Q)$, where $obs(t) \to^*_{Q;P}(\pi'_Q, t')$. A diagnosis Q is maximally informative (maxi-diagnosis) if no diagnosis Q' is more informative than Q.[8] Likewise, we can define a *minimal maximal informative* diagnosis (mini-maxi diagnosis):

Definition 6. *Let* $\langle P, obs(t), obs(t') \rangle$ *be a diagnostic problem with observations* $obs(t) = (\pi, t)$ *and* $obs(t') = (\pi', t')$*, and let* $obs(t) \to^*_{Q;P}(\pi'_Q, t')$*, given a qualification* Q*. Then* Q *is said to be a* maximally informative diagnosis *of* $\langle P, obs(t), obs(t') \rangle$ *iff (i)* $\pi' \approx \pi'_Q$*, and (ii)* $Var(\pi_Q)$ *is maximal among all diagnoses.*

Q is said to be a minimal maximally informative *diagnosis (mini-maxi diagnosis) iff the qualification Q is a minimal diagnosis among the maximally informative diagnoses.*

Mini-maxi diagnoses should be preferred if it is unlikely that a faulty plan step produces correct results. Quite surprisingly, as we have shown in a recent paper (see [17]), *mini-maxi* diagnoses can be found in polynomial time (polynomial in the size of the plan).

The following example gives an illustration:

Example 4. Reconsider the plan depicted in Fig. 2.a. If we only consider failing plan steps, then there are seven qualifications that are minimal diagnoses according to Definition 5. Among these seven diagnoses $Q = (\{s_2\}, \varnothing, \varnothing, \varnothing)$ is a *minimum* diagnosis, and $Q' = (\{s_3, s_7\}\varnothing, \varnothing, \varnothing)$ is a *mini-maxi* diagnosis. Let π'_Q denote the state derived at time $t = 3$ by using Q as a qualification. Then $Var(\pi'_Q) = \varnothing$, $Var(\pi'_{Q'}) = \{v_3\}$.

Consider a diagnosis Q of a plan with observations. Suppose that the qualification Q only consists of missing or duplicated actions and of violated constraints; i.e., $Q = (\varnothing, M, D, C)$. Then all plan steps are executed normally and the set of variables for which known values are predicted is maximal. Moreover, since the qualification Q is a diagnosis, these predicted values are compatible with the observations. Since coincidental compatibility of values is unlikely, this diagnosis must be preferred to any diagnosis in which less known values are predicted. Only plan steps that are qualified as failed reduce the predicted set of variables with known values. Hence, we can determine the missing and duplicated plan steps and the violated constraints by preferring mini-maxi diagnoses.

Example 5. Reconsider the plan depicted in Fig. 2.a. Suppose that changing the execution order of plan steps s_4 and s_7 enables us to correctly predict the value of variable v_4, and omitting plan step s_6 enables us to predict the value of variable v_2. Then $Q = (\{s_5\}, \{s_6\}, \varnothing, \{(s_7, s_4)\})$ is a qualification diagnosis. Figure 2.b depicts this diagnosis. Let π'_Q denote the state derived at time $t = 3$ by using the diagnosis Q. Then the set of correctly predicted variables given this diagnosis is: $Var(\pi'_Q) = \{v_2, v_3, v_4\}$.

Identifying Omitted and Duplicated Plan Steps. A plan step omitting diagnosis (M-diagnosis) and a plan step duplicating diagnosis (D-diagnosis) are defined by qualification diagnoses $Q = (\varnothing, M, \varnothing, \varnothing)$ and $Q = (\varnothing, \varnothing, D, \varnothing)$, respectively. It is easy to see that both M- and D-diagnosis are maximal informative diagnoses. They are both, in general, hard to compute:

---

[8] Note that a maximal informative diagnosis is also maximum informative diagnosis. Q is a maximum informative diagnosis if for no diagnosis Q': $|Var(\pi_{Q'})| > |Var(\pi_Q)|$.

Proposition 1. *Let $P = \langle \mathcal{O}, S, \prec \rangle$ be a plan with observations $obs(t) = (\pi, t)$ and $obs(t') = (\pi', t')$, where $t < t' \leq depth(P)$. Deciding whether an M-diagnosis exists as well as deciding whether a D-diagnosis exist is NP-hard.*

Proof. Easy reduction of KNAPSACK to an M- and to a D-diagnosis problem.[9]

Identifying Constraint Diagnoses. A constraint diagnosis is a qualification diagnosis $Q = (\varnothing, \varnothing, \varnothing, C)$. It is easy to see that every constraint diagnosis is a maximal informative diagnosis. It turns out that also these maxi-diagnoses are hard to compute:

Proposition 2. *Let $P = \langle \mathcal{O}, S, \prec \rangle$ be a plan with observations $obs(t) = (\pi, t)$ and $obs(t') = (\pi', t')$, where $t < t' \leq depth(P)$. Deciding whether a constraint diagnosis Q exists is NP-hard.*

Proof. Reduction of TSP to a C-diagnosis problem.[11]

3.2 Approximations

The above results are of course rather disappointing. However, assuming that the omitted or duplicated plan steps and constraint violations occur in unrelated parts of a plan (or occur only once), diagnoses can be determined efficiently. Given a diagnostic problem $\langle P, obs(t), obs(t') \rangle$ with observations $obs(t) = (\pi, t)$ and $obs(t') = (\pi', t')$, for each observed variable $v \in Var(\pi')$ at time point t' we can determine the set of plan steps and the set of precedence constraints on the value of the variable v at time point t' depends. Let $Dep^{steps}(v, t') \subseteq S$ and $Dep^{constr}(v, t') \subseteq \ll$ be the set of plan steps and the set of precedence constraints between pairs of plan steps, respectively, on which the value of the variable v at time point t' depends. The dependency sets $Dep^{steps}(v, t')$ of the observed variables in $Var(\pi')$ can be used to determine mini-maxi diagnoses in polynomial time.

A missing or duplicated plan step can also be determined using the dependency sets $Dep^{steps}(v, t')$. For each dependency set $Dep^{steps}(v, t')$ of an observed variable $v \in Var(\pi')$ of which the predicted value $\pi'_\varnothing(v)$ is incompatible with the observed value $\pi'(v)$, we can perform the following tests. Check for every plan step $s \in Dep^{steps}(v, t')$ whether omitting s or duplicating s enables us to predict compatible values for every observed variable $v' \in Var(\pi')$ such that $s \in Dep^{steps}_{PM,D}(v', t')$. Here $P^{M,D}$ denotes either the modified plan $P^{\{s\},\varnothing}$ or the modified plan $P^{\varnothing,\{s\}}$ depending on whether we check for the omission or duplication of the plan step s. Similarly we can use the constraints $s \ll s' \in Dep^{constr}(v, t')$ to check for constraint violations.

Note that a group of agents can efficiently determine the dependency sets $Dep^{steps}(v, t')$ and $Dep^{constr}(v, t')$. A multi-agent protocol for determining dependency sets in general diagnostic problems has been presented in [19].

4 Conclusion and Further Work

We have extended previous work on plan diagnosis in order to incorporate the identification of violations of the plan structure. This extension is particularly important for

---

[9] The proof is omitted due to lack of space. It can be found in [18].

multi-agent plan execution where such constraint violations can easily be caused by coordination errors. We have pointed out that, like maximally informative diagnosis of failing actions, constraint diagnosis and diagnosis of missing plan steps and duplicated plan steps also try to establish a maximally informative explanation of the observations made. Unlike a maximally informative diagnosis, however, identifying these M-, D- and C-diagnoses turns out to be an NP-hard problem. A heuristic that enables an efficient search for constraint diagnoses in some restricted cases has been presented.

In future work we intend to take the diagnosis one step further: By looking at the constraint violations an agent is responsible for, we may identify a pattern that indicates a flaw in the behavior of the agent.

References

1. Roos, N., Witteveen, C.: Diagnosis of plans and agents. In: Pĕchouček, M., Petta, P., Varga, L.Z. (eds.) CEEMAS 2005. LNCS (LNAI), vol. 3690, pp. 357–366. Springer, Heidelberg (2005)
2. Witteveen, C., Roos, N., van der Krogt, R., de Weerdt, M.: Diagnosis of single and multi-agent plans. In: AAMAS 2005, pp. 805–812 (2005)
3. de Jonge, F., Roos, N., Witteveen, C.: Primary and secondary plan diagnosis. In: 17th International Workshop on Principles of Diagnosis, DX'06, Universidad de Valladolid, pp. 133–140 (2006)
4. de Jonge, F., Roos, N., Witteveen, C.: Diagnosis of multi-agent plan execution. In: Fischer, K., Timm, I.J., André, E., Zhong, N. (eds.) MATES 2006. LNCS (LNAI), vol. 4196, pp. 86–97. Springer, Heidelberg (2006)
5. Kalech, M., Kaminka, G.A.: Towards model-based diagnosis of coordination failures. In: AAAI 2005, pp. 102–107 (2005)
6. Reiter, R.: A theory of diagnosis from first principles. Artificial Intelligence 32(1), 57–95 (1987)
7. Kleer, J.d., Williams, B.C.: Diagnosing multiple faults. Artificial Intelligence 32(1), 97–130 (1987)
8. Kalech, M., Kaminka, G.A.: On the design of social diagnosis algorithms for multi-agent teams. In: IJCAI-03, pp. 370–375 (2003)
9. Kalech, M., Kaminka, G.A.: Diagnosing a team of agents: Scaling-up. In: AAMAS 2005, pp. 249–255 (2005)
10. de Jonge, F., Roos, N.: Plan-execution health repair in a multi-agent system. In: Proc. 23rd Annual Workshop of the UK Planning and Scheduling SIG (PlanSIG 2004) (2004)
11. Carver, N., Lesser, V.: Domain monotonicity and the performance of local solutions strategies for CDPS-based distributed sensor interpretation and distributed diagnosis. Autonomous Agents and Multi-Agent Systems 6(1), 35–76 (2003)
12. Horling, B., Benyo, B., Lesser, V.: Using self-diagnosis to adapt organizational structures. In: Proc. 5th Int'l. Conf. on Autonomous Agents, pp. 529–536. ACM Press, New York (2001)
13. Baroni, P., Lamperti, G., Pogliano, P., Zanella, M.: Diagnosis of large active systems. Artificial Intelligence 110(1), 135–183 (1999)
14. Cassandras, C.G., Lafortune, S.: Introduction to Discrete Event Systems. Kluwer Academic Publishers, Dordrecht (1999)
15. Debouk, R., Lafortune, S., Teneketzis, D.: Coordinated decentralized protocols for failure diagnosis of discrete-event systems. Journal of Discrete Event Dynamical Systems: Theory and Application 10, 33–86 (2000)

16. Pencolé, Y., Cordier, M.: A formal framework for the decentralised diagnosis of large scale discrete event systems and its application to telecommunication networks. Artificial Intelligence 164(1-2), 121–170 (2005)
17. Roos, N., Witteveen, C.: Models and methods for plan diagnosis. In: Formal Approaches to Multi-Agent Systems (FAMAS'06), ECAI 2006, Workshop Notes (2006)
18. Roos, N., Witteveen, C.: Diagnosis of plan structure violations. Technical Report MICC 07-05, Universiteit Maastricht (2007)
19. Roos, N., ten Teije, A., Witteveen, C.: A protocol for multi-agent diagnosis with spatially distributed knowledge. In: AAMAS 2003, pp. 655–661 (2003)

Team Cooperation for Plan Recovery in Multi-agent Systems

Roberto Micalizio and Pietro Torasso

Università di Torino, corso Svizzera 187, Torino, Italy
{micalizio,torasso}@di.unito.it

Abstract. The paper addresses the problem of recovering the execution of a multi-agent plan when the occurrence of unexpected events (e.g. faults) may cause the failure of some actions. In our scenario actions are executed concurrently by a group of agents organized in teams and each agent performs a local control loop on the progress of the sub-plan it is responsible for. When an agent detects an action failure, the agent itself tries to repair (if possible) its own sub-plan and if this local recovery fails, , a more powerful recovery strategy at *team level* is invoked. Such a strategy is based on the cooperation of agents within the same team: the agent in trouble asks another teammate, properly selected, to cooperate for recovering from a particular action failure. The cooperation is aimed at achieving the goal assigned to the agents' team despite the action failure and to this end the agents exchange sub-goals and synthesize new plans.

1 Introduction

Within the AI community there is a growing interest in the development of *autonomous systems*; i.e., systems which are able to react to unexpected events. In general the autonomy is achieved by establishing a *closed loop of control feedback* (control loop in short), which involves many activities such as (re-)planning, (re-)scheduling, on-line monitoring and diagnosis and (re-) configuration. While the issues for establishing a control loop have found appropriate solutions when a single agent behaves as supervisor of a system (a significant example in the field is the Livingstone architecture proposed in the Remote Agent Experiment [1]), only recently there is a growing interest for establishing a control loop in a multi-agent scenario, where agents, organized in one or more teams, execute actions concurrently in a partially observable environment. Since the actual execution of a plan may be threatened [2] by the occurrence of unexpected events (e.g., faults in the functionalities of the agents), the task of executing a plan is critical and different Model-Based solutions for monitoring and diagnosing multi-agent plans have been proposed (see e.g., [3,4,5]). While these approaches provide solutions to the problems of detecting and explaining action failures, they do not explicitly address the problem of how these pieces of information can be exploited to overcome such failures.

The problem of recovering from an action failure is very complex and requires cooperation among agents and the ability of planning (and re-planning) under uncertainty. In fact, in most cases an action failure may have a huge impact on the whole plan, and not only on the specific sub-plan where the action failure has occurred. This propagation

P. Petta et al. (Eds.): MATES 2007, LNAI 4687, pp. 170–181, 2007.

of negative effects of an action failure makes unrealistic (in most cases) the invocation of a recovery procedure predefined for each type of action failure.

In [6] we have proposed a control architecture where each agent is responsible for establishing a closed loop of control over the execution of the actions it performs. Within this local control loop each agent has to detect the failure of its actions, and to recover (if possible) from these action failures. We now extend this architecture by exploiting the organization of the agents in teams[1] and by defining a more general level of control based on the notion of teammates. In particular, we discuss a plan recovery strategy at the team level, where an agent in trouble calls for the cooperation of another teammate for recovering from an action failure. During the process of plan recovery at team level, the two teammates cooperate for achieving the goal assigned to their team despite the occurrence of the action failure; to this end the two agents exchange each other their sub-goals and revise their sub-plans through a re-planning process.

The paper is organized as follows. In Sect. 2 the high-level architecture of the control loop is discussed; in Sect. 3 we describe the main characteristics of the multi-agent plans we deal with, while in Sect. 4 we briefly introduce the results inferred during the process of on-line supervision (monitoring + diagnosis) of a plan execution. In Sect. 5 we discuss the process of plan recovery at team level. Finally, in Sect. 6 we make some concluding remarks.

2   Control Loop Architecture

The architecture proposed in this paper is shown in Figure 1. We assume that a human user, possibly by exploiting different planning tools, synthesizes a global plan P, which achieves some desired, complex goal G. More precisely, the plan P is a completely instantiated multi-agent plan; the formal definition of P is given in the next section, for the time being it is sufficient to consider P as a classical Partial-Order-Plan (POP) where actions are expressed in a STRIPS-like language.

As soon as the global plan P has been constructed, the Dispatcher module decomposes P in as many sub-plans as agents available, assigning each sub-plan P_i to agent i. According to the plan P the Dispatcher organizes the agents in *teams* taking into account the sub-goals assigned to each agent and the resources allocated to them. For the sake of simplicity we assume that teams cannot change during execution of the plan. In the following, given the agent i, *team(i)* denotes the subset of agents in the same team of i. After this initial phase, each agent starts execution of its own local plan, therefore at each time instant multiple actions are executed concurrently. During the execution of their actions, agents receive observations about changes occurring in the environment; however each agent i receives just observations about its own status, hence the agents have a limited view of these changes occurred in the environment.

Observe that the agents may need the use of resources available in the environment. In principle, a subset of resources may be assigned to a specific team, however there may be resources that are shared among different teams. It follows that, even though each team considers just a portion of the global goal, the teams are not completely

---

[1] As discussed in [7], a multi-agent system represents an effective solution when it is structured so that just a small number of agents need to cooperate.

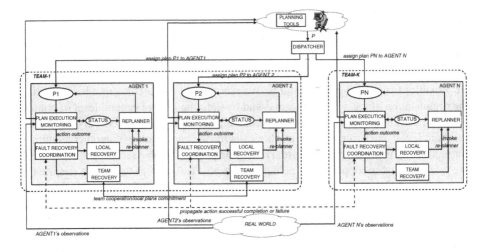

Fig. 1. The architecture of the control loop at the agent level and at the global level

independent of one another and cooperation or interaction among teams is possible (or even needed). The cooperation among agents, of the same or different teams, is achieved by means of *services* an agent provides to others. More precisely, a service is one of the effects of an action which results to be a precondition for other action(s).

Not only the execution of P, but also control of the plan is distributed among the agents, as each agent i performs a local control loop on the progress of its actions. This control loop at agent level involves a number of modules. The Plan Execution Monitoring module (PEM) estimates the current status of the agent and detects the outcome of the action the agent is executing on the basis of the observations from the environment. Every time an action outcome is determined, the Fault Recovery Coordination module (FRC) evaluates whether the outcome is nominal: if not, the FRC has to coordinate the recovery process: it invokes the Local Recovery (LR) module in order to repair (if possible) the failure by means of a new local plan (to do this, the LR module invokes the local Re-Planning module). Unfortunately such a local plan may not exist, i.e., single agents may not be able to autonomously overcome an action failure. When recovery at the local level fails, the FRC is responsible for activating the recovery at team level. To this end, the FRC invokes the Team Recovery (TR) module which establishes a cooperation with another agent in the same team (Figure 1 shows the communication channel between the TR modules of the agents $A1$ and $A2$, both in *team-1*, through which the cooperation is established). During plan recovery at team level, the involved agents exchange their sub-goals, synthesize new recovery plans and integrate them in their original plans in order to overcome, if possible, the action failure.

For the sake of simplicity we assume that in case plan recovery fails both at local and at team level, the FRC module of the agent in trouble informs the human user about the action failure. The user is responsible for adapting the global plan P and/or for revising the global goal G, by taking into account the actual health status of the agents in the systems; e.g., the global plan P could be revised by excluding the agent in trouble.

3   The Global Plan and the Local Plans

Global Plan. The global plan to be monitored is represented as partial order plan (POP), defined (e.g., [8]) as a directed acyclic graph, POP=$\langle A, <, C \rangle$, with: A the set of nodes representing the action instances the agents have to execute; $<$ a set of precedence links between actions (a precedence link $a \prec a'$ in $<$ indicates action a must precede execution of action a'); C a set of causal links of the form $l : a \xrightarrow{q} a'$, the link l indicates that action a provides action a' with the service q, where q is an atom occurring in the preconditions of a'. The class of multi-agent plans we deal with here is a subclass of the POP defined above. As in the POP case, we define P as the DAG $\langle A, <, C \rangle$, where A, $<$ and C have the same meanings, but we introduce the following requirements:

- Every action instance $a \in A$ is assigned to a specific agent $i \in T$.
- All the actions assigned to the same agent i are totally ordered, i.e., for any pair of actions a and a' assigned to i, either a precedes a' or a' precedes a must hold.
- Access to critical resources is ruled by means of causal links. If both the actions, a assigned to agent i, and a' assigned to agent j, require the same critical resource res, the causal link $l : a \xrightarrow{free(res)} a'$ imposes that a' must be executed after a; the link l states that action a provides a' with the service of freeing resource res.

A multi-agent plan instance P satisfying the previous requirements can be synthesized by exploiting the POMP planner proposed by Boutilier et al. in [9].

Local Plans. Given the global plan P, the Dispatcher module decomposes P into as many sub-plans as the number of the agents in the system. The decomposition is easy, involving the selection from P of all the actions an agent has to execute. Formally, the sub-plan for agent i is the tuple $P_i = \langle A_i, <_i, C_i, T_i^{in}, T_i^{out}, X_i^{in}, X_i^{out} \rangle$ where: A_i is the subset of actions in P agent i has to execute; $<_i$ is a total order relation defined over the actions in A_i; C_i is a set of causal links $a \xrightarrow{q} a'$ where both a and a' belong to A_i; T_i^{in} is a set of incoming causal links where a' belongs to A_i and a is assigned to another agent j in the same team of i (i.e., *team(i)=team(j)*); T_i^{out} is a set of outgoing causal links where a belongs to A_i and a' is assigned to another agent $j \in team(i)$; finally, X_i^{in} and X_i^{out} are analogous to T_i^{in} and T_i^{out}, respectively, but agent j belongs to another team ($j \notin team(i)$).

Primary Goals and Target Actions. Given an action $a \in A_i$, *primary*(a) denotes the set of effects of a such that every atom $q \in primary(a)$ satisfies at least one of the following conditions:

- $q \in G$, i.e., q is an atom which appears in the global goal G of P
- q is a service that agent i provides to another agent j, that is, there exists a causal link $l : a \xrightarrow{q} a'$, where $a \in A_i$ and $a' \in A_j$.

An action a such that *primary*$(a) \neq \emptyset$ is said a *target action*, otherwise it is said *simple*. We assume every simple action in the plan to provide (directly or indirectly) a target action with a service. The notion of target action plays a critical role in the process of plan recovery at team level; in fact when agent i detects a fault in its functionality preventing the execution of a target action a, the effects of a are the sub-goals that the agents i can send to another agent j ($j \in team(i)$) to recover from the failure of a.

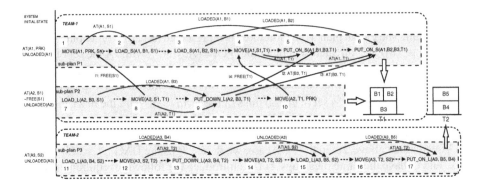

Fig. 2. The plan built by a POMP-like planner

Running Example. We will use a simple blocks world example to illustrate the basic
concepts of the proposal. Consider three agents $A1$, $A2$ and $A3$: $A1$ and $A2$, belonging
to the same team *team-1*, have to move three blocks $B1$, $B2$, $B3$ from a source $S1$ to
a target $T1$. They have to cooperate to achieve a specific configuration where the large
block $B3$ is put on the small blocks $B1$ and $B2$. Agent $A3$, the only member of *team-2*,
has to do a similar job moving blocks $B4$ and $B5$ from source $S2$ to destination $T2$
($B5$ must be placed on top of $B4$). We distinguish between two types of blocks: *small*
and *large*. Nominally, each agent can carry at most two small blocks or a large one.
The access to the source and target locations is constrained: just one agent at a time can
take (release) a block within them. A further location, PRK, is not constrained: this is
where the agents are positioned when they complete their sub-plans.

Figure 2 shows an instance of a multi-agent plan achieving the target configuration
of blocks. The global goal is decomposed into two sub-goals, $G1$ achieved by the agents
in *team-1*, and $G2$ assigned to *team-2*. The plan is a DAG: nodes correspond to actions,
edges to precedence (dashed) or causal (solid) links. Causal links are labeled with the
services an action provides to another; e.g., the causal link from action 2 to action 5 is
labeled with the service LOADED(A1,B1), which is both one of the effects of action
2 and one of the preconditions for the execution of action 5. The grey dashed rectangles
highlight the sub-plans the Dispatcher produces and assigns to the three agents. Sub-
plans P_1 and P_2 have causal dependent actions (causal links $l_1 \ldots l_4$), while plan P_3 is
completely independent from P_1 and P_2. It follows that a failure in P_1 (P_2) may affect
some actions in P_2 (P_1) and therefore may threaten achievement of the sub-goal $G1$.

4   Plan Execution Monitoring and Diagnosis

Due to space limitations, in this section we just introduce the basic concepts of the on-
line supervision task (monitoring + diagnosis), that each agent i has to perform over the
execution of the actions it is responsible for. A formal and detailed description of the
problem of supervising the plan execution has been addressed in [6,10].

Action Outcome. As discussed in [2], the actual execution of an action is threatened by the occurrence of unexpected events (e.g., faults). To supervise execution of a multi-agent plan, the PEM module thus has to be able to deal with not nominal action outcomes. In this paper, we assume that the outcome of an action consists of two sets: *achievedEffects* and *missedEffects*; the former maintains all the actions effects achieved by the agent, while the latter maintains all the missed action effects. An action is considered completed successfully only when *outcome(a).missedEffects*=$\emptyset$.

Extended Action Model. To keep track of the (possibly not nominal) outcome of actions an agent executes, we need an action model which represents both the nominal and the anomalous behavior of the action itself. For such a modeling task, in [10] we have proposed a relational representation to deal with the non deterministic effects of the actions caused by the possible occurrence of faults. In short, the extended model of an action a is a transition relation Δ_a, where every tuple $d \in \Delta_a$ models a possible change in the status of agent i, which may occur while i is executing a. Each tuple d has the form $d = \langle s_{t-1}, fault, obs, s_t \rangle$. In particular, s_{t-1} and s_t represent two agent states at time $t-1$ and t respectively, each state is a complete assignment of values to the status variables of agent i. $fault$ indicates which fault must occur in order to cause a change of status from s_{t-1} to s_t; of course, in the transitions which model the nominal behavior $fault$ is empty. Finally, obs is a set of observations received by i after the execution of a. For example, in our blocks world example the MOVE action can fail as a consequence of two types of faults: f-BRY and f-MOB. f-BRY affects the battery by reducing the level of power from the nominal *high* to the degraded *low*. An agent can complete a move action with power *low* iff the agent is empty or half loaded (i.e. the agent is carrying a small object only), the action fails otherwise. f-MOB affects the health status of the mobility functionality, which changes from the nominal *OK* to the anomalous *broken*; under this health status there is no way to complete the move action.

Agent Status. The status of agent i is represented by a set of status variables concerning for example the position of agent i and the health status of the functionalities of i (e.g., mobility and power). In [10] we have pointed out that the status of an agent can be predicted, at each time instant t, by exploiting the model of the action a the agent executes. However, since the action models are not deterministic and the system is only partially observable, the status of agent i cannot be precisely predicted; in general, instead, the agent status is just estimated by means of a set of alternative states assumed by i at time t; this set is known in literature as *belief state* and will be denoted as $\mathcal{B}_t^i$. As a consequence, in many cases, determining the health status of an agent is an hard task which requires diagnostic inferences (see [10]).

5   Plan Recovery at Team Level

5.1   The Basic Strategy

In the previous section we have sketched how an agent i can determine the outcome of actions it executes and how it can infer a diagnosis about the health status of its functionalities. We now show how these pieces of information can be used by agent i

to recover (if possible) from a detected action failure. In the control loop two different levels of recovery are considered: the one at the local level and the one at the team level.

Plan recovery at local level. When the occurrence of a fault f causes the failure of an action a executed by agent i, agent i has first to detect this failure and then try to synthesize a new local plan $NewP_i$ to achieve the same goals of the original local plan P_i independently of the actual health status of functionalities of agent i. Synthesis of the recovery plan $NewP_i$ is performed by invoking the Re-Planner module of agent i. Note that building $NewP_i$ is hard: in many cases such a plan $NewP_i$ may not exist, since the occurred fault may prevent the execution of some types of action ([6]).

Plan Recovery at Team Level. A more general recovery strategy consists in repairing the failure of action a, executed by agent i, by means of the help of another agent j, where the agents i and j are in the same team. This alternative strategy is referred to as *plan recovery at team level* (team recovery for short). Team recovery involves two cooperating agents: the first is said *requesting agent* since it sends a "request of help"; the second is said *cooperating agent* as it changes its own local plan to satisfy the incoming requests. For simplicity, we impose that at each time instant: 1) a requesting agent i cannot send multiple requests to different agents but can send only one request to a specific agent j and 2) a cooperating agent j can accept just a cooperation request per time; if an agent receives more cooperation requests at the same time we assume that the agent accepts only one request[2] and rejects all the others. However, the described solution can be extended to the more general case where these assumptions are relaxed. As it is reasonable, an agent cannot behave both as requesting and as cooperating agent at the same time. After these premises, in the following we discuss which pieces of information the requesting and the cooperation agents need to exchange and how an action failure can be recovered from.

For clarity, when introducing new concepts we exemplify them by referring to the plan in the blocks world introduced in Figure 2. In particular, assume action 8 fails as a consequence of the occurrence of fault f-BRY, thereby the move action cannot be completed, since agent $A2$ is fully loaded. It is then easy to see there is no way for agent $A2$ to move the block $B3$ from $S1$ to $T1$, i.e., recovery of plan P_2 at the local level fails.

Composing a Cooperation Request. We first discuss how a requesting agent i composes a cooperation request $\mathcal{R}$; essentially this task requires three steps: 1) selecting a cooperating agent in $team(i)$; 2) determining a set Q of services the cooperating agent has to obtain in lieu of agent i; and 3) synthesizing a new local plan $NewP_i$ for achieving a *safe status* where the resources currently used by agent i are released.

Selecting the Cooperating Agent. When agent i has to choose a cooperating agent in $team(i)$, the following policy is adopted. If the failed action a provides, directly or indirectly, a service to an action $a' \in A_j$ and $team(i) = team(j)$, then j is selected as cooperating agent; the cooperating agent is chosen randomly in $team(i)$ otherwise. The basic idea of this policy is that, if agent i can no longer provide agent j with a service q,

---

[2] In particular, the agent could choose the request that represents the closest threat in time.

agent j is called for achieving the service q on its own. In fact, without the availability of the service q, agent j cannot complete its local plan P_j, as q is a precondition of at least one action in P_j. On the contrary, when the effects of action a do not impact on the execution of other sub-plans (i.e., the effects of a are part of the global goal of the plan), the cooperating agent is chosen non deterministically[3] in $team(i)$. In our example, action 9 indirectly provides the actions 4 and 5 (both assigned to agent $A1$) with some services, therefore agent $A2$ chooses $A1$ as cooperating agent.

Determining the Set Q of Services. Once the cooperating agent j has been selected, the requesting agent i has to determine the set Q of services to be included in the cooperation request. It is important to note that the set Q must be inferred taking into account the notion of target action. In fact, the effects of a simple action are relevant just for the responsible agent, while the effects of target actions are meaningful for all agents in $team(i)$. In general, the request agent i determines the set Q of primary services to submit to the cooperating agent j as follows: agent i first selects the set *affectedTargetActions* containing all the target actions in A_i directly or indirectly affected by the failure of action a. The set Q is obtained as $\bigcup_{act \in affectedTargetActions} primary(act)$. Given the failure of action 9, we have that *affectedTargetActions*=$\{9\}$ and as a consequence $Q=\{\texttt{AT(B3,T1)}\}$.

Achieving a Safe Status. As a last step before the invocation of the cooperating agent j, the requesting agent i has to assess whether its current health status allows it to lead the system in a *safe status*, where all the resources and objects currently acquired by i are released and made available to other agents (in particular to agent j). Note that in order to get such a safe status, the agent i has to synthesize a new local plan $NewP_i$, which may undo some of the actions the agent i has already executed. Synthesis of $NewP_i$ may fail when some of the actions previously executed are not reversible or when the current health status of i prevents i to execute some particular action types; in both these situations team recovery fails immediately. In our example, the *safeStatus* the agent $A2$ has to get is the set of the atoms $\{\texttt{AT(B3, S1)}; \texttt{FREE(S1)}\}$. Since a large block can be unloaded even when the power of an agent is *low*, the $NewP_{A2}$ achieving *safeStatus* exists (Figure 5.a): it consists of unloading block $B3$ in position $S1$ and leaving the location $S1$.

Processing a cooperation request. Assuming that $NewP_i$ exists, the requesting agent i then sends a cooperation request $\mathcal{R}=\langle j, safeStatus, Q\rangle$ to the cooperating agent j. Note that the request $\mathcal{R}$ conveys two important pieces of information for the cooperating agent j; while Q represents the set of services j has to get for accomplishing the request, *safeStatus* indicates which resources and objects can be used to achieve Q. When agent j receives the request $\mathcal{R}$, it decides whether to serve $\mathcal{R}$ or not. In case it accepts to satisfy $\mathcal{R}$, agent j has to adjust its local plan P_j in two ways: 1) find a new plan that achieves *safeStatus* and 2) find a new plan that from *safeStatus* achieves Q. In other words,

---

[3] Currently the cooperating agent is randomly chosen. However, it is possible to devise more sophisticated solutions where the agent in trouble chooses the cooperating agent by reasoning about the current status of its teammates and of the resources. These solutions may be very computationally expensive since the agent has just a limited view of the system status and it may need to exchange a huge amount of information with each teammate.

Fault-Detection-Recovery(*outcome(a)*, $\mathcal{B}_t^i$, P_i) {

01 **if** (*outcome(a).missedEffects* $\neq \emptyset$) {

02      $NewP_i =$ **LocalRecovery**(*outcome(a)*, $\mathcal{B}_t^i$, P_i);

03   **if** ($NewP_i \neq \emptyset$) { $P_i = NewP_i$;   mark *a* as *re-planned*; }

04   **else** { $NewP_i =$**TeamRecovery-Request**(*outcome(a)*, $\mathcal{B}_t^i$, P_i);

05   **if** ($NewP_i \neq \emptyset$) { $P_i = NewP_i$;   mark *a* as *re-planned*; }

06   **else** mark *a* as *failed*; }}

07 **else** { mark *a* as *successfully-completed*

08   **if** (a request $\mathcal{R}$ has been received){

09          $NewP_i =$**TeamRecovery-Cooperation**($\mathcal{B}_t^i$, P_i, $\mathcal{R}$);

10   **if** ($NewP_i \neq \emptyset$) $P_i = NewP_i$; }}

11 **if** (*a* is marked as *failed*) {

12   **Propagate-Harmful-Effects-In-Global-Plan**(*a*, P_i);

13   ⟨ notify the user of the failure of action *a*⟩; }   }

Fig. 3. The algorithm for detection and recovery of a local plan failure

agent j first acquires the resources agent i has set in *safeStatus*, and it then plans for achieving the primary goals in Q.

Note that agent j may be itself impaired and therefore also not be able to perform some types of actions. Thus, a recovery plan may not exist; in this case, agent j notifies agent i about the failure of the team recovery process. In our simple example, since the health status of the cooperating agent $A1$ is OK ($A1$ behaves nominally), there exists a new local plan $NewP_{A1}$, shown in Figure 5.b: $A1$ first moves from its current position in PRK to the source $S1$; $A1$ then loads the block B3 and moves it to the desired position $T1$. With these steps, agent $A1$ has achieved the primary goal AT(B3,T1) the agent $A2$ was not able to. The plan $NewP_{A1}$ also includes the actions previously assigned to $A1$ in order to move both B1 and B2 from $S1$ to $T1$.

Plans Commitment. In case both $NewP_i$ and $NewP_j$ exist, team recovery ends with a commitment phase. In this phase, the two agents exchange their new local plans in order to properly set the causal links between the actions they have to execute. In our example, the actions agent $A2$ has to perform for leading the system to a *safeStatus* must precede those assigned to agent $A1$, which instead achieve the services in Q. Figure 5.c shows how the two agents set the causal links during the commitment phase: the plans are the new local plans the two agents $A1$ and $A2$ execute to achieve the sub-goal assigned them despite the occurrence of a fault in the battery of agent $A2$.

5.2   High-Level Algorithms

We now briefly describe the high-level algorithms of the two main modules involved in team level recovery: the Fault Recovery Coordination (FRC) and the Team Recovery (TR) modules (see the control loop architecture in Figure 3).

The Fault Recovery Coordination Module. The process of plan recovery is coordinated by the FRC module of each agent i. Given the outcome of the action a agent i has just executed, the FRC has the following tasks:

TeamRecovery-Request$(outcome(a), \mathcal{B}_t^i, P_i)\{$
01   *affectedTargetActions* = **FindTargetActions**(a, P_i);
02   $Q = \bigcup_{act \in affectedTargetActions} primary(targetAct)$;
03   j = **chooseCooperatingAgent**$(team(i), P_i)$;
04   *safeStatus* = **FindSafeStatusForAcquiredResources**$(a, \mathcal{B}_t^i)$;
05   $NewP_i$=**Replanner**$(\mathcal{B}_t^i, P_i, safeStatus)$;
06 **if** $NewP_i \neq \emptyset\{$
07      $\langle$ send the cooperation request $\mathcal{R} = \langle j, safeStatus, Q \rangle$ to $j \rangle$;
08      $\langle$ wait for the *replay* $\rangle$;
09   **if** (*replay* is *ok*) { **Plan-Commitment**(); **return** $NewP_i$; }
10 **else return** $\emptyset$; }

TeamRecovery-Cooperation$(\mathcal{B}_t^j, P_j)\{$
01   get the cooperation request $\mathcal{R} = \langle j, safeStatus, Q \rangle$
02   $TempP$=**Replanner**$(\mathcal{B}_t^j, P_j, safeStatus)$;
03   $NewP_j$=**Replanner**$(safeStatus, TempP, Q)$;
04 **if** $(NewP_j \neq \emptyset)\{$ $\langle$ send *ok* to *sender*$(\mathcal{R}) \rangle$; **Plan-Commitment**(); **return** $NewP_j$; }
05 **else** { $\langle$send *failure* to *sender*$(\mathcal{R}) \rangle$; **return** $\emptyset$; } }

Fig. 4. The algorithms for the team-level recovery

- *Activate plan recovery at local/team level* (lines 01-06): if the outcome of action a is not nominal ($outcome(a).missedEffects \neq \emptyset$), the FRC first invokes the **Local-Recovery** module [6] to recover from this failure via a local recovery plan $NewP_i$. If local recovery fails ($NewP_i$ is empty), the FRC activates team level recovery by invoking the **TeamRecovery-Request** function (Figure 4): agent i behaves as a requesting agent. Also in this case the recovery consists of a new local plan $NewP_i$ which overcomes the failure of a; if team recovery fails, $NewP_i$ is empty.
- *Accept a cooperation request* (07-10): If the current action a has been successfully completed, agent i can accept a cooperation request (function **TeamRecovery-Cooperation** in Figure 4). In this case, agent i behaves as a cooperating agent. When team recovery succeeds, the new local plan $NewP_i$ becomes the current plan of agent i, the plan P_i is not modified otherwise.
- *Propagate action failure* (11-13): if plan recovery fails both at local and at team level, the FRC module first propagates the failure of action a in the global plan (line 12): agent i informs the other agents that a subset of services cannot be achieved, and then notifies the human user of the failure of action a (line 13).

The Team Recovery Module. The behavior of the requesting agent i outlined in the algorithm **TeamRecovery-Request** of Figure 4 consists of the following main steps:

- *Preliminaries*(lines 01-05): Agent i first determines the cooperating agent j, the set Q of primary goals and the status *safeStatus*, as described previously. The agent then tries to synthesize a new local plan $NewP_i$ with the goal to achieve *safeStatus*: the **Replanner** module is invoked on the current agent status $\mathcal{B}_t^i$, the current local plan P_i, and the desired status *safeStatus*; the returned plan $NewP_i$ (if it exists) is a revised version of P_i including both the actions for getting *safeStatus* and the actions, previously included in P_i, not yet executed.

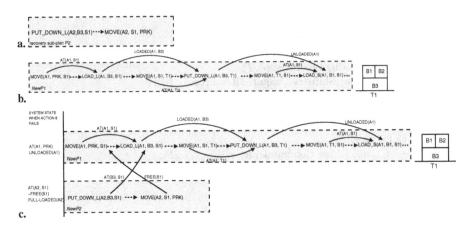

Fig. 5. The team recovery plan built to repair the failure of action MOVE(A2, S1, T1)

– *Team cooperation*(06-11): If $NewP_i$ exists, agent i sends a request to the cooperating agent j (line 07). Agent i awaits a reply from the cooperating agent j; if it is *ok*, recovery at team level succeeded, and agents i and j activate the plan commitment phase. Otherwise, team recovery failed and the function **TeamRecovery-Request** returns an empty recovery plan.

The behavior of the cooperating agent j outlined in the algorithm **TeamRecovery-Cooperation** of Figure 4 includes the following steps:

– *Accept a cooperation request* (line 01): j receives the request $\mathcal{R}$. item *Adjust the local plan*(02-03): to satisfy the request $\mathcal{R}$, agent j adjusts its current plan P_j in two ways: 1) j builds a new plan to get *safeStatus* (included in $\mathcal{R}$) from its current status $\mathcal{B}_t^j$ and 2) build another plan from *safeStatus* to a state where the services in Q are satisfied.
– *Sends a reply*(04-05): in the last part of the algorithm, the cooperating agent j sends the result of the cooperation to agent i and, if required, activates the plan commitment phase.

6   Discussion and Conclusions

We have discussed a strategy aimed at recovering the execution of a multi-agent plan from the occurrence of an action failure. Since the strategy is based on the cooperation between agents within the same team, we have referred to it as plan recovery at team level. The control architecture discussed in the paper represents an improvement over other approaches presented in the literature for multi-agent systems [3,4,10], as it does not only cover the detection of an action failure but addresses also the recovery step. While in [6] a local recovery strategy is discussed, (where each agent is responsible for recovering from the failure of the actions it executes), the introduction of team level recovery makes the process of plan repair more flexible and robust, since the team level recovery is able to overcome some failures which cannot be solved at the local level; as a consequence the amount of failures that the human user has to manage may be reduced considerably.

Given the complexity of the task, the work represents just a first step, as many problems remain open; e.g., the choice of the agent to be involved in team recovery could take into consideration its work load or the resources it is using. However, the present work has pointed out the essential role played by complex re-planning techniques as the basis for recovery.

Due to space limitations, the focus of this paper is on the methodological aspects of plan recovery at team level. As for implementation and performance issues, on-line monitoring and diagnosis of a multi-agent plan are addressed in [10] with a centralized approach, and in [5] with a distributed solution. In both these approaches we have advocated the use of the symbolic formalism of Ordered Binary Decision Diagrams (OBDDs) to efficiently encode action models and agent states. As concerns the re-planning task, we have implemented a solution similar to the one discussed in [11], which exploits an encoding of the actions via OBDD. The main difference to [11] is the use of extended action models during the re-planning phase. The adoption of OBDD plays a critical role for the efficiency of both, on-line monitoring and diagnosis as well as the re-planning step.

References

1. Muscettola, N., Nayak, P., Williams, B.: Remote agent: to boldly go where no AI system has gone before. Artificial Intelligence 103(1), 5–47 (1998)
2. Birnbaum, L., Collins, G., Freed, M., Krulwich, B.: Model-based diagnosis of planning failures. In: Proc. AAAI90, pp. 318–323. AAAI Press, Stanford (1990)
3. Witteveen, C., Roos, N., van der Krogt, R., de Weerdt, M.: Diagnosis of single and multi-agent plans. In: Proc. AAMAS05, pp. 805–812. ACM Press, New York (2005)
4. Kalech, M., Kaminka, G.: Towards model-based diagnosis of coordination failures. In: Proc. AAAI05, pp. 102–107. AAAI Press, Stanford (2005)
5. Micalizio, R., Torasso, P.: On-line monitoring of plan execution: A distributed approach. Knowledge-Based Systems 20(2), 134–142 (2007)
6. Micalizio, R., Torasso, P., Torta, G.: Intelligent supervision of plan execution in multi-agent systems. Internat. Transactions on Systems Science and Applications 1(3), 259–267 (2006)
7. Carver, N., Lesser, V.: Domain monotonicity and the performance of local solutions strategies for CDPS-based distributed sensor interpretation and distributed diagnosis. Journal of Autonomous Agents and Multi-Agent Systems 6(1), 35–76 (2003)
8. Kambhampati, S.: Refinement planning as a unifying framework for plan synthesis. AI Magazine 18(2), 67–97 (1997)
9. Boutilier, C., Brafman, R.I.: Partial-order planning with concurrent interacting actions. Journal of Artificial Intelligence Research 14, 105–136 (2001)
10. Micalizio, R., Torasso, P.: Diagnosis of multi-agent plans under partial observability. In: Proc. 18th Internat. Workshop on Principles of Diagnosis (DX07), pp. 346–353 (2007)
11. Jensen, R.M., Veloso, M.M.: Obdd-based universal planning for synchronized agents in non-deterministic domains. Journal of Artificial Intelligence Research 13, 189–226 (2000)

On the Behaviour of the TRSIM Model for Trust and Reputation*

Alberto Caballero, Juan A. Botía, and Antonio Gómez-Skarmeta

Universidad de Murcia. Campus Espinardo. Murcia. España
albe_cu@yahoo.com, {juanbot,skarmeta}@um.es

Abstract. We study here the behaviour of a trust and reputation model for agents in P2P environment, where agents act as providers or consumers of resources. We present partial results of the refinement process of our model in order to identify the suitable structure, functions, and parameters to correctly manage trust and reputation. We show some experimental results comparing several alternatives to obtain the quality of the response given the requirements, and the increase of the satisfaction of the recommended response when it uses a right way to estimate trust and reputation values using stored information about similar tasks.

1 Introduction

In previous works we define a trust and reputation model in a MAS to propose a suitable response for a consumer requirement in a P2P environment where agents can be consumer or provider of resources [1,2]. This model considers trust and reputation as emergent properties of direct interactions between agents, based on multiple interactions between two parties. In this model, trust is a belief an agent has about the performance of the other party to solve a given task, according to own knowledge. In other hand, reputation is related to the same belief but based on the opinions of other agents in the community.

Contrary to other models [3,4,5], where trust and reputation values are obtained as global values only associated to a peer, our model associates trust and reputation to the specification of the task that agents need to delegate. The performance of a given agent can be very different, according to the specification of the task that he executes or the requirements of the user that he represents.

Griffiths proposes a based-experience mechanism to model the trustworthiness of agents according to various criteria [6]. This work presents the notion of multi-dimensional trust to manage several facets of trust and combines them into a unique value, according to the preferences of the agent.

---

* This paper is supported by the Programme Alban scholarship No.E05D049799CU and also by the Spanish Ministry of Education and Science by the Research Project TIN-2005-08501-C03-02. Also, part of this work has been funded by the POPEYE Project, http://www.istpopeye.eu/. Contract No. IST-2006-034241.

P. Petta et al. (Eds.): MATES 2007, LNAI 4687, pp. 182–193, 2007.

Our model manages trust as a multidimensional concept too, depending on some predefined features related to the trust. However, it does not manages a unique value for each trust feature for a given agent, but it manages this values according to the preference of the user that agent represents. For instance, agent can provide very different download speeds for a given multimedia resource when the user preference is restricted by the deliver time or by the quality of the resource.

Also, it proposes to estimate trust values for tasks that the agent did not perform before, using knowledge about some similar one. For example, if a given agent needs to obtain the trust in another agent, it considers only the experiences related with the specification of this task (user requirements). If the agent does not have any information about the previous behaviour of its partner performing the specified task, the model gives the way to approximate trust and reputation values from the previous behaviour of agent performing similar tasks. Here, based on experimental results, we propose some ways to estimate trust and reputation from similar tasks.

Our model uses WSMO, a W3C standard proposal, as the base for definition of knowledge structures needed by the model: service requests and Web service response, basically [7,8]. Also, others domain-dependent elements, such as satisfaction of the task given the response, and similarity between two tasks (when the trust values for unknown tasks are obtained from trust values for similar tasks), are described by means of WSMO.

At present, the model is in a refinement and adjusting process, in order to find the most suitable definition for some of its functions and knowledge representations. The main objective of this paper is to propose and experimentally compare several alternatives for two functions of the model: satisfaction of the responses obtained after the execution of the contracted task; and the way to estimate trust and reputation values for unknown tasks.

The rest of the paper is organized as follows: Section 2 introduces the main characteristics of the model structure and general functionality, the approach used to estimate trust and reputation from similar tasks (Subsect. 2.1), and the definitions of domain-dependent functions (Subsect. 2.2). Section 3 compares experimental results to select a suitable way to obtain the satisfaction of a solution, and the way to estimate trust and reputation for unknown requested tasks using similarity between semantically specified tasks. Finally, in Sect. 4 we draw conclusions and discuss open issues.

2   Trust and Reputation Model Structure

Our model is composed by two information bases that each agent stores about the behaviour of the others, and a set of functions to operate with these bases. Following a distributed approach imposed by P2P environments, each agent manages its own bases of experiences. Functions produce values to guide the interactions between agents, based on trust and reputation concepts. Basically, the model is structured following the schema given in Fig. 1.

There are two bases of experiences to obtain trust and reputation values for a given task: base of experiences for trust (IET) and for reputation (IER). These values are produced by means of the right combination of some functions. First, by introspection of the bases of experiences, the model calculates direct trust (DT), reputation (R) and reliability of direct trust ($DTRL$), combined (like in REGRET [5]) to produce a unique value of trust, using the function T. This value, aggregated from direct trust and reputation, is used to select the partners in the interaction, to ask about the solution.

If the bases of experiences do not have information for a given task, the model obtain the values of trust (by means of function DT) and reputation (by means of function R) for a similar task and combines these values with the similarity degree between two tasks, given by function D. For that, the model uses functions IT and IR to select the partners in the interaction for both purposes.

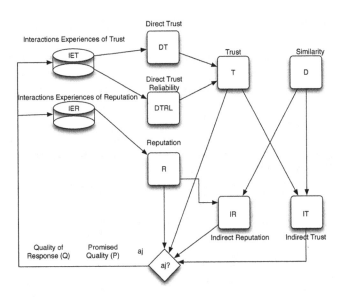

Fig. 1. Relationship between different parts of the model

The initiator agent interacts with the selected agent and solves his task with the response offered by the partner. In this moment, when interaction is finalized, the initiator agent evaluates the interaction, taking into account the solution w_j as response of the task s_k and the quality promised by the responder, at the beginning of the interaction, $ec_{i,j,k}$. This information may be used to update the base of experiences for trust. For that, our model gives two functions: fulfilment of the promised quality (P) and quality of the response (Q). (The definitions of functions P and Q are given in Sect. 2.2. The satisfaction degree, assigned to the responder agent, must be the combination of real quality of the solution (Q) and the fulfilment of the promised quality (P). This way, the proposed model avoids that an agent a_j, with a low promised quality $ec_{i,j,k}$ and a medium-quality solution for task s_k, may obtain a high satisfaction degree $et_{i,j,k}$.

Also, the model updates the base of experiences for reputation. This base has a unique value of reputation $er_{i,j,k}$ to indicate, according to experience of agent a_i, the reliability of agent a_j to give reputation information about other agents performing task s_k. The confidence of an agent a_j as recommender of others is increased or decreased following the variation of trust values on recommended agents (produced during the interaction). The value of the reputation at the end of the interaction $er_{i,j,k}$ will be better than the value at the beginning when the trust on recommended agents is improved during the interaction.

2.1 Obtaining Trust and Reputation from Previous Experiences on Similar Tasks

It is possible that an agent does not have information about performance of other agents for a given task. In this case, we propose to approximate the trust and reputation values using a similar task whose accomplishment has been previously done by known agents and requested by a_i. The model obtains this approximation using a similarity degree between the most similar well-known task and the unknown one. If there are not exist any similar task, the model assigns a predefined default value.

Our model defines the function D to obtain the similarity degree between two tasks from the comparison of the tasks attributes (please, see Sect. 2.2).

This way, combining the trust or reputation in the most similar task (s_p) with the similarity degree between the two tasks $D(s_k, s_p)$, we define indirect trust (IT) and indirect reputation (IR) functions to approximate direct trust or reputation values, respectively:

$$IT(a_i, a_j, s_k, s_p, IET_i)) = DT(a_i, a_j, s_p, IET_i) \oplus D(s_k, s_p),$$

$$IR(a_i, a_j, s_k, s_p, CR_{sup}(a_i, s_k)) = R(a_i, a_j, s_k, CR_{sup}(a_i, s_k)) \oplus D(s_k, s_p)$$

There are several ways to combine trust and reputation values with similarity. To simplify the notation, we use:

- IT to refer to $IT(a_i, a_j, s_k, s_p, IET_i))$,
- IR to refer to $IR(a_i, a_j, s_k, s_p, CR_{sup}(a_i, s_k))$,
- DT to refer to $DT(a_i, a_j, s_p, IET_i)$,
- R to refer to $R(a_i, a_j, s_k, CR_{sup}(a_i, s_k))$, and
- D to refer to $D(s_k, s_p)$

We may consider the following alternatives for the operator $\oplus$ to combine trust and reputation with similarity. They are defined in order to compare the performance because they seem the most trivial options according to the considerations and characteristics of our model:

$IT_a :\ IT = DT \cdot D$ $\qquad\qquad$ $IR = R \cdot D$

$IT_b :\ IT = \sin\left(\frac{\pi}{2} DT \cdot D\right)$ $\qquad$ $IR = \sin\left(\frac{\pi}{2} R \cdot D\right)$

$IT_c :\ IT = DT \cdot \sin\left(\frac{\pi}{2} D\right)$ $\qquad$ $IR = R \cdot \sin\left(\frac{\pi}{2} D\right)$

$IT_d :\ IT = \sin\left(\frac{\pi}{2} DT\right) \cdot \sin\left(\frac{\pi}{2} D\right)$ $\qquad$ $IR = \sin\left(\frac{\pi}{2} R\right) \cdot \sin\left(\frac{\pi}{2} D\right)$

$IT_e :\ IT = \frac{DT+D}{2}$ $\qquad\qquad$ $IR = \frac{R+D}{2}$

$IT_f :$ does not consider any estimation

The alternatives IT_a and IT_e combine trust/reputation with similarity following the multiplication and the arithmetic mean of these values, respectively. In spite of bearing them in mind, we think that these variants do not improve the satisfaction that produces the alternative IT_f (does not consider any estimation). IT_a produces smaller values than the factors, as both are in $[0,1]$. For very high values of trust/reputation and similarity, it can obtain average values of estimation. Hence, it is necessary a previous transformation of the values to combine. Alternative IT_e does not seem to be suitable either; is not viable to talk about the middle point between two values that represent different magnitudes.

The model must consider the estimation of the trust and reputation when there is a high degree of similarity between the tasks. The rest of the alternatives that we propose incorporate the function sin to amplify the value of the similarity, the trust/reputation, or their combination. The value of estimation must be as similar as possible to the original value for those cases where the similarity is very high. From the light of the experiments that we will introduce the most suitable variant seems to be IT_c.

Section 3.2 shows some experimental results comparing these alternatives.

2.2   Domain-Dependent Functions: Quality and Similarity

There are two functions in our model whose definition depends on the representations of tasks and responses: quality and similarity. The definition of these functions is based on the representation of domain concepts by means of WSMO. Each task request s_k and response w_j are described by the set of non-functional WSMO properties, and others added by the user, depending on the application domain [1].

For each property of request or response, the model must define a normalization function to make independent the domain of the real world values from model-managed values. The model uses values in the range $[0,1]$ to represent the convenience of the property, independent of the original property domain. A value near to 0 indicates a non-desired value in the original property, and values near to 1 indicate high-desired values in the original properties.

Quality of the Solution Given a Task. Our model uses two functions to evaluate the satisfaction of the initiator agent through the fulfilment of the promised quality and the quality of the solution according to the task.

The fulfilment of the promised quality indicates to what extent, the responder agent fulfils his agreement. Basically, the value of this function results from a comparison between the agreement quality $ec_{i,j,k}$ and the real quality of the given solution, denoted by $Q(w_j, s_k)$. To determine the fulfilment of the satisfaction agreement, we may define a function P:

$$P(ec_{i,j,k}, Q(w_j, s_k)) = \begin{cases} 1 & : \quad Q(w_j, s_k) \geq ec_{i,j,k} \\ 1 - (ec_{i,j,k} - Q(w_j, s_k)) & : \quad Q(w_j, s_k) < ec_{i,j,k} \end{cases}$$

The quality of the solution, denoted by $Q(w_j, s_k)$, indicates how much the response w_j satisfies the requirements specified in the task s_k. Calculation of this value is based on the comparison of both concepts.

According to the convenience of the value of each property, and following some ideas given by WSMO [8,7] we can to define a set of the most relevance attributes of a given concept. For each task (s_k) or response (w_j), we can split the good-valued attributes into the sets R_g and R_w, respectively.

If R_u is the set of properties used to define a task or response, then $R_g \subset R_u$ and $R_w \subset R_u$ consist of the most prominent attributes for each concept, according to the value of each attribute. To construct these sets, we consider that the attribute b_i of s_k (we denote with $s_k.b_i$) is a good-valued attribute and hence $b_i \in R_g$ if $s_k.b_i \geq \lambda_i$ (λ_i is a domain-dependent threshold value). In the same way, an attribute b_i of w_j is a good-valued and $b_i \in R_w$ if $w_j.b_i \geq \lambda_i$.

Using these sets we can define three alternatives to obtain the quality of the response w_j to satisfy the task s_k:

Q_a: following the WSMO Web service discovery process

$$Q(w_j, s_k) = \begin{cases} 1 & : \quad R_g = R_w & Match \\ 0.75 & : \quad R_g \subseteq R_w & Match \\ 0.5 & : \quad R_g \supseteq R_w & Partial Match \\ 0.5 & : \quad R_g \cap R_w \neq \emptyset & Partial Match \\ 0 & : \quad R_g \cap R_w = \emptyset & NoMatch \end{cases}$$

According to this definition, maximum satisfaction degree is obtained when all important (good-valued) attributes desired in goal s_k are important (good-valued) attributes in Web services w_j. Contrary, the worst satisfaction is obtained when no prominent attributes of goal s_k are satisfied by important attributes of Web service w_j.

Q_b: considering how many task attributes are satisfied by response

$$Q(w_j, s_k) = \sin\left(\frac{\pi}{2} \cdot \frac{|Q'_{w_j, s_k}|}{|R_u|}\right)$$

where R_u is the set of all properties of tasks and responses, $Q'_{w_j, s_k} \subset R_u$ is the set of these properties such that its values in the task s_k are less restrictive than the values in the response w_j:

$$Q'_{w_j, s_k} = \{b_i | b_i \in R_u, v_{s_k}(b_i) \leq v_{w_j}(b_i)\}$$

Satisfaction degree function is like a ratio between the satisfied s_k attributes and the total number of attributes R_u of any task or response. The maximum satisfaction degree is obtained when all (not only good-valued) attributes desired in goal s_k are satisfied by Web services w_j. Contrary, the worst satisfaction is obtained when none of them is satisfied.

Q_c: considering how many good-valued task attributes are satisfied

$$Q(w_j, s_k) = \sin\left(\frac{\pi}{2} \cdot \frac{|Q''_{w_j, s_k}|}{|R_g|}\right)$$

where R_g is the set of good-valued attributes of task s_k, $Q''_{w_j, s_k} \subset R_g$ is the set of these properties such that its values in the task s_k are less restrictive than the values in the response w_j, if the property is consider a good-valued for the response w_j:

$$Q''_{w_j, s_k} = \{b_i | b_i \in R_g, b_i \in R_w, v_{s_k}(b_i) \le v_{w_j}(b_i)\}$$

This alternative is similar to previous one. But, in this case, satisfaction is like a ratio between the satisfied s_k important attributes and the number of important attributes R_g of the task s_k. This is an intermediate case between the previous alternatives Q_a and Q_b.

A priori, we expect that Q_a does not produce the better values of satisfaction because it does consider only a few range of values of satisfaction (0, 0.5, 0.75, 1). It considers the satisfaction of groups of important attributes as a whole, but not the satisfaction of attributes independently.

In front of limitations of approach given by Q_a, we propose an alternative where the satisfaction produces a wider spectrum of values. Q_b considers the amount of task attributes that are satisfied by response, without taking into account the relevance of the attributes. This alternative should offer better values of satisfaction, because it is capable to represent in a better way the multitude of cases that occur.

On the other hand, Q_c is an intermediate case between Q_a and Q_b that takes into account the satisfaction of each attribute (like Q_b) but only of good-valued attributes (like Q_a).

Section 3.1 shows an experimental comparative between these alternatives.

Similarity Between Tasks (D). The similarity between two tasks s_k and s_p is obtained from the comparison of the task attributes.

$$D(s_k, s_p) = 1 - \frac{1}{n} \cdot \sum_{i=1}^{n} |s_{k_i} - s_{p_i}|$$

where n is the number of task attributes, s_{k_i} is the i-th attribute of task s_k, and s_{p_i} is the i-th attribute of task s_p.

The values produced by this function are real values between 0 and 1, where 0 indicates the lowest similarity (entirely different tasks) and 1 the highest similarity (equal tasks).

3 Experiments

We carried out some experiments in order to designate the best alternative for functions of the model. In the following we present most relevant results related with the way to obtain the quality of the response given a task, and the way to approximate trust and reputation using knowledge related with similar tasks.

These experiments took place over the same general conditions, using our own simulations in Java. We created 10 instances of agents, populating a community of agents with different responses. There were agents of several qualities, depending on the quality of its responses. Agents interacted during t=450 time steps. In each time step, one of them was selected to act as initiator in a negotiation with the rest. The WSMO goal of the initiator in the negotiation was a task selected from a predefined set of 10 different tasks. This task represented the requirement of the selected agent in the given time step.

The experiments were repeated 20 times and results averaged after that.

3.1 Alternatives to Measure the Quality

The experiment compares the evolution of the satisfaction for the solution recommended by the model (the response offered by the most reliable agent), for three different alternatives to obtain the satisfaction degree. In this case, we do not consider similarity between tasks, this means that the model does not estimate trust and reputation values for unknown tasks.

Figure 2 shows the satisfaction value of the responses given by the most reliable agent for each alternative. In each considered alternative, the satisfaction of recommended solution has stabilized after a small number of experiences. Best satisfaction values are obtained using Q_b, where the quality measure considers

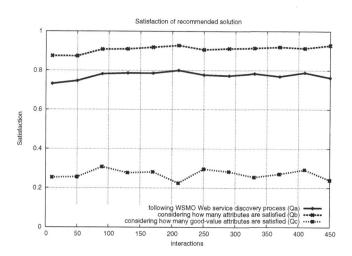

Fig. 2. Comparison of satisfaction degree of recommended solutions, for each alternative to obtain the quality of the response given the task

the amount of task attributes that are satisfied by the response. This alternative improves the satisfaction of the solution offered by the most reliable agents. It is the most suitable situation because the trust in the recommended agent is determined by the satisfaction degree stored in the bases of experiences. We use this alternative in the next experiments in order to adjust the model.

3.2   Alternatives to Estimate Trust and Reputation

When agents do not have any direct or indirect experience about the performance of other agents for a given task, they need to estimate trust and reputation values. In this way, the model proposes to use trust and reputation values associated with other task. For that, it gives a similarity function to determine which is the most similar task, in order to use it to approximate these values. Besides, the model needs to give the way to obtain the estimated values from similarity degree and the values for the most similar task. Section 2.1 gives some alternatives. This experiment compares them in order to determine the best way to estimate trust and reputation from a similar task. Here, the quality of the response is obtained using the best alternative proposed in the previous experiment (given by Q_b).

Figure 3 shows the satisfaction value of the responses given by the most reliable agent for each alternative. The satisfaction of the recommended solution, offered by the most reliable agent, using the alternative IT_c, is greater than the satisfaction produced by other alternatives. It is greater than values obtained without consider any approximation using similar tasks. Hence, we demonstrate that using similarity between tasks improves the selection process.

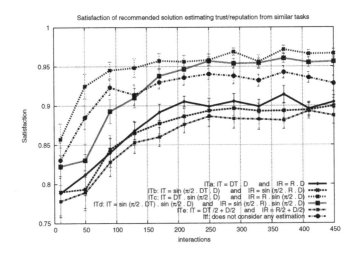

Fig. 3. Comparison of satisfaction degree of recommended solutions, for several alternatives to combine trust / reputation and similarity between task in order to estimate trust/reputation for unknown task

3.3   Evolution of Trust

The main objective of the trust and reputation model is to guide the response selection process. The model must select the response offered by high-reliable agent, but not in the response by itself because it is unknown.

It is important to know how trust values change when the model estimates trust and reputation from similar tasks. We analyze the evolution of trust values when the model uses these alternatives to combine trust and reputation with similarity. In this case, we study the evolution of trust of three types of agents. We classify the agents in accordance with the quality of the offered responses:

- $|R_w|$ near to $|R_u| \rightarrow$ HIGH
- $|R_w|$ near to $\frac{1}{2}|R_u| \rightarrow$ MEDIUM
- $|R_w|$ near to $0 \rightarrow$ LOW

Figure 4 shows trust evolution for three types of quality of the response that agents give, for each alternative to estimate trust/reputation for unknown task. All the alternatives behave of the same way: trust in high-quality agents is increased; trust in medium-quality agents do not shows a significative variation; and trust in low-quality agents is lightly decreased. This indicates that the estimation of trust and reputation values does not affect the evolution of trust values for any type of agent. The variation of trust values associated to a given agent is determined by the quality of the solution that it offers, but not in the way that model uses to estimate this value for unknown tasks.

Also, Fig. 4 give evidence about the capability of the model to represent the quality of agents using trust values. The model shows a differentiated behaviour in front of different types of agents. It increases trust in agents with response of appreciated quality, to keep the values in medium-quality agents and to penalize the low-quality agents.

In high-quality agent figure (Fig. 4.a), trust evolves from a default value (given by model at the beginning of simulation) to a value near to 1. It means that this type of agent offers good responses and, consequently, agents increase their associated trust value. Figure 4.b shows how that model keeps the trust around an average value for agents with a medium-quality response. Trust in low-quality agents (4.c) behaves in a similar way, but with a little decrease. The model penalizes the bad solutions decreasing the trust for agent that gives it.

Concluding, these experiments show that satisfaction in the response is increased when the model estimates trust and reputation for unknown tasks in a suitable way. The combination of trust and reputation with similarity between task using the alternative IT_c (please, see Sect. 2.1) enhances the satisfaction of recommended response. This alternative produces greater satisfaction values than the alternative when system does not use any approximation of trust and reputation. Also, this way to estimate trust and reputation has a desired differentiated behaviour according to the quality of the response given by each agent. Agents with a high-quality response increase its trust.

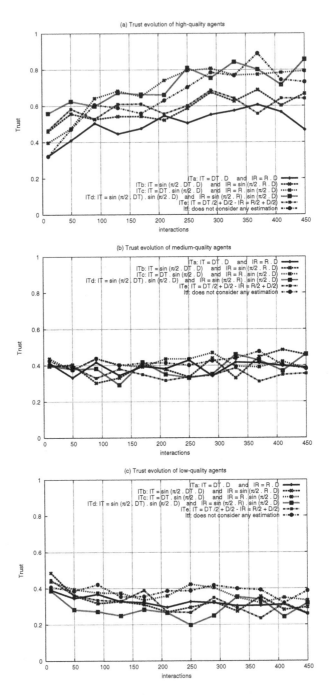

Fig. 4. Trust evolution of different types of agents (a: high-quality, b: medium-quality, c: low-quality), using several alternatives to combine trust/reputation and similarity between task in order to estimate trust/reputation for unknown task

4   Conclusions and Future Work

Trust and reputation information can be different depending on the specified task or requirement. Nevertheless, if the model ignores the behaviour of the service for a given task, the values of trust can be approximated using the similarity degree between this and a well known task. Our proposed model increases the satisfaction of the recommended response when it uses a suitable way to combine trust and reputation with similarity, with respect to cases in which it does not use any estimation. The proposed way is capable to show different behaviours according to the quality of the response offered by agents. Nevertheless, we need to do some experiments where the quality of the agent response changes during the experiment, in order to prove the adaptability of the model.

We intend to define and prove some alternatives for other functions of the system (i.e. an array of agents for asking them about trust and reputation, bases of experience updating process, etc.), in order to identify the parameters that affect the system performance and their high-recommended values.

References

1. Caballero, A., Botía, J., Skarmeta, A.: Trust and Reputation Model based on WSMO. In: Falcone, R., Barber, S., Sabater-Mir, J., Singh, M. (eds.) Proc. Ninth Workshop on Trust in Agent Societies at AAMAS, pp. 9–18 (May 2006)
2. Caballero, A., Botía, J., Skarmeta, A.: A New Model for Trust and Reputation Management with an Ontology Based Approach for Similarity Between Tasks. In: Fischer, K., Timm, I.J., André, E., Zhong, N. (eds.) MATES 2006. LNCS (LNAI), vol. 4196, pp. 172–183. Springer, Heidelberg (2006)
3. Golbeck, J., Hendler, J.: Filmtrust: Movie recommendations using trust in web-based social networks. In: Proc. of the IEEE Consumer Communications and Networking Conference, January 2006, vol. 1, pp. 282–286. IEEE Computer Society Press, Los Alamitos (2006)
4. Marti, S.: Trust and Reputation in Peer-to-Peer Networks. PhD thesis, Stanford University (2005)
5. Sabater, J., Sierra, C.: REGRET: reputation in gregarious societies. In: Müller, J.P., André, E., Sen, S., Frasson, C. (eds.) Proceedings of the Fifth International Conference on Autonomous Agents, Montreal, Canada, pp. 194–195. ACM Press, New York (2001)
6. Griffiths, N.: Task Delegation Using Experience-Based Multi-Dimensional Trust. In: AAMAS '05: Proceedings of the Fourth International Joint Conference on Autonomous Agents and Multiagent Systems, pp. 489–496. ACM Press, New York (2005)
7. WSMO Team: Web Service Modeling Ontology (WSMO). W3C (2005), http://www.w3.org/Submission/WSMO/
8. de Bruijn, J., Lausen, H., Krummenacher, R., Polleres, A., Predoiu, L., Kifer, M., Fensel, D.: D16.1v0.2 The Web Service Modeling Language WSML. WSML Final Draft March 20, 2005. W3C (2005), http://www.wsmo.org/TR/d16/d16.1/v0.2

Implementing ReGreT in a Decentralized Multi-agent Environment

Stefan König[1], Sven Kaffille[2], and Guido Wirtz[2]

[1] University of Bayreuth
Chair of Information Systems Management
stefan.koenig@uni-bayreuth.de
[2] University of Bamberg
Distributed and Mobile Systems Group
{sven.kaffille,guido.wirtz}@wiai.uni-bamberg.de

Abstract. Since the last decade reputation management has been examined as a possible foundation for trust establishment and trust dissemination in distributed artificial intelligence. While the systems are distributed the reputation management systems are in most cases centralized. This paper describes the implementation of the ReGreT approach to trust and reputation management in Multi-Agent Systems in a decentralized environment, where the services which provide reputation management are also distributed.

1 Introduction

Since the last decade the concept of trust has received much attention by computer scientists. Especially in distributed artificial intelligence (DAI) many researchers have discovered trust as a concept to deal with probably malicious interaction partners.

One goal of DAI is to provide autonomous and flexible open Multi-Agent Systems (MAS). In MAS autonomous agents interact, while there exists no central global control. This fact requires that agents are able to choose partners by selecting a trustworthy partner (which nevertheless may be harmful), as harmful agents cannot be generally excluded from a MAS.

Trust is a highly vague concept [1] that has no single common definition agreed on yet, but there are many definitions available. Most of the definitions agree that trust is highly subjective and context-dependent. In this paper we do not try to create a new definition of trust, but base our work on already available definitions, namely the ones provided in the work about ReGreT [2]. A concept closely related to trust is reputation which is used in ReGreT, as well. Reputation can be used as one source of information to estimate the trustworthiness of an agent. While trust is a subjective concept, reputation is a measure of an agent's trustworthiness a group of other agents shares [3].

In order to allow fast dissemination of reputation a central entity is often employed for reputation management, which stores reputation of agents as records

P. Petta et al. (Eds.): MATES 2007, LNAI 4687, pp. 194–205, 2007.

of recommendations. In fast growing MAS a central (physical) entity may become a performance bottleneck, as its resources are limited, and also a single point to compromise reputation management. In order to ensure that resources for reputation management grow with the number of parties that participate in the MAS, we proposed in [4] a physically decentralized reputation management based on peer-to-peer concepts which is provided in cooperation by all agent platforms, that are part of the MAS. Logically all agents and agent platforms can use this reputation management like a centralized entity. The peer-to-peer foundations of our reputation management account for data consistency and integrity and provide a distributed authentication mechanism based on PGP-like [5] mechanisms. They provide security facilities for reputation management which operates on top of these.

The initial implementation of this reputation management employed only a simple reputation metric and understanding of reputation. Therefore we adopted a well known approach to trust and reputation management [2] to our implementation. This also adds a feature, that allows collection of subjective information by single agents, to ease implementation of trust. This paper describes how this approach can be implemented using our decentralized infrastructure.

For this purpose the next section relates our work to other reputation management systems. The following Sect. 3 sketches ReGreT and concepts that have been incorporated into our work. Section 4 describes how ReGreT can be implemented based on our proposed infrastructure. The last Sect. 5 discusses limitations and advantages of our reputation management scheme, as well as directions for future research.

2 Related Work

There are two approaches we see in close relation to our approach. The first approach is described in [6]. Instead of `Chord` [7] which is used in our approach it uses the decentralized storage method `P-Grid`. In this approach only information on dishonest interactions is considered as relevant and the result of a reputation calculation yields only a result that indicates if an agent is untrustworthy (0) or trustworthy (1). In our system all interactions are considered relevant to be able to get a more concise impression of agent behavior. In our approach the metric to calculate reputation of an agent is not an integral part of the system, but can be exchanged as required by the application using our system. But [6] reveals also some facts in common with our system. The reputation data is globally available and also scalability issues are addressed similar to our approach using `Chord`.

The second approach, called AVALANCHE, is based on ideas of the Institute for Computer Science and Social Studies of Freiburg, Germany (see e.g. [8]). One part of this project is a reputation mechanism. This approach has a sanction component that prevents contacting agents with low reputation like our system does with platforms. However, in AVALANCHE the metrics are hardwired where in our work the metrics are exchangeable. But the main difference is that AVALANCHE uses a physical central trusted entity, while our approach employs a logical central entity, which is physically distributed and therefore our approach has no single point, that can be attacked to disrupt reputation management. An approach, which is very simular to our approach can be found in the PACE architecture [9]. This implementation differs in some details of the trust- and reputation mechanism's implementation.

While many approaches rely only on a single kind of information to estimate trustworthiness of other agents, we decided to elaborate our work ([4]) in direction of ReGreT, which incorporates different information sources. We chose the ReGreT framework, as it has been developed by examining (see [10]) other trust and reputation management systems and incorporating the best practices from the examined approaches.

3   The ReGreT Approach

This section will introduce the ReGreT approach as it is proposed by Sabater and Sierra in [10], [2] and [11]. In order to decide on the trustworthiness of an interaction partner, ReGreT relies on direct experiences an agent can gain, witness, and social information. These information sources are described in this section in line with how they are stored (data bases) and how they are processed by the different modules of ReGreT to determine trust. At the end of this section we justify, why we decided to extend our previous work by the ReGreT approach. Figure 1 provides an overview of ReGreT and its components, which are explained in the following. Direct experiences are, without any doubt, the most reliable and relevant information about other agents. This kind of information arises after a interaction between two agents. Depending on the metrics used

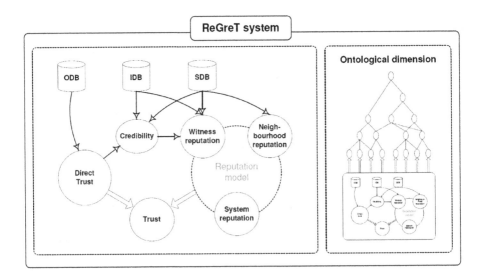

Fig. 1. The ReGreT Approach (see also [10], p. 42)

in the specific reputation model, this can be either positive, negative or both types of information. Thus ReGreT uses a continuous metric between 0 and 1, all kinds of experiences can be represented within this interval. Some reputation models also mention the observation of transactions between other agents.

Witness or word-of-mouth information comes from other agents. This information is based on their direct experiences and information received from others. This kind of information is not as trustworthy as the direct information mentioned above. Every piece of witness information has some uncertainty around itself. More detailed and extensive approaches, like the advancement of ReGreT, called Repage [12], have different modules to specify these two sources of witness reputation. ReGreT does not differentiate between these two sources.

The third and last information source of ReGreT is the social information. The knowledge used here is generated from the relations between the system members or the roles, which they play in the (artificial) society. This kind of information is based on the adoption that agents' behavior is influenced by the role or roles the agents play within the society. This information is available and meaningful only after a couple of transactions. Before that no social structure of the system members can be identified. Sabater and Sierra [13] suppose that this kind of information source will become more and more important because of the increasing complexity of Multi-Agent-Systems.

Following the three information sources, the ReGreT model employs three data bases, the "outcomes data base"(ODB) for own experiences with other agents, the "information data base"(IDB) for storage of witness information, and the "sociograms data base"(SDB) to represent social structures.

For simplicity the ODB does not distinguish between direct interaction and direct observation in terms of reliability of information. Direct trust is context dependent, so ReGreT stores "the direct trust agent a has in agent b in a specific context to perform a specific action" [10]. The outcome of an interaction is defined as a tuple including the trusting agent, the trusted agent and the issues of the contract between the agents. Furthermore the tuple contains the fulfillment level, which has been achieved, and the interaction time stamp. The context is defined by the issues of the contract, that are used to determine the behavioral aspects that are relevant in the context.

The IDB is very similar to the ODB, but contains the outcomes observed by other agents. It contains tuples which have the same structure as the tuples in ODB, but they are annotated with the identifier of the agent, that provided the information.

The information included in the SDB is also stored with the help of tuples. These tuples consist of the relation type, the two agents and the intensity of this relation. The data of SDB are the basis of three ReGreT modules, which are described in the following subsection.

Orthogonal to the information and data bases described so far, another kind of information is considered. This information specifies the relation between different contexts of the domain, in which ReGreT is applied. Therefore it is called ontological dimension. It allows to transfer trust and reputation values from one context to a more complex context.

For data processing of the different information sources, the ReGreT model provides modules. The *direct trust* $(DT_{a \to b}(\varphi))$ module processes the direct experiences of an agent. The problem with solely relying on direct trust is that it is not always available, as the trusting agent may never have had an interaction or too few interactions with the trusted agent (i.e. the reliability of direct trust is low). Therefore ReGreT also relies on reputation $(R_{a \to b}(\varphi))$. As the calculation of the reputation value is more complex than the calculation of the trust value from the ODB, the *reputation model* is divided in three parts: "If the reputation is calculated from the information coming from witness we talk about the *witness reputation*, if the reputation is calculated using the information extracted from the social relations between partners we are talking about the *neighborhood reputation*. Finally, reputation based on roles and general properties is modeled by the *system reputation*." ([10] p. 43) Each of these modules delivers two values: The trust/reputation value and the reliability of this value. The modular architecture allows the agents to choose what kind of trust and reputation values they want to focus on. Furthermore the model provides information about almost new agents in the system, and new agents, in return, can use the model to get information about the system's social structure.

The *direct trust* module of ReGreT focuses on the direct interactions, in contrast to the complete *trust* module, which also depends on opinions and observations of third party agents. The information regarding direct interactions is always context-dependent and is linked to a certain behavioral aspect. Direct trust $DT_{a \to b}(\varphi)$ can be calculated by weighted mean, whereas a and b being agents and φ being the context the information is based on. More formally the calculation of direct trust is formulated as

$$DT_{a \to b}(\varphi) = \sum_{o_i \in ODB^{a,b}_{gr(\varphi)}} \rho(t, t_i) * Imp(o_i, \varphi) \qquad (1)$$

whereas $ODB^{a,b}_{gr(\varphi)}$ ensures selection of all outcomes that are relevant for context φ, $\rho(t, t_i)$ is a weight, which increases with interactions closer to the current time t, and $Imp(o_i, \varphi)$ is a function, which calculates the trust value regarding information about the related context. The implementation of this function depends on the agent. Furthermore ReGreT employs reliability of these values. Reliability of ratings is calculated dependent on the quantity and the variability of the different rating values (see [10] p. 46 et seq.) provided. *Witness reputation* is estimated from information provided by other agents, which gained experience with the target agent in the past. *Neighborhood reputation* accounts for the social environment of the target agent. It is a kind of prejudice as it is not directly based on earlier interactions. *System reputation* is based on objective observations like the role the agent fulfills in the society or company. To calculate the reliability of witness reputation values, the model provides a *credibility module*. These values have to be evaluated together with information about the witnessing agent as its social relations. This module provides a kind of meta-belief about a given reputation value and eases its interpretation.

System reputation is, compared to the other reputation modules, the easiest one to calculate, as ReGreT assumes that this information is known or directly observable by all members of the system or its groups. Therefore this is an available data source even for new agents in the society, whereas e.g. the neighborhood reputation requires a deep knowledge of the system, as its calculation is based on fuzzy rules. Witness reputation (value and reliability), is calculated from the trust values the witnesses assigned to the target agent for a certain context, the credibility of the witness. From a sociological point of view this model is not complete, but it seems to provide a good compromise between the complexity and the requirements needed in artificial societies. For a more detailed description and discussion of the reputation model see [10, pp 47-60].

Based on the three reputation types mentioned and *default reputation*, which is always available even if the other reputation types cannot provide meaningful values, an overall reputation value can be calculated. If all reputation types are available, witness reputation is weighted stronger than the neighborhood which is weighted stronger than the system reputation which again is weighted stronger than default reputation. The next step of consolidation is the integration of knowledge from the trust module with the knowledge from the reputation module. If an agent has more reliable value based on its own direct interactions, it uses that value to generate its image. If not, it falls back to the reputation values (see [10, p. 60]).

The *ontological dimension* of a domain completes the model. Any module can use this information. This module allows agents to calculate trust and reputation values from information of related contexts. With this module all modules can combine single trust and reputation values from one specific context to values of a more complex context, which is related to the specific contexts by a weighted ontological relationship. Each related context has to be considered while aggregating the trust and reputation values with help of a weighted mean.

In this section we had a closer look at the ReGreT approach. Now it is necessary to justify, why this approach is worth implementing in our environment. Regarding trust it respects subjectivity, as the implementation of the Imp-function is dependent on the agent, and dependency on context, as each context can be described by certain properties, that become part of the contract between interaction partners. These properties constitute a kind of objective part of the context. The properties that are relevant in a context are known by all agents interested in that context. Subjectivity is created by how individual agents weigh these properties. This allows a more meaningful creation of reputation values than just communicating plain reputation values. Furthermore the ontological dimension allows (partial) transfer of trust and reputation from one context to another, so that eventually trust and reputation information can be created faster for contexts, in which no interactions have occurred, so far.

4   Implementing ReGreT as a Decentralized Mechanism

In this section we describe how the ReGreT concepts have been implemented into our proposed decentralized reputation management system. For this purpose we first summarize our earlier work and its properties.

4.1   Foundations for ReGreT Implementation

To support really open MAS, in [4] we developed a physically decentralized architecture, that facilitates the provision of logically centralized services. The central goal is to distribute the load for agent management services as e.g. directory services [14], agent authentication, and also reputation management among the participating hosts, which constitute a platform for an open MAS. These hosts provide an execution environment to software agents, which can use the provided services. The distribution of services among all participants is based on Peer-to-Peer (P2P) technologies. At the core of our reputation management service a Java implementation [15] of the distributed hash table (DHT) Chord [7] is employed.

Our distributed reputation management service was designed to store ratings which agents can provide for other agents. Each single agent can use these ratings to estimate trustworthiness of other agents. All agents of the open MAS have shared access to all ratings stored by our system. As a context for the ratings we just considered the roles an agent can play in a MAS e.g. in cooperate problem solving [16] processes.

In order to achieve this goal we identified a set of requirements, which have to be met in a physically completely decentralized environment with no global control. A distributed authentication mechanism has to be implemented to enable the unique identification of hosts and agents, to facilitate attribution of ratings to the right agent(s). Distributing the data within a DHT may lead to data consistency problems, that have to be addressed. Agents must be enabled to rate each other only in case they really interacted. Different attacks on the system by hosts and agents have to be counter-measured, as e.g. denial of service or manipulation of ratings by hosts, and faking of ratings by agents.

The authentication mechanism has been implemented by means of a PGP-like key infrastructure, which is provided and also used by our modified Chord DHT implementation, that has an authentication-based join protocol. The data consistency and manipulation problems have also been addressed by adaptation of the DHT and implementing different subsystems on each host, that counter-measure different attacks. In order to meet all requirements we developed an architecture with four layers, that has to be implemented on each host (Fig. 2). Each layer performs different kinds of tasks and provides its functionality to the layer above or directly below. The top layer just provides a facade of the reputation management system to the agents executed by a host. The lowest layer provides communication facilities for the DHT and subsystems on higher layers. On the layer above the communication facilities a service providing communication services to other services and a service managing data stored in and retrieved from the DHT is located. These are used by another layer of services, which are responsible for cryptographic concerns (security service) like authentication and data integrity, data consistency (platform service), interaction and agent tracking (lease service), and reputation calculation.

Agents executed on a host are enabled to retrieve the ratings on a per agent and role (context) basis. The reputation service provides means to calculate a

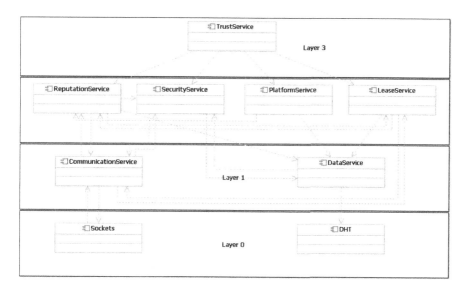

Fig. 2. Architecture of local services on each host

reputation value from these ratings. Our architecture was designed to facilitate the exchange of this reputation service and the representation of the rating values as different application domains may require different values and representation of reputation.

The focus of this paper lies on the reputation service, that is exchanged by a reputation service that implements the ReGreT approach. For this purpose different problems have to be addressed, which are discussed along with the implementation of ReGreT in our architecture. The main modifications of ReGreT to implement it as a completely decentralized mechanism can be subsumed to the following topics: the missing direct observation possibility, the missing information about the society and the different way to manage credibility.

Figure 3 presents an overview of our reputation service implementation and how the information sources have been changed. The ODB, and the data base for the ontological relations become part of a so called *local data manager*, that is instantiated for each single agent and provided to it by our reputation management service. As it may not be possible or too expensive in a P2P system to observe interactions between other agents for relevant trust contexts, the ODB stores only information about direct interactions and no information about observed interactions of a target agent in a certain context. This information is the source of the credibility module. In contrast to ReGreT, not the number of interactions it has processed or observed influences the reliability of direct trust, but the deviation of an agent's estimation of trust before an interaction from the outcome of the interaction. This seems to be useful as in our ODB fewer entries exist than in the original one. The data manager also stores the experiences with other agents in their role as evaluators (meta-belief) into the ODB, which becomes relevant for evaluating witness' credibility.

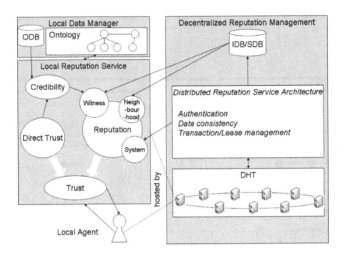

Fig. 3. Architecture of ReGreT implementation

The ontological dimension is provided by the local data manager as well. Our implementation allows to define associations between and composition of roles agents can play in the relevant domain. We distinguish between association and composition, as for a composition reputation values for all roles that take part in a composition must be present to allow calculation of meaningful values, but for associations only one role of all known associations to the target role must have reputation values assigned to allow a meaningful transfer of reputation values. The associations and compositions are annotated with weights that are used to transfer a trust value and its reliability from one context to another. These weights have usually to be defined by a domain expert. Our reputation management service allows adjustment of these weights at runtime, so that agents can eventually adapt these values to a changing environment.

The IDB, in the original approach responsible for importing other agents' beliefs, is replaced by an interface to adapt the DHT. In contrast to the ideas of Sierra and Sabater, no other agent is contacted to collect its experiences, as they can be requested from the underlying DHT. A big advantage of a *logically centralized* data management is the ubiquitous availability of data on the one hand and the data security through distribution on the other hand. No agent has a local IDB and it is logically shared among all agents, while being *physically decentralized*. Therefore an agent must not reason about which witnesses to contact in order to obtain relevant ratings. All ratings relevant for the context can be obtained from the DHT by a single request. The original ReGreT approach proposes analyzing the deviation of the witness' ratings to determine the witness' credibility. Weighted with this credibility the agents' beliefs are aggregated. But this proceeding cannot be realized with the current version of the plugin. The data sets needed for this calculation cannot be retrieved from the DHT. Instead of that, agent credibility is implemented as a personal belief about another agent and held in the ODB. The agent's evaluation of the target before interaction takes place is compared with

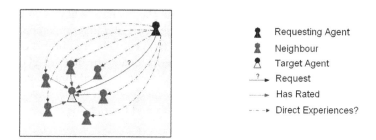

Fig. 4. Implementing Neighborhood Reputation

the own experience gained through interaction. After this comparison the agent rates the evaluator in its role as evaluator.

The information contained in the SDB cannot be provided to an agent when it enters the system as the system is completely distributed and open. The social relations may be not directly observable and may constantly change. Implementing neighborhood reputation is a more difficult challenge, because our reputation management service provides no possibility to generate information about the society and there is no central unit to analyze all social interactions between the society members. To generate the information, another way has to be found (see also figure 4): The requesting agent tries to get information about the former interaction partners of the target. So it requests the ratings of others about the target agent in the target context from the P2P system and the contexts with an ontological correlation (line with question mark in Fig. 4). Based on these data structures, the requesting agent can identify the agents which have interacted with the target agent (solid lines). Then the personal experiences with these identified agents (dotted lines) are used to calculate a neighborhood-reputation value. Only a subset of possible relationships can be identified in this manner, more precisely, only the interactions that concern the target agent in the target contexts. To complete the proceeding, the ratings the target agent has evaluated other agents with in the target context should be examined, as well. This information is not directly available in the DHT and therefore currently not accounted for. It could be retrieved by examining all ratings of all agents in the target context, but this proceeding is expensive as these data have not been stored explicitly (e.g. with a unique identifier assigned) in our DHT.

In order to calculate a trust value the target agent and the target context has to be provided to our reputation management system. First of all, contexts with an ontological relation are identified. Thus, the following procedure is executed for all identified contexts. If there are many direct experiences available and they are reliable, the reputation values are less important in the aggregation of direct experiences with reputation beliefs at the end. Therefore if direct experiences are highly reliable, the evaluation of agent reputation is omitted, as the retrieval of ratings from the underlying DHT is expensive. To calculate the reputation value the witness reputation can be requested directly from the underlying P2P network. While the neighborhood reputation is calculated as shown above, the system reputation includes information about the agent's behavior in the past. This includes e.g. his willingness to renew its leases. All different elements of reputation are weighted regarding the reliability (respectively credibility) of the single values. The final aggregation of values is performed according to ReGreT. The reputation service has been implemented in Java to be easily integrated in our previous work. Classes corresponding to each module of ReGreT have been implemented, as well as for the local data manager and the ontology representation.

5   Conclusion and Future Work

In this paper we investigated and presented how the ReGreT approach, one of the most matured trust and reputation mechanisms, can be implemented in our decentralized multi-agent environment. Some minor modifications had to be made regarding the collection of social information, as it cannot be assumed that all relationships between agents are observable in a distributed computing environment. We also adjusted the understanding and implementation of the ontological dimensions. We were able to provide a Java implementation, which has been successfully tested with a simple example application.

The future directions for extension and research we see are twofold. One direction is to further evaluate and refine the trust and reputation mechanism on the agent level. Therefore the next step is to evaluate the impact of our modifications to the original ReGreT approach with help of simulations similar to the simulations in [10]. There are also discussions if a plain mathematical approach to trust and reputation can really model it (see e.g. [17]) or if a cognitive approach is needed. Currently there is a successor of ReGreT, called Repage [12]. It uses a cognitive approach using the latest results from psychology. For our architecture and implementation it has to be evaluated how a cognitive approach can complement our framework, as we assume that in a computational environment a cognitive approach will depend on the mathematical approaches used to estimate how far the required beliefs can be attributed to an agent under consideration for being trusted.

Another direction of extension regards the DHT layer of our reputation management service. As we already have reputation for single hosts, regarding the performance of the host for storage reliability, this can be further advanced, as we also need reputation regarding routing in the DHT. Therefore it has to be tested, if an approach using social links as suggested by Marti et al.[18] is applicable for our DHT layer.

References

1. Marsh, S.P.: Formalising Trust as a Computational Concept. PhD thesis, University of Stirling (April 1994)
2. Sabater, J., Sierra, C.: REGRET: Reputation in gregarious societies. In: Müller, J.P., Andre, E., Sen, S., Frasson, C. (eds.) Proceedings of the Fifth International Conference on Autonomous Agents, Montreal, Canada, pp. 194–195. ACM Press, New York (2001)

3. Conte, R., Paolucci, M.: Reputation in Artificial Societies: Social Beliefs for Social Order. Kluwer Academic Publishers, Norwell, MA (2002)
4. Grünert, A., Hudert, S., König, S., Kaffille, S., Wirtz, G.: Decentralized Reputation Management for cooperating Software Agents in open Multi-Agent Systems. International Transactions on Systems Science and Applications 1(4), 363–368 (2006)
5. Garfinkel, S.: PGP: Pretty Good Privacy. O'Reilly (1994)
6. Aberer, K., Despotovic, Z.: Managing Trust in a Peer-2-Peer Information System. In: Paques, H., Liu, L., Grossman, D. (eds.) Proceedings of the Tenth International Conference on Information and Knowledge Management (CIKM01), pp. 310–317. ACM Press, New York (2001)
7. Stoica, I., Morris, R., Karger, D., Kaashoek, M.F., Balakrishnan, H.: Chord: A Scalable Peer-to-Peer Lookup Service for Internet Applications. In: Proceedings of the 2001 conference on applications, technologies, architectures, and protocols for computer communications, pp. 149–160. ACM Press, New York (2001)
8. Padovan, B., Sackmann, S., Eymann, T., Pippow, I.: A Prototype for an Agent based Secure Electronic Marketplace Including Reputation Tracking Mechanisms. In: Proceedings of the 34th Annual Hawaii International Conference on System Sciences (HICSS-34), vol. 7, p. 7008. IEEE Computer Society, Washington, DC (2001)
9. Suryanarayana, G., Diallo, M.H., Erenkrantz, J.R., Taylor, R.N.: Architectural Support for Trust Models in Decentralized Applications. In: ICSE '06: Proceedings of the 28th international conference on Software engineering, pp. 52–61. ACM Press, New York (2006)
10. Sabater, J.: Trust and Reputation for Agent Societies. PhD thesis, Institut d'Investigacio en Intelligencia Artificial (IIIA) (2003)
11. Sabater, J., Sierra, C.: Social ReGreT, a reputation model based on social relations. SIGecom Exch. 3(1), 44–56 (2002)
12. Sabater, J., Paolucci, M., Conte, R.: Repage: REPutation and ImAGE Among Limited Autonomous Partners. Journal of Artificial Societies and Social Simulation 9(2), 3 (2006)
13. Sabater, J., Sierra, C.: Review on Computational Trust and Reputation Models. Artif. Intell. Rev. 24(1), 33–60 (2005)
14. Kaffille, S., Loesing, K., Wirtz, G.: Distributed Service Discovery with Guarantees in Peer-to-Peer Networks Using Distributed Hashtables. In: Arabnia, H.R. (ed.) The 2005 International Conference on Parallel and Distributed Processing Techniques and Applications, CSREA Press, pp. 578–584 (2005)
15. Kaffille, S., Loesing, K.: Open Chord version 1.0.2 - User's Manual. Lehrstuhl für Praktische Informatik, Fakultät WIAI, Otto-Friedrich Universität Bamberg, Feldkirchenstraße 21, 96047 Bamberg (2006)
16. Wooldridge, M.J., Jennings, N.R.: Cooperative Problem Solving. Journal of Logic and Computation 9(4), 563–592 (1999)
17. Castelfranchi, C., Falcone, R.: Principles of Trust for MAS: Cognitive Anatomy, Social Importance, and Quantification. In: Demazeau, Y. (ed.) Proceedings of the Third International Conference on Multiagent Systems, ICMAS 1998, pp. 72–79. IEEE Computer Society, Los Alamitos (1998)
18. Marti, S., Ganesan, P., Garcia-Molina, H.: DHT Routing Using Social Links. In: 3rd International Workshop on Peer-to-Peer Systems, pp. 100–111 (2004)

Author Index

Aldewereld, Huib   61

Benamrane, Nacéra   49
Botía, Juan A.   182
Braubach, Lars   85
Busquets, Dídac   109

Cabac, Lawrence   1
Caballero, Alberto   182
Chiu, Chung-Cheng   37

de Jonge, Femke   61
Dikenelli, Oguz   13

Goknil, Arda   13
Gómez-Skarmeta, Antonio   182

Hamraz, Seyed Hamid   98

Kaffille, Sven   194
Kardas, Geylani   13
Katasonov, Artem   25
Klügl, Franziska   145
König, Stefan   194

León Soto, Esteban   73
López, Beatriz   109

Mao, Xiaoyu   133
Micalizio, Roberto   170
Minaei-Bidgoli, Behrouz   98
Muñoz, Víctor   109
Murillo, Javier   109

Nassane, Samir   49

Pokahr, Alexander   85
Punch, William F.   98

Rindsfüser, Guido   145
Roos, Nico   61, 133, 157

Schuldt, Arne   121
Soo, Von-Wun   37

ter Mors, Adriaan   133
Terziyan, Vagan   25
Topaloglu, N. Yasemin   13
Torasso, Pietro   170

Werner, Sven   121
Wirtz, Guido   194
Witteveen, Cees   133, 157

Lecture Notes in Artificial Intelligence (LNAI)

Vol. 4733: R. Basili, M.T. Pazienza (Eds.), AI*IA 2007: Artificial Intelligence and Human-Oriented Computing. XVII, 858 pages. 2007.

Vol. 4720: B. Konev, F. Wolter (Eds.), Frontiers of Combining Systems. X, 283 pages. 2007.

Vol. 4702: J.N. Kok, J. Koronacki, R. López de Mántaras, S. Matwin, D. Mladenič, A. Skowron (Eds.), Knowledge Discovery in Databases: PKDD 2007. XXIV, 640 pages. 2007.

Vol. 4701: J.N. Kok, J. Koronacki, R.L.d. Mantaras, S. Matwin, D. Mladenič, A. Skowron (Eds.), Machine Learning: ECML 2007. XXII, 809 pages. 2007.

Vol. 4694: B. Apolloni, R.J. Howlett, L. Jain (Eds.), Knowledge-Based Intelligent Information and Engineering Systems, Part III. XXIX, 1126 pages. 2007.

Vol. 4693: B. Apolloni, R.J. Howlett, L. Jain (Eds.), Knowledge-Based Intelligent Information and Engineering Systems, Part II. XXXII, 1380 pages. 2007.

Vol. 4692: B. Apolloni, R.J. Howlett, L. Jain (Eds.), Knowledge-Based Intelligent Information and Engineering Systems, Part I. LV, 882 pages. 2007.

Vol. 4687: P. Petta, J.P. Müller, M. Klusch, M. Georgeff (Eds.), Multiagent System Technologies. X, 207 pages. 2007.

Vol. 4682: D.-S. Huang, L. Heutte, M. Loog (Eds.), Advanced Intelligent Computing Theories and Applications. XXVII, 1373 pages. 2007.

Vol. 4676: M. Klusch, K. Hindriks, M.P. Papazoglou, L. Sterling (Eds.), Cooperative Information Agents XI. XI, 361 pages. 2007.

Vol. 4667: J. Hertzberg, M. Beetz, R. Englert (Eds.), KI 2007: Advances in Artificial Intelligence. IX, 516 pages. 2007.

Vol. 4660: S. Džeroski, J. Todorovski (Eds.), Computational Discovery of Scientific Knowledge. X, 327 pages. 2007.

Vol. 4659: V. Mařík, V. Vyatkin, A.W. Colombo (Eds.), Holonic and Multi-Agent Systems for Manufacturing. VIII, 456 pages. 2007.

Vol. 4651: F. Azevedo, P. Barahona, F. Fages, F. Rossi (Eds.), Recent Advances in Constraints. VIII, 185 pages. 2007.

Vol. 4648: F. Almeida e Costa, L.M. Rocha, E. Costa, I. Harvey, A. Coutinho (Eds.), Advances in Artificial Life. XVIII, 1215 pages. 2007.

Vol. 4635: B. Kokinov, D.C. Richardson, T.R. Roth-Berghofer, L. Vieu (Eds.), Modeling and Using Context. XIV, 574 pages. 2007.

Vol. 4632: R. Alhajj, H. Gao, X. Li, J. Li, O.R. Zaïane (Eds.), Advanced Data Mining and Applications. XV, 634 pages. 2007.

Vol. 4629: V. Matoušek, P. Mautner (Eds.), Text, Speech and Dialogue. XVII, 663 pages. 2007.

Vol. 4626: R.O. Weber, M.M. Richter (Eds.), Case-Based Reasoning Research and Development. XIII, 534 pages. 2007.

Vol. 4617: V. Torra, Y. Narukawa, Y. Yoshida (Eds.), Modeling Decisions for Artificial Intelligence. XII, 502 pages. 2007.

Vol. 4612: I. Miguel, W. Ruml (Eds.), Abstraction, Reformulation, and Approximation. XI, 418 pages. 2007.

Vol. 4604: U. Priss, S. Polovina, R. Hill (Eds.), Conceptual Structures: Knowledge Architectures for Smart Applications. XII, 514 pages. 2007.

Vol. 4603: F. Pfenning (Ed.), Automated Deduction – CADE-21. XII, 522 pages. 2007.

Vol. 4597: P. Perner (Ed.), Advances in Data Mining. XI, 353 pages. 2007.

Vol. 4594: R. Bellazzi, A. Abu-Hanna, J. Hunter (Eds.), Artificial Intelligence in Medicine. XVI, 509 pages. 2007.

Vol. 4585: M. Kryszkiewicz, J.F. Peters, H. Rybinski, A. Skowron (Eds.), Rough Sets and Intelligent Systems Paradigms. XIX, 836 pages. 2007.

Vol. 4578: F. Masulli, S. Mitra, G. Pasi (Eds.), Applications of Fuzzy Sets Theory. XVIII, 693 pages. 2007.

Vol. 4573: M. Kauers, M. Kerber, R. Miner, W. Windsteiger (Eds.), Towards Mechanized Mathematical Assistants. XIII, 407 pages. 2007.

Vol. 4571: P. Perner (Ed.), Machine Learning and Data Mining in Pattern Recognition. XIV, 913 pages. 2007.

Vol. 4570: H.G. Okuno, M. Ali (Eds.), New Trends in Applied Artificial Intelligence. XXI, 1194 pages. 2007.

Vol. 4565: D.D. Schmorrow, L.M. Reeves (Eds.), Foundations of Augmented Cognition. XIX, 450 pages. 2007.

Vol. 4562: D. Harris (Ed.), Engineering Psychology and Cognitive Ergonomics. XXIII, 879 pages. 2007.

Vol. 4548: N. Olivetti (Ed.), Automated Reasoning with Analytic Tableaux and Related Methods. X, 245 pages. 2007.

Vol. 4539: N.H. Bshouty, C. Gentile (Eds.), Learning Theory. XII, 634 pages. 2007.

Vol. 4529: P. Melin, O. Castillo, L.T. Aguilar, J. Kacprzyk, W. Pedrycz (Eds.), Foundations of Fuzzy Logic and Soft Computing. XIX, 830 pages. 2007.

Vol. 4520: M.V. Butz, O. Sigaud, G. Pezzulo, G. Baldassarre (Eds.), Anticipatory Behavior in Adaptive Learning Systems. X, 379 pages. 2007.

Vol. 4511: C. Conati, K. McCoy, G. Paliouras (Eds.), User Modeling 2007. XVI, 487 pages. 2007.

Vol. 4509: Z. Kobti, D. Wu (Eds.), Advances in Artificial Intelligence. XII, 552 pages. 2007.

Vol. 4496: N.T. Nguyen, A. Grzech, R.J. Howlett, L.C. Jain (Eds.), Agent and Multi-Agent Systems: Technologies and Applications. XXI, 1046 pages. 2007.

Vol. 4483: C. Baral, G. Brewka, J. Schlipf (Eds.), Logic Programming and Nonmonotonic Reasoning. IX, 327 pages. 2007.

Vol. 4482: A. An, J. Stefanowski, S. Ramanna, C.J. Butz, W. Pedrycz, G. Wang (Eds.), Rough Sets, Fuzzy Sets, Data Mining and Granular Computing. XIV, 585 pages. 2007.

Vol. 4481: J. Yao, P. Lingras, W.-Z. Wu, M. Szczuka, N.J. Cercone, D. Ślęzak (Eds.), Rough Sets and Knowledge Technology. XIV, 576 pages. 2007.

Vol. 4476: V. Gorodetsky, C. Zhang, V.A. Skormin, L. Cao (Eds.), Autonomous Intelligent Systems: Multi-Agents and Data Mining. XIII, 323 pages. 2007.

Vol. 4456: Y. Wang, Y.-m. Cheung, H. Liu (Eds.), Computational Intelligence and Security. XXIII, 1118 pages. 2007.

Vol. 4455: S. Muggleton, R. Otero, A. Tamaddoni-Nezhad (Eds.), Inductive Logic Programming. XII, 456 pages. 2007.

Vol. 4452: M. Fasli, O. Shehory (Eds.), Agent-Mediated Electronic Commerce. VIII, 249 pages. 2007.

Vol. 4451: T.S. Huang, A. Nijholt, M. Pantic, A. Pentland (Eds.), Artifical Intelligence for Human Computing. XVI, 359 pages. 2007.

Vol. 4441: C. Müller (Ed.), Speaker Classification. X, 309 pages. 2007.

Vol. 4438: L. Maicher, A. Sigel, L.M. Garshol (Eds.), Leveraging the Semantics of Topic Maps. X, 257 pages. 2007.

Vol. 4434: G. Lakemeyer, E. Sklar, D.G. Sorrenti, T. Takahashi (Eds.), RoboCup 2006: Robot Soccer World Cup X. XIII, 566 pages. 2007.

Vol. 4429: R. Lu, J.H. Siekmann, C. Ullrich (Eds.), Cognitive Systems. X, 161 pages. 2007.

Vol. 4428: S. Edelkamp, A. Lomuscio (Eds.), Model Checking and Artificial Intelligence. IX, 185 pages. 2007.

Vol. 4426: Z.-H. Zhou, H. Li, Q. Yang (Eds.), Advances in Knowledge Discovery and Data Mining. XXV, 1161 pages. 2007.

Vol. 4411: R.H. Bordini, M. Dastani, J. Dix, A.E.F. Seghrouchni (Eds.), Programming Multi-Agent Systems. XIV, 249 pages. 2007.

Vol. 4410: A. Branco (Ed.), Anaphora: Analysis, Algorithms and Applications. X, 191 pages. 2007.

Vol. 4399: T. Kovacs, X. Llorà, K. Takadama, P.L. Lanzi, W. Stolzmann, S.W. Wilson (Eds.), Learning Classifier Systems. XII, 345 pages. 2007.

Vol. 4390: S.O. Kuznetsov, S. Schmidt (Eds.), Formal Concept Analysis. X, 329 pages. 2007.

Vol. 4389: D. Weyns, H. Van Dyke Parunak, F. Michel (Eds.), Environments for Multi-Agent Systems III. X, 273 pages. 2007.

Vol. 4386: P. Noriega, J. Vázquez-Salceda, G. Boella, O. Boissier, V. Dignum, N. Fornara, E. Matson (Eds.), Coordination, Organizations, Institutions, and Norms in Agent Systems II. XI, 373 pages. 2007.

Vol. 4384: T. Washio, K. Satoh, H. Takeda, A. Inokuchi (Eds.), New Frontiers in Artificial Intelligence. IX, 401 pages. 2007.

Vol. 4371: K. Inoue, K. Satoh, F. Toni (Eds.), Computational Logic in Multi-Agent Systems. X, 315 pages. 2007.

Vol. 4369: M. Umeda, A. Wolf, O. Bartenstein, U. Geske, D. Seipel, O. Takata (Eds.), Declarative Programming for Knowledge Management. X, 229 pages. 2006.

Vol. 4343: C. Müller (Ed.), Speaker Classification I. X, 355 pages. 2007.

Vol. 4342: H. de Swart, E. Orłowska, G. Schmidt, M. Roubens (Eds.), Theory and Applications of Relational Structures as Knowledge Instruments II. X, 373 pages. 2006.

Vol. 4335: S.A. Brueckner, S. Hassas, M. Jelasity, D. Yamins (Eds.), Engineering Self-Organising Systems. XII, 212 pages. 2007.

Vol. 4334: B. Beckert, R. Hähnle, P.H. Schmitt (Eds.), Verification of Object-Oriented Software. XXIX, 658 pages. 2007.

Vol. 4333: U. Reimer, D. Karagiannis (Eds.), Practical Aspects of Knowledge Management. XII, 338 pages. 2006.

Vol. 4327: M. Baldoni, U. Endriss (Eds.), Declarative Agent Languages and Technologies IV. VIII, 257 pages. 2006.

Vol. 4314: C. Freksa, M. Kohlhase, K. Schill (Eds.), KI 2006: Advances in Artificial Intelligence. XII, 458 pages. 2007.

Vol. 4304: A. Sattar, B.-h. Kang (Eds.), AI 2006: Advances in Artificial Intelligence. XXVII, 1303 pages. 2006.

Vol. 4303: A. Hoffmann, B.-h. Kang, D. Richards, S. Tsumoto (Eds.), Advances in Knowledge Acquisition and Management. XI, 259 pages. 2006.

Vol. 4293: A. Gelbukh, C.A. Reyes-Garcia (Eds.), MICAI 2006: Advances in Artificial Intelligence. XXVIII, 1232 pages. 2006.

Vol. 4289: M. Ackermann, B. Berendt, M. Grobelnik, A. Hotho, D. Mladenič, G. Semeraro, M. Spiliopoulou, G. Stumme, V. Svátek, M. van Someren (Eds.), Semantics, Web and Mining. X, 197 pages. 2006.

Vol. 4285: Y. Matsumoto, R.W. Sproat, K.-F. Wong, M. Zhang (Eds.), Computer Processing of Oriental Languages. XVII, 544 pages. 2006.

Vol. 4274: Q. Huo, B. Ma, E.-S. Chng, H. Li (Eds.), Chinese Spoken Language Processing. XXIV, 805 pages. 2006.